Investment Decisions, Economic Forecasting,
and Public Policy

INVESTMENT DECISIONS, ECONOMIC FORECASTING, and PUBLIC POLICY

JOHN R. MEYER
Professor of Economics
Harvard University

ROBERT R. GLAUBER
Doctoral Research Fellow
Harvard Graduate School of
Business Administration

DIVISION OF RESEARCH
GRADUATE SCHOOL OF BUSINESS ADMINISTRATION
HARVARD UNIVERSITY
Boston · 1964

Foreword

Former Dean Donald K. David used to refer frequently to the role of statistics, economics, and other social sciences in a graduate school of business administration as being quite analogous to the role of the biological and physical sciences in contributing to the primary functions of a medical school. Increasingly over the last decade or so, a growing number of able economists have been concerned to adapt and elaborate earlier theories and to develop new theoretical structures which would provide more adequate and reliable explanations of the economic aspects of the behavior of business firms, and which would be more directly useful in dealing with important problems faced by the business executive. These developments are exemplified in much of the work in what is called econometrics — the development of economic theories in *testable* forms and their associated statistical evaluation — and by major contributions to the development of methods of mathematical programming, production smoothing and inventory control, and forecasting.

The present study falls squarely in this growing tradition. In the early chapters, the authors briefly review the major theoretical generalizations regarding business investment behavior, and they advance a more complex and eclectic "accelerator-residual funds" theory which they believe *should* be more adequate. They then carefully review its adequacy in terms of the evidence of twelve postwar years of experience under widely varying conditions of liquidity, profitability, capacity pressures, inflation or price weakness, prosperity or recession, as well as ease or tightness in money markets, and stagnant or buoyant stock markets. In the statistical work, both time series for the manufacturing sector and cross-sections of firms in some twenty separate industry groupings are examined. These results should be directly useful to business organizations needing to forecast plant and equipment expenditures either as a critical component of their forecasts of general business conditions which affect many aspects of their planning, or, more specifically for companies in heavy goods industries, as one of the direct determinants of their own sales. The results of these chapters will be of interest to other economists working on similar problems and to economists and others concerned with the implications of the findings for such broader issues as the relative effectiveness of monetary policy and changes in tax rates on consumers or on business in stabilizing business fluctuations and encouraging a higher and more sustained level of business investment. These results also throw further light on the operation of profits and the profit motive in an important set of business decisions.

The other main focus of the study is on methodological issues. The authors are especially concerned with the subtle problems involved in the use of time-series data, both in efforts to test and choose among alternative theoretical generalizations or "models" of investment behavior, and in the distinct and more general problem of using available data for the purpose of getting the best forecast of not-yet-observed future levels of activity. In dealing with the problems raised by highly intercorrelated explanatory variables, the authors propose and test the forecasting efficiency of a technique of constrained estimation which adopts mathematical programming procedures. The authors also deal with the relationships of these new methods both to established "classical" procedures and to the "Bayesian" analysis being developed by Professors Raiffa and Schlaifer of this Faculty.

The authors also present a valuable analysis of the purpose and evaluation of economic forecasts, and illustrate empirically the several important points made. They particularly emphasize that what is the best forecast (and therefore the best forecasting procedure) depends essentially on the decision maker's *objectives*, the *context* of the decisions which will be affected by the forecasts, and the *evaluation* of the *consequences* of the different decisions which depend on the forecasts.

This particular study is a part of a broader program of research in the area of "Profits and the Functioning of the Economy" which has been financed by a generous grant from the Rockefeller Foundation to the Harvard Business School. This broad program, under the direction of Professor Lintner, has consisted of a series of interrelated studies focusing on particular decisions by management in which profits play a key role either as a source of funds or as expected returns which provide incentives to take action. Professor Meyer, of the Harvard Department of Economics, has worked closely with members of this Faculty on many aspects of this broad program of research, and with the collaboration first of Professor Edwin Kuh of the Massachusetts Institute of Technology and more recently of Robert R. Glauber, currently a doctoral research fellow at this School, he has focused his own work on the determinants of investment outlays of corporations. The financial support for this particular study has come almost entirely from the Rockefeller Foundation grant to the School, and we wish to express for the School its appreciation of the support for this program of research.

BERTRAND FOX
Director of Research

JOHN LINTNER
Professor of Business Administration

Soldiers Field
Boston, Massachusetts
November 1963

Preface

When the research for this study was first undertaken, more years ago than I now wish to admit, it was very simple in concept. Essentially, it was to be an extension of earlier empirical cross-section studies of business investment behavior undertaken by Edwin Kuh and myself and published under the title of *The Investment Decision: An Empirical Inquiry*. Indeed, an appropriate title for this work as originally conceived would have been *The Investment Decision Revisited*. These simple origins, however, were somewhere lost in the process of completing the research.

The final version, in fact, tends to involve itself in three highly related but yet distinct topics. The first of these, not unsurprisingly and also fortunately from the standpoint of initial commitments, is still the investment decision analyzed with cross-section data. The second is a concern with matters of statistical methodology, in particular the possible adaptation of certain decision theory and subjective estimation concepts to econometrics or, more precisely, the possible use of *a priori* information to improve parameter estimation techniques (as contrasted with hypothesis testing) in economics. The third is an elaboration of the investment models in time-series applications with particular emphasis on economic forecasting.

This extension in the scope of the study has been the result of many influences and factors. The interest in subjective estimation and decision theory, for example, is mainly due to Professor Robert Schlaifer of the Harvard Business School. I was fortunate enough, seven years ago, to be engaged jointly with him in another more mundane task in which we usually ended each work day with an hour or two of private discussion and debate on the general philosophy of statistical estimation procedures. In these discussions he vigorously challenged all the conventional wisdom of objective statistical estimation.

It has only been very recently, long after most of the basic researches for this book were completed, that I have had an oppor-

ix

tunity to reconsider systematically the developments in Professor Schlaifer's thinking, as found in *Applied Statistical Decision Theory*, written by him in collaboration with Professor Howard Raiffa. In making this reassessment and comparing it with the work in this study, I was somewhat surprised to learn how my own reaction to their challenges of objective statistical methods had been more to reject probability models as such in economics, or at least become skeptical of their applicability, rather than to accept subjective models.

The expanded interest in time-series and forecasting problems had several sources. First, there was a feeling of dissatisfaction with the brief (one short chapter) treatment of these problems in *The Investment Decision*. For reasons Kuh and I have explained elsewhere, these efforts proved quite abortive, mainly because of the complex problems involved in reconciling the results of cross-section investigations with time-series analyses. Progress made on solving these problems in this study proved to be disappointingly small, but any progress in this difficult area is worthy of effort.

Additional motivation to expand the study to encompass a more thorough consideration of time-series analyses also came from Professors John Lintner and James Duesenbury. Besides being important sources of general information and insight on business behavior, their interest in problems of economic forecasting proved quite contagious and this, in turn, almost intrinsically leads to a consideration of time-series problems. These same interests were also furthered by a reading of Professor Henrí Theil's excellent and highly suggestive study, *Forecasting and Economic Policy*, an exercise, incidentally, which also led to consideration of the formal inter-relationships between decision theory, subjective estimation procedures, and economic forecasting. Professor Theil's presence on the Harvard campus as a Visiting Professor during the spring of 1960 was helpful in cultivating these interests, but it should be pointed out that some of the parallels between the work reported here and that undertaken recently by Professor Theil and his associates at Rotterdam (particular mention in this connection should be made of Arnold Zoellner's contributions) is essentially fortuitous. We did not know of their work until February 1961 when most of the basic drafts and calculations for this study had already been completed and they were similarly uninformed about our undertakings. In the same vein, I should add that similarities that exist between this work and Professor Kuh's recently published and very fine study, *Capital Stock Growth: A Micro-Econometric Approach*, are the results only of our earlier collaboration and continuing common interests. We saw only parts of each other's work before essentially all the drafting had been completed — but we, of course, had many conversations at the luncheon table and on other occasions so that some pronounced parallels do exist in our approaches. Finally, it is quite obvious that this work bears many signs of Professor Guy Orcutt's influences and teaching, which, in fact, provided much of the inspiration for this undertaking. Needless to say, those acknowledged here in no way bear responsibility for our errors; those remain exclusively our property!

Other factors leading to an extension of the study beyond its original scope were the energy, zest, and intellectual caliber of my collaborator, Robert Glauber. I first became acquainted with him in the spring of 1959, when he was a sophomore in Harvard College and serving as my research assistant, doing routine programming and data processing. Later he wrote his Senior Honors Thesis under my direction; in this he developed some of the decision theory and forecasting implications of the investment behavior analyses reported in this study. This thesis, incidentally, won the Allyn Young prize as the best Senior Honors Thesis submitted to the Harvard Department of Economics by the class of 1961. Chapters 8 and 9 in this book represent extended versions of his thesis work. Long before he reached this thesis writing stage, however, his research assistance had ceased to be merely routine. His contributions, therefore, are to be found throughout. In fact, only the errors and cantankerous views on policy and theory, a debility acquired strictly with age, remain exclusively mine!

JOHN R. MEYER

November 1963

Acknowledgments

To the already considerable list of people to whom we have previously expressed our intellectual debts of gratitude in the Preface, I should like to add one further name. While Professor Meyer was away last year, I had several extensive discussions with Professor Howard Raiffa of the Harvard Business School concerning the theoretical material in Chapters 8 and 9. His comments were particularly helpful in clarifying the comparison between our methods and those developed by the Bayesians. Of course, Professor Raiffa has no responsibility for what errors might remain.

The energetic and diligent secretarial assistance of Miss Nancy Eichenberger and Miss Sarah James, who typed and retyped the various drafts, was indispensable. The index, always a difficult job, was compiled with painstaking care by Miss Beatrice Rogers. Finally, Miss Ruth Norton of the Harvard Business School's Division of Research shepherded the manuscript through the intricacies of publication, tolerantly accepting our last minute revisions.

The major source of the financing for this project was a grant from the Rockefeller Foundation to the Harvard Business School for the study of "Profits and the Functioning of the Economy." The expenses involved in collecting the cross-section sample of American manufacturing firms for the years 1951–1954 were in large measure defrayed by funds provided by the McGraw-Hill Publishing Company. The Ford Foundation, through its grant to the Harvard Department of Economics for making small research grants, supplied the funds necessary to perform the final computations and clerical and secretarial chores associated with finishing the book.

Most of Professor Meyer's first drafting was carried out during the academic year 1958–1959 when he was the recipient of a Guggenheim Foundation Fellowship. A Ford Foundation Research Professorship for the academic year 1952–1953 provided him with the time necessary for much of the final revisions of the manuscript. My share of the re-drafting was completed last year while I was studying under a Ford Foundation Pre-Doctoral Fellowship in Business and Economics.

ROBERT R. GLAUBER

Contents

Figures and Tables

Chapter **I** | *The Issues*

It is hardly an overstatement to assert that the theory and measurement of investment behavior is one of the most controversial areas of professional economic study.[1] The disputations have several sources.

First, the subject is inherently difficult and complex. Involved are such influences as uncertainty, managerial preference patterns, imperfect knowledge, and risk. These have not been customarily or easily incorporated into conventional economic theories. And modern theory has only made a modest start on the problem.

[1] Business investment decisions have been the subject of much economic research, both conceptual and empirical, in recent years. Because of the quantity of documentation required, no attempt has been made in this study to reference these materials systematically. A reasonably thorough bibliography for the period up through about the middle of 1956 can be found in John R. Meyer and Edwin Kuh, *The Investment Decision: An Empirical Inquiry* (Cambridge: Harvard University Press, 1957), pp. 269–277. A selected list of some of the more important contributions since that time will be found in the bibliography on investment decisions reported at the end of this book. All of the materials listed there have had, incidentally, an impact on the discussion of investment concepts contained in this and the next chapter. References have been given in the text, of course, wherever direct quotation or special discussions of other works have been presented. Similarly, all references dealing with technical statistical procedures are given in the text.

1

Second, the available data are not always of the highest quality or of the type needed. Even today little is known about such key investment factors as the "true rate" of economic obsolescence of most manufacturing equipment or what constitutes a correct or even good measure of capacity utilization. Also, many of the issues could be resolved only by performing comparisons of behavior over time. Unfortunately, as is often the case in economics, nature has not been kind enough to perform historical experiments of sufficient variety to discriminate adequately among the many competing hypotheses. In the jargon of economic statistics, the data are too collinear.

Third, specific theories, concepts, or views of investment behavior have become intimately associated with "justifications" for particular tax and fiscal programs. They thus become intellectual accessories or committed participants in some of the most sensitive and motivated of public policy discussions.

Under the circumstances it is perhaps remarkable that any intelligent and reasonably dispassionate discussion of the issues has taken place or that any pattern can be discerned. In fact, a simple yet comprehensive scheme for categorizing the issues and participants in these disputes is difficult to establish. At least one fundamental cleavage, however, can be discerned. Specifically, there are those who believe that investment patterns can be described adequately by fairly simple theory and there are those who do not.

The adherents to the simple approach are as a rule today mainly advocates of some form of "acceleration concept" in which investment outlays are considered to be a function of the rate of change of output or, alternatively, of "capacity utilization." Once, in a bygone and apparently less complex age, the "simplicity school" also numbered among its adherents classicists or, better, neo-classicists who felt that investment, like most economic activity, was determined primarily by the price mechanism, the relevant price for investment decisions being the interest rate at which business managers could borrow. This classical point of view has been, however, the object of much criticism and adverse empirical evidence. Few proponents of its primacy will still step forward. Today, indeed, it is counted as something of a revival when the interest rate is even asserted to have at least *some* influence on investment outlays.

Another view, also once prominently represented in the "simplicity school," was that associated with the concept of the marginal efficiency of capital. In pristine, nonempirical form, this theory was not terribly exceptionable: it merely asserted that investments in a free-enterprise setting were mainly motivated by the desire and the calculated expectation of profit. Translated to a form suitable for empirical testing, the expectation of profit usually was asserted to be equal to the most recent profit experience. Stated in this form, inadequacies and exceptions soon were noted. For example, the explanatory power of such profit models often was not very great. In extenuation it was sometimes argued that past or current profits merely measured the supply of investment funds and not the expectation of investment rewards. Furthermore, it became at least moderately fashionable to argue that profits should be converted into a purer measure of the flow of free money (by, say, adding in depreciation and subtracting dividends) to improve the explanatory power of profits in investment models. Needless to say, discriminating between these two profit-type theories was rather difficult with the available empirical data, nature's limited variety of historical experiments being the major problem. The advocates of the marginal efficiency approach have never been driven though to the same extremely defensive posture as the interest-rate classicists. For the most part they have not conceded the primacy of their variable, only its possible exclusiveness.

The other group, the nonsimplifiers, are, of course, synthesizers or eclectics and, as befits their character, this group is at least as fully heterogeneous as the simplifiers. The eclectics argue that many considerations can and often do exert an important influence on investment demand. They insist that new product introduction and product improvements, cost reduction, and considerations of market or competitive strategy are just a few of many examples of the important influences on investment that are often independent of simple profit, interest rate, and capacity-output relationships. Under some conditions, moreover, certain constraints are said to place effective limits on an investment program, no matter how desirable. An oft-cited constraint, for example, is the availability of internal financing, a constraint which is said to have its origins in, among other sources, the seemingly strong aversion on the part of professional managements toward the kind of risk involved in extensive debt financing. Other constraints also have been cited, as, for example, simple scarcity in some cases of trained management to supervise and administer more than a certain rate of expansion.

These "other-motivated" investments are, of course, closely akin to what often has been termed by economists "exogenous" investment. These investments have earned the label "exogenous" because their demand is ostensibly generated by noneconomic considerations or influences outside the immediate economic system; e.g., discovery of new technologies. Whether their generation is really this independent is a difficult and complex question. The problem, however, is not their generation alone but also how they tend to be financed over time. In short, the eclectic feels that investment must be considered in a broader framework and, in particular, in a framework that takes account of *both* supply and demand influences on the investment decision.

The major issues of investment theory can be rather readily summarized, in fact, within a very simple supply and demand framework.[2] The first step is establishing a supply of funds schedule, a schedule that represents both internal and external sources. Disagreements on the nature of the supply function tend to take two forms. Either supply characteristics are totally ignored, as in most of the simplified approaches and particularly in the naive acceleration theories, or there is argument over the exact shape of the supply of funds function. The central dispute about shape is whether or not a kink or discontinuity occurs at the point where internal sources of funds (profits, depreciation expenses, business capital gains, etc.) join the supply of external funds (new equity and bond issues, bank loans, etc.). One school would contend that businessmen look upon external funds as considerably more expensive than any and all internal sources, thus creating a discontinuity at the point where internal funds are exhausted. Those arguing for a

---

[2] Both the approach and much of the analysis presented here are in accord with the position of James S. Duesenberry, *Business Cycles and Economic Growth* (New York: McGraw-Hill Book Company, 1958). An extended and diagrammatic discussion of these same points can be found in Edwin Kuh and John R. Meyer, "Investment, Liquidity, and Monetary Policy," in *Impacts of Monetary Policy*, Commission on Money and Credit Research Monographs Vol. 10 (Englewood Cliffs, New Jersey: Prentice-Hall, 1963).

discontinuity in the supply schedule also insist that the valuation businessmen place on internal funds is not closely related to market rates for external funds. By contrast, those arguing against the discontinuity position would say that businessmen must rationally place the same valuation on internal and external fund sources and therefore that the supply of funds function is likely to be quite elastic and continuous, at least within relevant ranges.

On the demand side, the controversy centers on the exact specification of variables to be entered as determinants of investment demand. For example, even among those who would simplify there is considerable disagreement over exactly which variable or variables best gauge the level of activity influences on demand. At one extreme, in the simplest acceleration theory, changes in the level of activity are considered to be the best measure of these influences. In slightly more complex formulations of the accelerator concept, the level of activity is measured relative to some ability to produce or some measure of productive capacity. On the other hand, in a marginal efficiency of capital approach, some measure of profits or change in the level of profits is taken as the best measure of the general level of investment demands. The ultimate complexity is advanced by some eclectics who would insist that one or more of these measures, and some additional ones as well, should be included in any reasonably adequate model.

The controversy over the interest elasticity of investment demand does not center much upon the question of alternatives but, rather, whether in fact any such interest elasticity exists and, particularly, whether it is at all significant. For example, those adhering to simple acceleration explanations, whether of a capacity or a change in the level of activity type, implicitly or explicitly impute a zero elasticity. Basically, they deny the possibility that short-run variations in investments are made, at least in any important amounts, for *any* purpose other than responding to an expansion of production levels. However, if other reasons for investing such as cost reduction and product improvement are admitted (and are assumed to be not simply trend-related or autonomous), it seems reasonable to suppose that investment serving these other objectives might be potentially interest sensitive. Accordingly, an eclectic theorist is at least likely to admit the possibility of the interest rate being related with investment demands. The marginal efficiency approach also recognizes interest influences on investment since it is the interest rate that serves as the factor for obtaining the present value of expected future profits. However, because in the usual empirical application (and it is empirical applications that are of central concern here) the expected profit figures are not available and current or recent profits are used instead, the interest rate enters these empirical models mainly as an additional and separate variable. A marginal efficiency advocate also would insist, of course, that other motives for investment can be incorporated into his theory by simply noting that these other possibilities influence profit expectations. In a strictly conceptual sense this is true. However, the approach is notable for its dearth of specific recommendations on how to proceed with an actual empirical test of these implications.

An additional, and very important, issue concerning supply and demand relationships has been raised in recent discussions, particularly by those adopting the eclectic approach. This is the relationship, if any, between shifts in the supply and demand functions, a particularly crucial question being whether shifts in the two functions are positively synchronized with one another. The existence or nonexistence of synchronization is important since if (a) the shifts are synchronized, (b) the supply function is discontinuous, and (c) the demand function normally cuts the supply function somewhere near the discontinuity, the question of whether investment demand is interest elastic becomes academic or superfluous (because the demand function would be almost continuously "operating against" a relatively inelastic supply function). Since internal business funds can be described to a fair degree of approximation as the sum of retained earnings, depreciation expense, and excess cash assets, those arguing for synchronization would point out that the most volatile portion of this sum is retained earnings which, in turn, tends to be closely tied to the level of activity. This, they would argue, also is the main determinant of shifts in investment demand. Since shifts in the two functions have a common cause or are related to a common underlying variable, synchronization should follow almost automatically. Clearly, assertion of the contrary case, nonsynchronization, involves denying one or more of the underlying assumptions.

In sum, the initial question about investment behavior is whether the investment process is complex and, specifically, complex enough to involve *both* demand and supply problems. If this is answered affirmatively, then a number of additional issues arise which can be best summarized by the following four questions: [3]

(1) To what extent is investment demand interest elastic?
(2) What constitutes the best measure of the general level of investment demand?
(3) Is the supply of investment funds discontinuous (or at least substantially less elastic in some portions) because of different business valuations being placed on internal and external funds?
(4) To what degree are shifts in the investment demand and supply functions positively synchronized?

Those adopting an eclectic approach to the study of business investment behavior consider all these questions pertinent and also not necessarily answerable to any degree of accuracy at the moment. In short, they place the business investment decision in a context of many very different constraints, motives, and reasons for desiring new productive equipment and they are not certain that they completely understand all the mechanisms by which these forces work.

In full agreement with that eclecticism, in the pages that follow attention will center on the question of what might be the dominant decision rule or rules followed by manufacturers in establishing investment programs under various circumstances. The suggestion will be made that an accelerator or a capacity-output relationship would seem to be the key factor in establishing short-run investment budgets when capacity is fully utilized and, contrarily, the level of cash funds flowing into the firm from current operations is the prime determinant when capacity is less than fully utilized. In terms of the supply and demand framework just outlined, this means that investment demands are expected to outpace the supply of internal funds in business upswings (or that no serious discontinuity exists in the supply function at such times) and that the main determinant of the level of investment demands is some measure of capacity utilization.

---

[3] Some of these questions clearly would arise in even the most simple of investment theories, the only notable exception being the most naive accelerator theories. However, it is the achievement of the eclectic approach that it has brought all these issues forward for discussion.

By contrast, in business downswings, it is hypothesized that a discontinuity exists in the supply of funds function and that investment demand is more or less synchronized with the internal supply of funds, cutting the supply function near the point of discontinuity. The rudiments of this rather eclectic theory have been sketched out previously under the title of "the residual funds theory of investment." [4]   A more suggestive or accurate name might have been "an accelerator-residual funds theory of investment" since such a label would emphasize the theory's essence, the discontinuity in investment behavior which occurs at the point where full utilization of capacity is achieved.   A more complete summary and elaboration of this theory, as well as a summary of the empirical findings on which its development was based, are presented in the next chapter.

[4] Meyer and Kuh, *The Investment Decision*, Chapter 13.

Chapter **II** | *The Accelerator-Residual Funds Hypothesis*

I. *Introduction*

Empirical relationships observed in business behavior can be classified as of two types. First, there are those that are more long than short run, often noncausally defined and therefore best measured by interdependence statistics, and related to underlying policy objectives chosen by individual firms. Such relationships might be described as "behavioral" or motivational and will be analyzed and alluded to only peripherally in this study. The second type of relationships can be characterized as mechanistic, temporal, relatively short-run in character, and these are often attributable to administrative rules used for simplifying the internal control of business operations. These relationships will here be termed "mechanistic." Mechanistic relationships should be evidenced by reasonably high correlations between the specified variables and, in addition, a consistent intertemporal or interindustry behavioral pattern should be observable in the empirical results. The search for relationships of this second type as they relate to business investment decisions is the central concern of this study.

The objective is to specify and test various hypotheses about the relationship between certain measures of business performance, which are assumed to be beyond the full control of the firm and industry, and managerial policy decisions to commit liquid assets to plant and equipment investments. The ultimate objective is to determine if certain rules dominate the short-run investment relationships of United States manufacturing corporations and if these relationships can be used to specify a simple, more accurate forecasting model of investment aggregates than is now available.

Accordingly, a more or less traditional approach to the investigation of econometric relationships in business data has been adopted in this study; traditional, first, in using groups defined by industry and product characteristics for analysis; second, in emphasizing mechanistic, causal relationships; third, in using the conventional statistical tools of econometric analysis, regression, and correlation. Despite many shortcomings, this traditional approach can be justified on at least two counts: (1) the results produced are readily contrastable with previous results; and (2) a control is established for better evaluation of results obtained by using alternative methods. Furthermore, empirical regularities observable by traditional methods may have an intrinsic value of their own, at a minimum making some potential contribution to the better specification of aggregate models for the study of economic policies and forecasts.

As a first step in this attempt to obtain better investment relationships by traditional econometric methods, a theoretical framework within which the search will be executed is developed in this chapter. In essence, existing knowledge about investment behavior will be utilized to make further search for behavioral regularities more efficient. The major source of previous knowledge for this effort is an earlier empirical study of investment behavior relating mainly to the years 1946–1950 in which 75 different industry-years or groups of cross-section data were analyzed and a few brief analyses of time-series data also were undertaken.[1] This choice of source materials provides continuity and facilitates comparison between the earlier and later empirical results. (This earlier study was conducted by one of the present authors, John Meyer, and Edwin Kuh and henceforth will be referred to as the Meyer-Kuh study.)

Section II of this chapter presents a brief summary of the major findings of the Meyer-Kuh study while Section III sets forth a model, the so-called accelerator-residual funds hypothesis, that serves

[1] Meyer and Kuh, *The Investment Decision.*

as a means of systematically organizing these findings. In Section IV, the interpretative discussion of models is further expanded to consider the meaning of so-called "distributed lag" formulations of the underlying hypotheses. Finally, a summary is presented in Section V.

II. *The 1946–1950 Investment Experience*

A typically behavioral or nonmechanistic finding of the Meyer-Kuh study was the so-called "senility effect." This described a tendency for firms that have once lagged behind in the competitive race to remain behind. The senility effect was evidenced in the 75 different industry-years of experience analyzed by a preponderance of negative partial correlations between the age of a firm's capital stock (as measured by the relative size of depreciation reserves) and investment outlays. A negative relationship of this kind runs counter to at least some *a priori* expectations since the older a firm's capital equipment the greater the expected possibilities might be for making cost reducing investments. Some firms apparently choose to operate with old or outdated capital equipment as a matter of deliberate policy, low investment rates associated with old capital merely constituting a continuation of established policy.

The age of the capital stock also was positively correlated with the size of the net liquidity stock held by the firm. A hoarding of liquid funds combined with a conservative expansion policy could be construed as a sign of an excessively cautious, defensive behavior or as an indication that more favorable capital goods prices were expected in the near future. At least during the 1946–1950 period a small group of manufacturing firms seemed to exist that had an older than average physical plant, a relatively low investment rate, and a substantial hoard of liquid assets.

A second behavioral finding was the general prevalence of financial conservatism among United States manufacturing firms included in the study sample. This finding was, of course, not surprising, corroborating as it did earlier work on corporation financial practices. During the 1946–1950 period financial conservatism manifested itself mainly in a strong reluctance to use external funds to finance expansion. Where outside funds were used, a preference existed for debt to equity financing; short-term bank loans, more-over, were employed more often than long-term debt. There was also some tendency, especially at the extremes of the sample observations, for the use of outside funds to be positively related to the extent of market competition within the industry and the over-all rate of industry growth. These two conditions, of course, can be interrelated; growth industries are sometimes also, though certainly not necessarily, highly competitive.

As a third structural finding, small firms' investments also were found to be more sensitive than those of large firms to the level of available internal funds and the general business climate. Small firms' internal or investment growth rates (as contrasted with external or merger growth) exceeded those of larger firms during the years 1946 through 1950 for every year except 1949. That this latter year was the one year of recession during the sample period was considered at least suggestive.

While small firms were incrementally more sensitive to internal fund flows in their investment planning, on the average they also used more outside financing than large firms throughout the 1946–1950 period. Notable exceptions were firms in growth industries in 1949, for which outside financing might have been highly desired during a recession. Finally, there was a slight, though unmistakable, tendency for the partial correlations between investment and the liquidity flow variables, net profits and depreciation expense, to be more significant for small than for large firms.

The most important temporal or mechanistic relationships pertained to the different performances of the capacity utilization and profit variables at different stages of the business cycle. The capacity variable provided the best explanation of investment during the years 1946–1948 when the economy was expanding and financing was plentiful. On the other hand, capacity had a very loose relationship with investment in the recession year of 1949 and the mixed recession and war boom year of 1950. In these latter two years the liquidity flow variables, profit and depreciation expense, evidenced a closer correlation with investment.

Furthermore, these liquidity flow-investment relationships seemed attributable more to financial than expectational influences. Not only did the profit variable behave much the same as the relatively pure liquidity flow measure, depreciation expense, but the comparative performance of the profit variable in different industries was negatively related, at least to a limited extent, to the average change over the previous year in the industry's profit and liquidity stock holdings. In addition, no relationship was discernible between the performance of the profit variable and average capacity utilization or sales change in an industry — two variables which might be expected to have some influence on expectations.

In the long run, by contrast, investment consistently tended to be more closely related to technological needs, as defined by the capacity utilization variable, than to financial requirements. It might be argued, of course, that a need to maintain some sort of approximate output to sales ratio in the long run is almost tautological in the absence of marked technological change.

The depreciation expense variable also showed an influence on investment that was apparently independent of physical depreciation or possible replacement needs. A mechanistic tendency seemed to exist to reinvest that portion of the internal fund flow (or cash throwoff) that was classified as depreciation expense. A differentiation between depreciation expense and other internal funds is not too easy to explain on strictly rational grounds since the depreciation figure is essentially an artificial accounting construct. Accordingly, it was hypothesized that cash realizations earmarked as depreciation allowances might have a privileged position as a source of investment funds, perhaps because depreciation allowances are less pervious than profits to either stockholder demands for larger dividends or labor demands for higher wages.

There were also some purely negative findings of interest. For example, no regular relationship, either over time or by industry, could be found between the rate of investment and the *stock* (as contrasted with *flow*) of liquid assets. Similarly, there seemed to be no systematic behavioral connection between debt or equity position and investment. In particular, little verification could be found for the "principle of increasing risk" that, broadly speaking, hypothesizes a negative relation between investment and the debt to equity ratio of a firm. In fact, what little relationship that was observable between these variables appeared to be positive rather than negative. A similar negativity characterized attempts to verify the strong market share competition hypothesis that investment increases when sales decline under certain circumstances of oligopolistic rivalry.

Similarly, no differentiation was possible between sales and profit influences on investment. These two variables were so closely correlated in the 1946–1950 cross-section samples that they could effectively be considered the same variable for statistical purposes. This, unfortunately, prevented including them simultaneously in the same regression model and made it impossible to test effectively certain conflicting hypotheses about the relative influence of the two variables on investment. What little independent variation that did exist indicated that sales behaved, as might have been expected, like a crossbreed between capacity-accelerator and profit measures.

Null results also characterized a time-series analysis, based on annual aggregates, 1920 to 1951, of the connections between investment and certain price and interest rate variables. The only systematic time relationship was between an industry's total investment and an index of stock market prices for the same industry. Since no notable lag was observable between improvement of stock prices and increased investment expenditures, the existence of a positive relationship between these two variables seemed to be best explained by the role that the stock market might play in forming business expectations.

III. *The Model*

The accelerator-residual funds hypothesis is almost solely concerned with the mechanistic, temporal, and short-run relationships between investment outlays and current measures of a firm's performance. The emphasis is upon the relatively short-run or transitional adjustments made in investment programs in response to changes in a firm's immediate environment and achievements.

The essential elements of the theory can be described — at the risk, however, of some oversimplification — in the simple terms of so-called "comparative statics." In such a format, the accelerator-residual funds theory has three equilibrium conditions: (1) that an optimal or least-cost relationship exists between available productive capacity and the individual firm's average output; (2) that the dividend to net profit ratio is at a specified, long-run target level; and (3) that investment is confined to a level that requires little or no outside financing and implicitly has as its objective goals other than increasing productive capacity as such.[2] If this equilibrium is disturbed by an increase in demand (that is, by an increase in the average output that the firm could expect to sell), profits would increase but dividends would rise only gradually and after a lapse of time. The dividend to profit ratio therefore would fall below the long-run target or equilibrium level. The resulting increase in retained earnings, augmented under certain circumstances by outside borrowing, would be used to expand productive capacity until the optimal relationship between capital and output was restored. When the optimal capacity relationship was re-established, dividends would be increased until the target payout level was again achieved (to the extent that stockholder pressures had not already forced this objective). At this point, a new, higher level equilibrium position would be reached corresponding to the enlarged output.

The rate of adjustment between these two equilibria would be influenced by competitive, financial, expectational, and institutional considerations. For example, the more competitive the industry, the more quickly the adjustment should be performed; that is, with competition there would be less use of order backlogs as substitutes for expanded productive capacity. Similarly, the more confidence there was that the increased demand would be permanent, the more rapidly should the new capital equipment be put in place. One possible indicator of such confidence would be if the stock market quickly reflected the increased earnings in improved equity prices. Similarly, for firms in "growth" industries there might be a generally greater *expectation* that increased demand would be a permanent circumstance. In competitive and growth situations, therefore, the

[2] Beyond those mentioned earlier, there are several other opportunities for noncapacity-oriented investment: for example, mergers that lead to a diversification of the company's product line, thereby improving its defense against recession. In the same vein, the liquid assets of the corporation may be built up during these periods as an insurance against any future downturn in business activity. The above choices might be described in terms of the relative marginal profitability of each. Such an approach, however, is probably not too realistic because the choices involved are likely to be large and discontinuous and based on rather vague expectations about the future.

rate of adjustment should be somewhat quicker than otherwise; furthermore, in such circumstances more of the adjustment might be financed from outside funds.

Investment taking place under expanding, fully utilized capacity conditions is thus mainly for the purpose of maintaining optimal productive relationships between capital and output. In periods of less than full utilization of capacity, by contrast, the objectives would be many and diversified.[3] For instance, one of the most important might be cost reduction. Investments aimed at achieving cost reductions might be accompanied, of course, by an incidental expansion of productive capacity, but this would not be considered a major objective. New, more efficient equipment often can be operated more cheaply well below rated capacity than old, anti-quated equipment can be operated at full capacity. Excess capacity may also be desired because it constitutes a good defense against potential entry and prepares the firm for the next general expansion in business activity. Obviously, competition (or its threat) and good growth prospects should stimulate investments of this type, just as they stimulate more rapid expenditure on new productive capacity under expansionary conditions.

Investment under less than full utilization conditions might also be made on product development and research. This kind of invest-ment, of course, may modify the capital output coefficients whose constancy is so important to simple accelerator theories of invest-ment. Again, expenditures of this kind should be positively related to industry growth and the existence of competition, perhaps with the Schumpeterian-type of qualification that the competition is oligopolistic or workable and not too intense.

As already noted, the investment purposes being served during periods of under-capacity utilization are, in many instances, similar to those described as "exogenously generated" in the literature on business cycles. An implication of the accelerator-residual funds

[3] Extremely suggestive and generally compatible evidence on this point can be found in the annual surveys of business investment plans conducted by the McGraw-Hill Department of Economics and reported in *Business Week*. For example, in recent surveys the question has been asked: How much of the planned investment is for expanding productive output and how much for other purposes? The answers generally have confirmed the cyclical pattern postulated here.

theory is that even though the demand for this kind of investment may be exogenously determined, the actual timing of the investment outlays (including inventories and working capital outlays as well as plant and equipment expenditures) may be endogenously determined because of financial, managerial, or other constraints.

Whatever the character of the investments, under circumstances of less than full-capacity utilization total investment would be limited by hypothesis to a level not in excess of the funds internally available after conventional dividend demands have been met. In essence, the difference between internally available funds and the conventional dividend payment is taken as a first approximation to the investment budget for *all* purposes under these circumstances while upward deviations occur only under expansionary circumstances, especially when that expansion occurs in competitive or growth industries. Downward deviations may be imposed when expectations are pessimistic and an increase in the stock of liquid funds is considered desirable. Such adverse conditions, moreover, should be most likely in the early stages of a cyclical downturn.

While the accelerator-residual funds theory places heavy emphasis on the flow of funds as a determinant of the capital budget, it does not imply or connote that the flow of funds is necessarily or always a crucial constraint on investment. Specifically, the theory is not meant to be a variation on the current fashion in economists' theories of the firm in which growth maximization supplants profit maximization in the "objective function" and profits and debt levels assume the roles of constraints. Contrarily, as stated in the original summary of the hypothesis, "the profit motive, closely linked in a world of oligopolistic markets to long-run retention of market share and trade position, remains the central wellspring of entrepreneurial action." [4]

As the exposition in terms of comparative statics should make evident, moreover, the controlling constraint on growth in the accelerator-residual funds hypothesis is the firm's demand function, just as in conventional Marshallian or neoclassical theory. In keeping with these conventional origins, the definition of the demand function is established by a specification of markets in which the

---

[4] Meyer and Kuh, the final sentence of the final chapter, p. 205.

firm's management feels competent to compete and by the extent to which the firm normally has shared in these markets. The ultimate constraint, therefore, is management skill which limits the set of markets and the market shares that determine the firm's demand function. The accelerator-residual funds hypothesis asserts that during periods of expansion, investment is carried to the point where growth and profit maximums specified by these demand constraints are fully satisfied and required financing is *then* arranged in as conservative a manner as possible, mainly so as to minimize managerial risk.[5] Of course, if considerable external financing is required to meet these profit opportunities and a particular management has a high degree of risk aversion, growth may be constrained by financial considerations; however, such occurrences would seem to be rare in true growth situations.

Any process of risk minimization is also necessarily constrained. Clearly, minimum financial risk for the management would be achieved by exclusive reliance on original equity and subsequent retention of earnings. Stockholder pressures, though, usually will prevent a 100% retention policy. Furthermore, even 100% of earnings often may not be sufficient to finance the investments required for profit maximization, particularly in growth and competitive situations. Finally, even if the target dividend payout ratio has been set so as to yield sufficient retained earnings to finance investment needs on the average over the cycle, these calculations can be easily upset by unforeseen and unpredictable developments and funds can be insufficient at particular periods, like a cyclical peak. Accordingly, even the most conservative of managements may resort sometimes to outside financing. External financing, however, will be most common in growth and competitive circumstances since it is in these circumstances that retained earnings usually will fall short of the investment required for profit maximization.

---

[5] The implication in this formulation that investment is not dependent upon debt but that, if anything, debt is dependent upon investment runs counter, of course, to many conventional notions about the relationship of investment to financial patterns. That the proposition advanced here is empirically based, *at least within the range of present corporate financial practices*, seems supported (a) by the generally negative results obtained when attempts are made to corroborate the "increasing risk" debt hypotheses; and (b) the usually positive relationships that are found between debt levels and investment whenever any relationship at all is discernible. For evidence on these points see Chapter VI below.

In a cyclical downturn or nonexpansionary period, on the other hand, the accelerator-residual funds hypothesis avers that the dividend payout ratio and investment aspirations are such that internally generated funds are generally sufficient for investment needs. The direction of causation in the recessionary short-run model primarily runs from availability of funds to investment. By contrast, during periods of expansion and near-capacity utilization, profits influence investment mainly through expectational influences and financing is more a function of investment and funds retention.[6] This asymmetry in the relationship of financial considerations to the investment decision is a crucial aspect of the theory.

In notational form, the more mechanistic aspects of the accelerator-residual funds theory, particularly as these relate to the empirical qualities of the model, might be summarized as follows.

Let: I = investment in productive capacity;

C = a measure of capacity needed for optimal, lowest cost operations at the expected output level;

K = the existing stock of capital goods, measured in the same units as C;

p = the sales price of the commodity produced (or some appropriate index of prices if more than one commodity is produced);

ATC_0 = the lowest attainable average total cost per unit of output (again, an index if more than one commodity is produced);

p/ATC_0 = a very rough measure of market power or lack of competition;

$\bar{S}'$ = the average increase in *sales* over a specified number of years in the past, taken as a measure of growth;

E' = the increase (say, over the last year) in the company's or, better, the industry's equity share prices on the stock market, taken as a measure of business confidence;

P = net profits after all charges but before dividends, i.e, net income to surplus;

[6] For an interesting formulation and test of the accelerator-residual funds hypothesis in which the rate of external borrowing is the dependent variable, see W. H. Locke Anderson, "A Regression Study of Manufacturing Finance," paper presented at Meeting of the Econometric Society, St. Louis, December 1960. Abstract in *Econometrica*, Vol. 29, No. 3 (July 1961), p. 455.

D = depreciation charges on current account;
V = total cash dividend payments.

Then, if $\dfrac{C}{K} \geqslant 1.0$ (i.e., capacity is fully or more than fully utilized):

(II.1) $I = f_1(C, p/ATC_0, D, \bar{S}', E')$.

If capacity is not fully utilized $\left(\dfrac{C}{K} < 1.0\right)$:

(II.2) $I = f_2(P - V, D,$ and possibly $\bar{S}'$ and E' as well).

Further, if depreciation expense is hypothesized *not* to have a greater influence on investment than other forms of internal financing, D should be eliminated from (II.1) and (II.2) rewritten as follows:

(II.3) $I = f_3(P + D - V, \bar{S}', E')$.

All variables would be expected to have positive signs except p/ATC_0, which should be negative.

In most empirical applications the minimum attainable costs needed for p/ATC_0 will not be known, nor will it usually be easy to derive a suitable price index for the multiple product firms that characterize modern manufacturing operations. Therefore, in cross-section analyses, profits as a percentage of sales, gross fixed assets, or some other measure of output or total investment may have to be accepted as a proxy measure of p/ATC_0 and none of these profit variable proxies will be particularly satisfactory. For one thing, profits also measure several other factors that influence investment and these influences generally have a positive effect on investment, just the opposite of the hypothesized relationship if profits are accepted as a measure of market power. Given these countervailing effects, observed regression or correlation relationships between profits and investment could be slight or even negative during periods of rapid expansion; that is, when model (II.1) is hypothesized to hold.

An alternative and probably superior approach to measuring market competition would be to associate differences in market structure with differences in industry characteristics. In fact, the extent or prevalence of competition is a variable that is evaluated mainly in terms of behavior in a given product market and is therefore somewhat more intelligible as an industry than an individual firm variable.

Similar remarks apply almost as forcibly to the growth variable, $\bar{S}'$, particularly to the extent that the growth prospects are a function of the industry's rather than the firm's own experiences. However, the essential aspect of growth from the investment standpoint probably is its effect on expectations. Accordingly, different degrees of past sales growth success realized by different firms in an industry might give rise to different responses to short-run overutilization of capacity or recent sales changes. On cross-section samples the simplest and most promising measure of an individual firm's previous sales achievements is probably its present absolute sales position or some average of recent sales experience. In essence, an absolute sales variable in a cross-section analysis is more a measure of the longer-run position of the firm while the capacity variable, normalized in terms of an individual firm's experience, and changes in sales are more measures of shorter-run influences.

The cross-section analysis problem of separating short-run from long-run influence is also difficult with profit and profit related variables. As already noted, the simple or unmodified profit variable is usually closely related to sales in cross-section samples and, therefore, like sales is probably a measure of many long-run influences. The total cash throwoff, net profits plus depreciation expense, unquestionably reflects similar characteristics. However, subtraction of the dividend payment from either profits or cash throwoff could materially alter the picture. For example, in cross-section data observed profit levels may be considered to be the sum of permanent and transitory influences and it is not unreasonable to suppose that the dividend payment is based mainly on the permanent component. Indeed, the dividend payment itself seems to have a strong tendency toward stability and lack of transitory elements. As such, subtraction of the dividend payment from profits probably reduces the relative importance of covariation attributable to the permanent component in the profit and cash throwoff variables. The adjusted or after dividend profit or cash throwoff variables therefore might be measures more of short-run and transitory influences.

The models of the accelerator-residual funds hypothesis employed in the actual empirical analyses reported in subsequent pages are more or less like (II.1), (II.2), and (II.3) above except that profits, absolute sales, and the changes in sales are used instead of the difficult to define and estimate p/ATC_0 and $\bar{S}'$ variables. In addition, almost all of the actual empirical models are cast in a so-called distributed-lag format by including lagged investment as an additional explanatory variable. Inclusion of a lagged value of the dependent variable as an independent variable raises a number of questions about interpretation and estimation procedures which are discussed in the next section.

IV. *Lagged Investment as an Explanatory Variable*

Several interpretations can be assigned to a lagged value of the dependent variable used as an explanatory variable in an econometric model. One of the more common is to assume the existence of a distributed lag in one of the other explanatory variables and use the lagged dependent variable as a representation of these effects. For example, investment might be hypothesized to be a function of sales, change in sales, or profit levels not of just the current period or the period before but of the past several periods. However, because of multicollinearity and other statistical problems,[7] it is usually not considered desirable to include a large number of lagged values of any one explanatory variable in a regression model. A simple way to circumvent these problems derives from the fact that the value of the dependent variable lagged one period would be a function of the same lagged values of the explanatory variable as the current dependent variable except for one additional term, the most ancient value of the explanatory variable, and one less term, the most recent value of the explanatory variable. If, in addition, the importance of the explanatory variable declines the more time that has elapsed (and preferably declines in a geometric pattern), a reasonably good approximation to a distributed-lag structure can be obtained by using only two explanatory variables, the current value of the origi-

---

[7] For further elaboration on these problems, see Leendert Marinus Koyck, *Distributed Lags and Investment Analysis* (Amsterdam: North-Holland Publishing Co., 1954), and L. R. Klein, "The Estimation of Distributed Lags," *Econometrica*, Vol. 26, No. 4 (October 1958), pp. 553–565.

nal explanatory variable and a lagged value of the dependent variable. Algebraically this argument can be summarized as follows.

Let:
$$I_t = X_t + \sum_{j=1}^{N} \lambda^j X_{t-j} \cong X_t + \lambda I_{t-1}$$

since
$$\lambda I_{t-1} \cong \sum_{j=1}^{N} \lambda^j X_{t-j}$$

where I is the dependent variable, X is the "distributed lag" explanatory variable, $0 < \lambda < 1$, and N is the number of periods of experience previous to the present one having an influence on I_t.

To take a more explicit example, investment might be hypothesized to be described by the sum of historical relationships between changes in sales (taken as a causal factor) and investment. Starting with no capital whatsoever, the firm's expansion through investment outlays would occur only when stimulated by an increase in sales and the investment outlay at any point in time would depend on a complex weighted sum of previous sales changes. Rather than regressing on all these lagged values, the statistical problem could be simplified by letting I_{t-1} represent all the lagged sales changes previous to the most recent, a permissible procedure as long as the influence of previous sales changes declined exponentially or approximately so.

This simple accelerator formulation bears, moreover, a relationship to the original distributed lag formulations as applied to investment models by Koyck.[8] Koyck began by hypothesizing that the whole adjustment path of K is approximated by an exponential curve so that:

$$K_t = \sum_{j=0}^{\infty} \alpha_0 \lambda^j S_{t-j}$$

where, as before, K designates capital stock, S sales, and α_0 is a fixed capital coefficient. Koyck then deduces what he terms a "simple relationship" for the change in K, denoted by K', which can be taken (temporarily overlooking any measurement difficulties) as equal to investment, I.

[8] Koyck, *op. cit.*, Chapter II.

Thus:
$$K_{t+1} = \alpha_0 S_{t+1} + \alpha_0\lambda S_t + \alpha_0\lambda^2 S_{t-1} + \cdots$$
$$\lambda K_t = \alpha_0\lambda S_t + \alpha_0\lambda^2 S_{t-1} + \cdots$$
$$K_{t+1} - \lambda K_t = \alpha_0 S_{t+1}$$

or
$$K_{t+1} - K_t = \alpha_0 S_{t+1} - (1 - \lambda)K_t = I_{t+1}$$

or
$$I_{t+1} = \alpha_0 S_{t+1} - BK_t$$

where $B = 1 - \lambda$. Investment, in short, is hypothesized to be a function of current sales and lagged capital stock. One method of obtaining the alternative distributed lag accelerator formulation, that is, investment as a function of the current change in sales and lagged investment, is to difference, so to speak, "earlier" in the ·proceedings. Thus assume:

$$I_{t+1} = K'_{t+1} = \alpha_0 S'_{t+1} + \alpha_0\lambda S'_t + \alpha_0\lambda^2 S'_{t-1} + \cdots$$

then
$$\lambda I_t = \alpha_0\lambda S'_t + \alpha_0\lambda^2 S'_{t-1} + \cdots$$

and
$$I_{t+1} = \alpha_0 S'_{t+1} + \lambda I_t.$$

An alternative, and in many respects simpler, rationalization for including a lagged value of the dependent variable as an explanatory variable can be obtained by formulating hypotheses directly about the variable to be estimated in terms of target levels that are realized or achieved only with a lag. The Lintner dividend hypothesis and some of Nerlove's agricultural functions are excellent examples of such models.[9] In these formulations attention usually centers directly on the dependent variable as a policy variable to be controlled and the policy objective is stated in terms of a *desired flow rather than a stock*. For investment the basic hypothesis would be that investment itself is to be set at some desired level and there would be no direct concern with the capital stock as such.

A great advantage of this approach in investment studies is that it accommodates a wider spectrum of possible reasons for undertaking investment outlays than any simple stock adjustment model, particularly if the latter is technologically defined. Thus, a "flow approach" directly incorporates the fact that investments can be

[9] John Lintner, "The Determinants of Corporate Savings," in Walter W. Heller, Francis M. Boddy, and Carl L. Nelson, eds., *Savings in the Modern Economy* (Minneapolis: University of Minnesota Press, 1953), and Marc Nerlove, *Distributed Lags and Demand Analysis for Agricultural and Other Commodities*, U.S. Department of Agriculture Handbook No. 141 (1958).

made for other reasons than adjusting capital stock to some optimum level and makes it possible for investment outlays to occur in periods of declining sales for reasons other than a distributed lag influence of long-previous sales changes.   The flow approach, in short, lends itself to an eclectic approach to investment theorizing.

This does not mean, of course, that discrepancies between desired and existing stocks might not influence investment decisions.   As in the accelerator-residual funds theory just propounded they might under certain circumstances even become the dominant influence. Nor does it deny that a *long-run* relationship usually must exist between levels of output and capital stock.   That is, the assertion that *short-run* investment outlays are sometimes adjusted to considerations other than the need for additional productive capacity does not constitute a denial of the proposition that it is necessary (technology and product assumed reasonably constant) for the capital stock to be adjusted in the long run to the level of output. What the flow approach does deny is that the short-run movements toward these long-run capacity-output equilibria are strictly a weighted function of previous sales changes and are never influenced by other considerations, such as product innovation, cost reduction, and competitive strategy, ingredients which have been argued previously to be possible elements in a good investment model.

A target level-lagged adjustment interpretation can be applied readily to the accelerator-residual funds theory.   In a nonexpansionary period, the basic hypothesis of the residual funds theory is that desired investment equals some percentage of a specified fund flow.   If we assume that the appropriate fund flow is some measure of the net available cash, say $P + D - V$, and use the subscript d to denote a desired level, the basic relationship can be expressed as follows:

$$I_d = \alpha(P + D - V)$$

where α is the target ratio of funds to be spent on investment. Delay in realizing the desired goal can be expressed by subtracting lagged investment from both sides of the preceding equation; similarly, actual investment can be substituted for desired investment by introducing a new parameter, B, a coefficient of adjustment.

Thus:

$$I_d - I_{t-1} = \alpha(P + D - V) - I_{t-1}$$

and

$$I_t - I_{t-1} = B[\alpha(P + D - V) - I_{t-1}].$$

Also, lagged investment can be cleared from the lefthand side of the equation with the following simplification:

$$I_t = \alpha B(P + D - V) + (1 - B)I_{t-1}.$$

An important aspect of this formulation is that the lagged value of the dependent variable enters the equation on its own merit rather than as a proxy for other variables. Consequently, there are no automatic statistical bias problems to be considered, whereas there can be with distributed lag formulations, and usually will be when analyzing a distributed lag model with time series data.

A reaction coefficient type model, differing a bit from the above version, can be developed for the expansionary or accelerator oriented formulations of the accelerator-residual funds model. For example, a target investment rate could be defined by applying a simple capital coefficient to the sales variable, following usual procedures for formulating acceleration hypotheses. As before, a delay could be assumed between adjusting to the technologically defined desired investment level and the realized level. For example, by hypothesis let:

$$K_{dt} = \alpha S_t$$

where K_{dt} is desired capital stock at time t, S_t is sales at that same time, and α is the usual capital coefficient. Then

$$I_{dt} = K'_{dt} = \alpha S_t - K_{t-1}$$

where I_{dt} is the desired investment level, K'_{dt} designates the desired change in capital stock, and K_{t-1} represents the capital stock at the *end* of the previous period. A conventional lagged adjustment hypothesis is to assume that actual investment, say I_t, deviates from the desired by some constant proportion (usually called the reaction coefficient) of the discrepancy between actual and desired capital stock. Thus if B is the reaction coefficient:

$$I_t = B[\alpha S_t - K_{t-1}].$$

In this formulation, of course, lagged investment does not enter as an explanatory variable.[10]

An equally plausible hypothesis about the lagged adjustment might be that it is the rate of investment itself that is difficult to increase. Accordingly, the delay in adjustment would not be proportional to the gap between desired and actual capital stock but to the gap between the desired rate of investment and the previously achieved rate. In short, the absolute size of the "adjustment chore" does not matter but rather the discrepancy between the needed adjustment and how fast the adjustments have been made previously. In this case,

$$I_{dt} - I_{t-1} = \alpha S_t - K_{t-1} - I_{t-1}$$
$$I_t - I_{t-1} = B\left[\alpha S_t - K_{t-1} - I_{t-1}\right]$$
$$I_t = \alpha B S_t - B K_{t-1} + (1 - B)I_{t-1}$$

and lagged investment enters as an explanatory variable. If α were thought to be roughly the same for all observations in a cross-section sample, more than enough information to estimate B and α could be obtained by simply regressing I_t on S_t, and K_{t-1}, and I_{t-1}.[11]

A slightly different approach to the estimation of α and B is needed if a capacity variable, C, is employed which is distinctive to each firm. In a cross-section study use of such a variable basically implies that some doubts are retained about the constancy of α over the sample group, regardless of how carefully the group may have been defined so as to eliminate heterogeneous technologies and practices. Basically the use of the capacity variable amounts to specifying a unique α for each firm. For example, in the 1946–1950 study the following type of capacity variable was used:

$$C_{it} = R_{Ii}S_t = \left[(K/S) \text{ minimum, } 1947–1950\right] S_t$$

[10] This reaction coefficient is, of course, similar to those hypothesized by R. M. Goodwin, "The Nonlinear Accelerator and the Persistence of Business Cycles," *Econometrica*, Vol. 19, No. 1 (January 1951), pp. 1–17, and Hollis B. Chenery, "Over Capacity and the Acceleration Principle," *Econometrica*, Vol. 20, No. 1 (January 1952), pp. 1–28.

[11] If, however, K_{t-1} has been used as a deflator, its coefficient would be hidden in the constant term in the equation until, or unless $1/K_{t-1}$ was also introduced in which case the original constant would be the coefficient of $1/K_{t-1}$ and the "observed constant" would be B. Thus, for simple regression models without $1/K_{t-1}$ in cross-section analysis the relevant or best estimate of B would be the regression coefficient of I_{t-1}, subtracted from one.

where i designates the ith firm and K is the capital stock (as measured by gross fixed assets) at the end of the period in which the K/S minimum is achieved. Therefore R_{Ii} can be interpreted as an estimate of α_i where this "capital coefficient" is unique to each firm. The "uniqueness" of each α_i, that is, interfirm differences in this parameter, can be attributed to many causes: for example, residual differences in the technologies employed within the sample group, differences in the assessment of the competitive situation or differences in the cyclical fluctuations in output experienced by the firms that lead to different evaluations attached to having standby capacity, etc. The use of R_{Ii} as an estimate of α_i is also a special illustration of the technique of so-called extraneous estimation. If the lagged adjustment is again assumed proportional to the discrepancy between currently desired and previously attained investment, an accelerator model with capacity used as an explanatory variable becomes:

$$I_d - I_{t-1} = C_t - K_{t-1} - I_{t-1}$$
$$I_t - I_{t-1} = B[(C_t - K_{t-1}) - I_{t-1}]$$
$$I_t = BC_t - BK_{t-1} + (1 - B)I_{t-1}$$

since now $C_t = \alpha S_t$.[12]

V. *Conclusion*

It would be more than brash to suggest that the theory, as just briefly outlined, encompasses all the diversity and complications that occur in business investment decisions in the modern American economy. Indeed, encompassing all these complexities is not necessarily a valid objective. The real question is whether the model reflects a wide and important range of reality, particularly in the manufacturing industries to which it is expressly addressed. At

[12] If this hypothesis holds, interestingly enough, the regression coefficients obtained by regressing I_t and C_t, $1/K_{t-1}$, and I_{t-1} and using K_{t-1} as a deflator, should result in the C variable's regression parameter being roughly equal to the regression constant and one less the parameter for I_{t-1}. A discussion of the general problems of estimation bias that may arise from certain specification errors when using cross-section data to estimate lagged adjustment models can be found in Yehuda Grunfeld, "The Interpretation of Cross Section Estimates in a Dynamic Model," *Econometrica*, Vol. 29, No. 3 (July 1961), pp. 397–404.

this point it is impossible to say whether the model really meets this test. Much more empirical evidence is necessary before any firm conclusions on this point can be reached and only a start is made at answering this empirical question in the pages that follow. In particular, a good deal more should be known about the ability of the model to predict aggregate investment behavior over time in a way that is useful for policy purposes. However, on the bases of the evidence presented here and in the earlier Meyer-Kuh study, the hypothesis at least appears to be suggestive and worth further testing. Too, the model appears at least as compatible with existing or available empirical evidence as any alternative theory of investment behavior — though this may be faint praise.

One unresolved problem of particular difficulty is how best to account for continuity or cumulative effects observable in investment processes. If the emphasis is placed on cumulation and the adjustment of a capital stock to levels of the explanatory variables, the empirical implementation of the model can be facilitated by assuming fixed weights or a particular pattern of weights for lagged values of explanatory variables. If the emphasis is instead on continuity in the flow of new capital or investment, a lagged value of the dependent investment variable provides a very direct, flexible, and independent measure of these effects. A flow format has the further advantage, at least from the standpoint of this study, of being somewhat more compatible with an eclectic approach to defining the determinants of investment.[13]

---

[13] Given uncertainty about the autoregressive properties of these models, the generally very high observed multiple correlations in the time-series analyses (see Chapter 7), and the emphasis on forecasting in this study, little gain seems attainable from employing methods designed to obtain statistically consistent estimates of the parameters associated with lagged investment when autocorrelated error terms exist. Determination of error autocorrelation in these cases is complicated, moreover, by the fact that the usual tests are biased. A more thorough treatment of these points can be found in T. Wilson and L. Taylor, "Estimation of Models with a Lagged Dependent Variable," a paper presented at the Cleveland meetings of the Econometric Society, September 1963.

Chapter **III** | *Notes on Samples and Variables*

I. *The Samples: Sources and Characteristics*

The samples used in this study are of two distinct types, cross sections and time series. The cross-section samples are composed of observations on a number of individual firms at one point in time. By contrast, the time-series samples are composed of observations over time of aggregates of individuals grouped by industrial or product sectors.

That cross-section and time-series samples are not the same and cannot always be expected to measure identical types of behavior hardly can be overemphasized. For example, hypotheses about long-term consumer or producer adjustments to different goals, especially when the adjustments are subject to the Marshallian or neoclassical constraints of static technology and preferences, are not readily tested by most time-series data. When the time period covered by the sample is relatively short, as it usually is in economics, there often will not be sufficient "experience" represented in the data for accurate inferences. The longer the time period included in a given sample, on the other hand, the greater the possibility of structural shifts, nonlinearities, or other modifications in behavior occurring that cannot be encompassed in a conveniently simple econometric model. In fact, such shifts in behavior patterns are often so difficult to handle in an empirical model that many time-series studies are based on relatively short series even when longer series are available; for example, it is not uncommon to analyze pre-World War II and postwar data separately. As a further handicap, most time-series samples used in economics are composed of aggregate figures that do not reflect much of the covariation that is indispensable for testing certain micro-hypotheses.

Hypotheses about variables that vary primarily over time, by contrast, usually cannot be tested conveniently with cross-section data. Cross-section samples emphasize inter-individual differences. Some of these differences will be long-run and fairly permanent in character; others will be short-run and transitory. While the behavioral relationships associated with short-run, transitory changes usually will be reflected in time-series data too, the longer-run, more permanent inter-individual differences often are not observable in time-series data. It is this greater possibility of testing hypotheses about long-run relationships that mainly differentiates the cross-section from the time-series study.

Care must be exercised when using cross sections to insure, in fact, that long-run and short-run effects are not indiscriminately mingled. Under certain conditions, such intermingling can give rise to a bias in cross-section results usually labeled as the "regression fallacy." [1] There are two basic methods of eliminating or minimizing this bias. The first is to take steps to insure that the variance of transitory or short-run effects is small compared with the variance of long-run influences. In many cross sections this condition may be met almost automatically; in other cases, averaging of cross-section observations over a number of years may prove helpful. [2] A second approach is to introduce an additional variable that measures, at least approximately, the extent of either the

[1] This use of the term "regression fallacy" has been popularized in economics by Milton Friedman, *A Theory of the Consumption Function.* A study by the National Bureau of Economic Research, New York. (Princeton: Princeton University Press, 1957).

[2] For suggestions along this line, see John Johnston, *Statistical Cost Analysis* (New York: McGraw-Hill Book Company, 1960), Chapter VI, and John R. Meyer and Gerald Kraft, "The Evaluation of Statistical Costing Techniques as Applied in the Transportation Industry," *American Economic Review*, Vol. 51, No. 2 (May 1961), pp. 313–334.

transient or permanent influences or, alternatively, that provides a method of separating short-run and long-run effects. The introduction of capital stock variables in cross-section cost studies is an example of an attempt at such separation; similarly, first difference variables or lagged values of the dependent variable used as an explanatory variable often will prove helpful. In the present study, transient influences have been controlled mainly by the second approach, that is, by introducing additional variables that are, hopefully, related and identifiable with either permanent or transient influences.

The cross-section samples used in the present study are composed primarily of large manufacturing firms and, in particular, large manufacturing firms in industries with relatively high capital intensity and investment rates. The time periods covered are the years 1951 through 1954. The specific manufacturing industries included are: textiles, chemicals, petroleum, rubber, primary iron and steel, fabricated metal products, electrical machinery, other machinery, motor vehicles and equipment, and pulp and paper. In most respects the present sample is very similar to that employed in the 1946–1950 investment study by Meyer and Kuh.[3] The basic sources of data in both cases were the Securities and Exchange Commission Form 10K and publicly available company reports. The SEC reports provided needed information on investment outlays and also provided an opportunity to obtain information which is normally reported on company statements but occasionally is omitted, especially by smaller firms. With the exception of the investment data, and an occasional missing figure, the data came from company reports as found in Moody's or Standard and Poor's Industrial Manuals.

One major departure from the data collection and sampling procedures used in the earlier investment study was to exclude from *all years* of the sample any firm that was involved in a relatively

---

[3] A full description of the sample used in the earlier study, and therefore in essence also of the present sample, will be found in Meyer and Kuh, *The Investment Decision*, Chapter 3. Additional information on the characteristics of the sample can be obtained from descriptions of the "SEC segment" of the Federal Trade Commission — Securities and Exchange Commission quarterly sample of manufacturing corporations described in the FTC–SEC *Quarterly Financial Reports: U.S. Manufacturing Corporations.*

large merger at any time during the period of study. In the earlier sample, firms involved in mergers were excluded only for the year in which the merger took place. This complete exclusion was done to achieve a sample that was absolutely identical in its composition throughout the four-year period. Thus, no year-to-year differences in observed behavioral characteristics can possibly be attributed to differences in the sample.[4]

Sample homogeneity for all four years of the study was achieved, obviously, at the expense of reducing the number of observations that otherwise might have been available for any one year. Compared with the cross-section sample used in the 1946–1950 study, however, this reduction was more than offset by three developments. First, the availability of greater financial resources for financing clerical operations in the present study made it possible to exhaust completely the entire list of firms publicly registered with the SEC. Second, a marked increase occurred in certain industries in the number of firms publicly registered with the SEC between 1946 and 1951. Finally, firms whose investments for any given year exceeded more than .5 of their existing gross fixed assets at the beginning of the year were not excluded from the present study, whereas they were excluded from the earlier study. Before adopting this revised procedure, a careful comparison was made for every year in the sample of the simple correlations obtained by including or excluding these rapid growth firms for five test industries: pulp and paper, heavy chemicals, heavy steel, heavy electrical equipment, and basic textiles. In few cases did the simple correlations vary by more than .02 and seldom was the difference that large. The effect on partial regression and correlation estimates would be correspondingly small. Accordingly, the inclusion of firms with investment growth rates greater than .5 was considered to be of little practical importance and was abandoned as a procedure that unnecessarily complicated the computations.

The increase in the number of publicly registered firms, the more

---

[4] Similarly, the occasional firm that changed its reportorial habits during the four-year period so that complete sets of data were available for some years but not for others were also excluded from the sample for all four years; the net effect of this action, however, was quite small because most firms that failed to report needed data for one year of a study also failed to report it for all years.

exhaustive search for data, and the inclusion of firms with investment rates in excess of .5 substantially augmented the number of
available observations in the 1951–1954 sample compared with the
1946–1950 sample in two industries, metal fabricated products and
other machinery. This in turn made it possible to reconsider the
appropriateness of the industry groups used in the 1946–1950 study.

Defining the appropriate sample group is perhaps the most difficult
practical problem in using cross-section samples. The grouping
problem is not, of course, unique to cross-section studies. The
greater number of observations normally available in cross-section
samples does complicate the problem, though, by substantially
increasing the number of feasible or seemingly logical groupings.
Cross-section samples usually will be comprised of several hundred
observations. In time-series applications, by contrast (especially
those based on annual aggregates), the total of available observations rarely exceeds 30 in number. Under such circumstances, an
obvious division into two groups, such as prewar and postwar, often
may exhaust the range of feasible alternatives and also provide a
reasonably satisfactory solution to the grouping problem.

For the study of business behavior the appropriate sample group
usually must have some sort of relationship initially to an industry
or product grouping. The cross-section stratification problem is to
determine what modifications in traditional industry or product
groups might be desirable or appropriate in light of the objectives
of the study. One obviously desirable property for any sample
group is that it have homogeneous behavioral characteristics with
respect to the particular kind of behavior being studied. For an
investment study, for example, individuals included within a particular group should not be widely divergent in the expected values of
their investment relationships or parameters.

One method of trying to improve the behavioral homogeneity of
industry groups is to employ a variable that is known to have a
particularly important or sensitive influence in the behavioral relationship under study and test it for its variance in alternative groupings, those groupings yielding a minimum within-group variance
being selected for further study. In the present case, the capital
to output ratio is a variable that might be expected to have a substantial, technologically defined relationship to investment.   In

both this and the previous investment study, therefore, basic Standard Industrial Classification and Securities and Exchange Commission definitions of industry groups were altered so as to achieve a reduction in the within-group variance of the capital to output ratio. For the 1951–1954 sample, the increase in the number of available observations permitted a subdivision of the over-all sample into slightly more narrowly or homogeneously defined industry groups than seemed possible with the 1946–1950 sample. Explicitly, 15 industry groupings always were employed in the earlier study and 19 in the present study. In addition, the electronics industry has been extensively used in this study, despite a very small number of observations, whereas it was used only in the big with small firm comparisons in the original study; therefore the total number of industries in the present work is for many purposes 20.

Ten of the 15 industries used in the original study were left as they were before; these were pulp and paper, light chemicals, heavy chemicals, petroleum, rubber, light electrical machinery, heavy electrical machinery, machine tools, basic textiles, and other textiles. Thus, five industries of the original study were regrouped to form nine industries in the present study. These five were heavy steel, metal products, other machinery, motor vehicles and suppliers, and household durables. The nine industries created from these five industries were heavy steel; fabricated metal products (rivets, screws, wire, roller bearings, and similar products); special industrial machinery; general industrial machinery; heavy equipment, engines, and turbines; air conditioning, heating, and similar equipment; household durables; auto fabricators; and auto parts and accessories. A schematic summary of the industry alterations is shown in Figure III–1; breadth of the different arrows in the figure roughly corresponds to the approximate number of firms represented in each redistribution.

Two important effects of the industry redistributions were to split the other machinery industry into three almost equal groups and the motor vehicles and suppliers industry into two groups, one large in numbers (auto parts and accessories) and one small (auto fabricators). The fabricated metal products industry was divided into two major and three minor groups; the main result was to separate the machinery and larger sheet metal product suppliers

FIGURE III–1

A Comparison of Industry Groups Used in 1946–1950
and 1951–1954 Studies

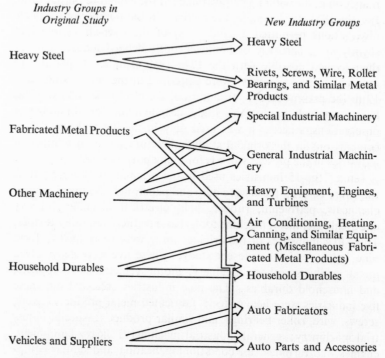

*Industry Groups in
Original Study*

New Industry Groups

from the manufacturers of the "smaller" sheet metal products like
rivets, wire, screws, and roller bearings. The two major groups
created from the fabricated metal products industry thus are described as "rivets, screws, wire, roller bearings, and similar metal
products producers" and "air conditioning, heating, canning, and
similar equipment manufacturers." The rivets, screws, etc., group
is substantially the more homogeneous of the two and subsequently
is described simply as "fabricated metal products." Three small
splinter groups from fabricated metal products were allocated to
general industrial machinery, household durables, and auto parts
and accessories. Household durables, like vehicles and suppliers,
was broken into two subgroups, one large and one quite small.

The heavy steel industry was only slightly modified; to be exact, three firms were moved from heavy steel into the fabricated metal products group. A more exact statement of the various industries' composition will be found in Appendix A where a listing by industry group is provided of the individual firms in the sample.

Even with the finer industry stratification of the 1951–1954 sample, it must be recognized that each of the industry sample groups probably still contains a number of heterogeneous or highly divergent observations. Unfortunately for the economist as a statistician, different policy or managerial characteristics may give rise to different behavioral patterns for firms that are identical in capital utilization, product, technological, and other economic characteristics. Some of the remaining behavioral heterogeneity might be removed, of course, by redefining or including more variables. Similarly, the use of normative ratios, first differences, and other such devices is a possible means of removing some inter-firm differences. Several attempts of this type were made as part of this study and are described subsequently; these efforts, however, have not been completely successful.

On the other hand, it is the grossest sort of misunderstanding of the character of the cross-section samples used in this study to claim that no controls over heterogeneous elements have been attained. For example, it is simply not true that the procedures used here are akin to comparing the investment behavior of "flower sellers" with an industrial firm.[5] A major objective of the "grouping exercises" just described was to eliminate such absurd comparisons.

In contrast with the cross-section data, the time-series samples used in this study are simple and relatively conventional in character. The most important single source of data for the time-series analyses was the Federal Trade Commission — Securities and Exchange Commission, *Quarterly Financial Report: U.S. Manufacturing Corporations*. These data were adjusted to compensate for changes in the sample size during the period under study.[6] Other sources of time-

---

[5] As stated by R. Eisner and R. Strotz in a study, "The Determinants of Business Investment," *Impacts of Monetary Policy*, Commission on Money and Credit Research Monographs (Englewood Cliffs: Prentice Hall, 1963).

[6] The splicing was performed by Professor W. H. Locke Anderson of the University of Michigan who generously made the corrected data available for this study.

series data were Moody's AAA industrial bond rates, Standard and Poor's common stock price index, series on industrial manufacturing capacity published by the McGraw-Hill Publishing Company,[7] the Federal Reserve Board's index of manufacturing production, and the *Survey of Current Business* (which was the primary source for the dependent variable, corporate investment expenditures for new plant and equipment).

It was deemed advisable to deflate all money variables in the time-series analyses (except the interest rate and stock price variables which were obviously of a different character) to reduce the possibility of spurious results due to price changes. The deflator used was formed from the *Survey of Current Business* implicit price deflators for producers' durable equipment and new construction (non-residential), the former weighted twice and the latter once.[8] The weighting reflects the approximate relative importance of the two series in total investment expenditures. All the time-series data are on a quarterly basis.

II. *The Variables: Definitions and Properties* [9]

As just noted, the cross-section variables used in this study are based mainly upon balance sheet and income statements reported to stockholders. The only notable exception to this rule is the investment variable which, as indicated in the previous section, was taken from the Securities and Exchange Commission Form 10K. In keeping with these origins the variables used in this study have been defined in customary accounting terms. Thus, the terminology used in Table III-1, which presents a summary of the cross-section variables used in this study, is the same as might be used in any standard introductory accounting textbook. A substantial effort

[7] For the capacity series, see McGraw-Hill Publishing Co., *Business Plans for New Plants and Equipment* (New York: 1959 and 1960). The annual capacity series was interpolated to a quarterly basis by using the SEC–OBE investment series taken from the *Survey of Current Business.*

[8] This deflator closely parallels the one used by Franco Modigliani and H. M. Wiengartner, "Forecasting Uses of Anticipatory Data on Investment and Sales," *Quarterly Journal of Economics*, Vol. 72, No. 1 (February 1958), pp. 23–54.

[9] The choice of variables is explained more fully in the next chapter.

also has been made to keep the variables simple in character. The only complexity is attributable to the manner in which the various underlying component parts have been synthesized or manipulated into new variables. Therefore an attempt also has been made to build up systematically definitions of the variables in terms of component values that would be obtained directly from underlying income statements or balance sheets.

The most complex of the variables are those involving "achievement ratios" for individual firms. Three such ratios are employed in the present study: R_{Yi}, R_{Ri}, R_{Ii}. The first of these, R_{Yi}, represents the smallest inventory to sales ratio on which an individual firm operated during the 1951–1954 period. Similarly, R_{Ri} is the minimum accounts receivable to sales ratio for each particular firm during the years 1951–1954. Finally, R_{Ii} is the minimum capital to output ratio (as measured by the ratio of gross fixed assets to sales) attained by each particular firm during the four-year period. In each case the minimum ratio pertains only to one firm. The effect of using these ratios is, therefore, to normalize each firm's observation in terms of its own performance or achievement. These ratio variables are not used as explanatory or dependent variables themselves but are employed instrumentally with other variables (in the present case always sales or change in sales) to define new variables that are used directly in the study. The capacity variable C_i is an illustrative case.

The capacity variable, C_i, has, incidentally, been the subject of considerable confusion in discussions of the 1946–1950 investment study in which it was first employed. This variable, deflated, is the quotient of two terms: the current level of sales, S_t, divided by the first of the same year's stock of gross fixed assets, K_{t-1}, divided by the ratio of sales to the *end* of the same year's stock of gross fixed assets in the year when that ratio was highest; this latter term or divisor is, of course, $1/R_{Ii}$. Denoting by t_0 the year in which S_t/K_t attains its peak value, then for the ith firm

$$R_{Ii} = \frac{K_{it_0}}{S_{it_0}}$$

and the C_i variable for any year, t, can be represented algebraically as:

$$C_{it} = \frac{\frac{S_{it}}{K_{it-1}}}{\frac{1}{R_{Ii}}} = \frac{S_{it}}{K_{it-1}} \cdot R_{Ii} = \frac{S_{it}}{K_{it-1}} \cdot \frac{K_{it_0}}{S_{it_0}}.$$

An important complication arises when R_{Ii} occurs in the same year as the year under analysis, since in this case

$$R_{Ii} = \frac{K_{it}}{S_{it}}$$

and

$$C_{it} = \frac{\frac{S_{it}}{K_{it-1}}}{\frac{S_{it}}{K_{it}}} = \frac{K_{it}}{K_{it-1}}.$$

Under such circumstances, if $K_t = I_t + K_{t-1}$ (or $K_t' = I_t$) for all observations in the sample, it is obvious that regressing I_t on C_t should yield a high correlation, unity to be exact. More generally, and as pointed out in the earlier investment study, there would be reasons for suspecting a comparison of correlations between C_t and I_t in different industries and years if: (1) there was a tendency for $\frac{S_{it_0}}{K_{it_0}}$ to congregate or bunch heavily in certain industry-years and these were the industry years when the correlation between C_t and I_t were highest; and (2) there really was a close identity between I_t and K_t', that is, between investment outlays and changes in gross fixed assets. It must be emphasized that these two conditions must hold simultaneously for the C_t with I_t correlation to be considered spurious.

The second of these two required conditions is the more likely, though it is not an absolute certainty. I_t will differ from K_t' on a cross-section sample for several reasons. For example, different firms can follow different accounting practices with respect to capital retirements. Similarly, firms with identical investment outlay can record different changes in gross fixed assets because one firm might be involved in a merger while the other was not, or because one acquired real estate or land while the other did not. Many other reasons might be advanced as to why I_t might not equal K_t'. *It should be noted that all these differences flow from the fact that*

K_t' *takes account of all sorts of influences and acts besides those strictly attributable to the decision to invest.* The obvious corollary is that K_t' is a very poor variable to use as a dependent variable or as a measure of investment in a study of investment behavior,[10] as occasionally has been done. If nothing else, use of such a "proxy measure" for investment builds in a bias toward finding a high correlation between investment and change in sales since the extreme K_t' and S_t' observations often will be generated by the same common cause, namely merger, which has nothing to do with most investment theories.

An interesting, but incorrect, attempt [11] has been made to explain the high 1946 I_t with C_t correlations recorded in the earlier investment study on the grounds that the C_t variable is always dominated by the capital ratio in its composition. Explicitly, again denoting by t_0 the year in which R_{Ii} occurs, the capacity variable for the jth year preceding t_0 could be rewritten as:

$$C_{t_0-j} = \frac{K_{t_0}}{K_{t_0-j-1}} \cdot \frac{S_{t_0-j}}{S_{t_0}}$$

where the subscript referring to the ith firm has been suppressed for clarity. Conversely, for the jth year following t_0

$$C_{t_0+j} = \frac{K_{t_0}}{K_{t_0+j-1}} \cdot \frac{S_{t_0+j}}{S_{t_0}},$$

the only difference being that all minus signs before the j have now been converted into pluses.

If, of course, the capital stock *were not* multiplied by the sales ratio, then high positive correlations should be expected between C

---

[10] To illustrate the point that changes in gross fixed assets and investment are not identical, annual investment was correlated with annual changes in gross fixed assets for 14 of the 15 industries included in the earlier investment study. (Data for the fifteenth industry, light chemicals, were out on loan at the time computations were performed.) Because size effects tend to dominate cross-section samples, making most correlations between undeflated variables quite high, simple correlations were also computed between annual investment and the sales levels as a check. In only 6 of the 14 industries were the investment with change in gross fixed assets correlations higher than between investment and sales. It could be argued, therefore, that sales is a better proxy of investment than change in gross fixed assets in a majority of manufacturing industries.

[11] Eisner and Strotz, "The Determinants of Business Investment."

and I for years prior to t_0, since without the sales ratio C is merely the rate of growth of capital stock between $t_0 - j - 1$ and t_0 and I_{t_0-j} is one of the years of investment contributing to that growth. Conversely, if the sales effect can be ignored, negative correlations should be expected between C and I for years after j because K_{t_0}/K_{t_0+j-1} then would be the inverse of the rate of growth of capital stock. This, in turn, would explain why high correlations between C and I were found for 1946 in the earlier study and not for 1949 and 1950.

Unfortunately for this whole argument, its basic assumption is not met: the sales ratio is included in the variable. Furthermore, or more exactly, there is every reason to expect that the variance of the sales ratio across the cross-section samples would be at least as great as that for the gross fixed assets ratio *so that the sales ratio should have as much influence on the final value of C as the gross fixed assets ratio.* In economic terms, the sales ratio is, of course, the inverse of the rate of growth in sales for years before t_0 and the rate itself for years after. The value of C therefore depends on whether the capital stock or sales grew more quickly between years $t_0 - j$ or $t_0 + j$. For example, if C were greater than unity for a year before t_0 it could be inferred that sales did not grow as fast as gross fixed assets between the year $t_0 - j$ and t_0; this, in turn, would suggest that the capital stock must have been overworked (been used beyond the desired capacity level) in year $t_0 - j$. Conversely, if C had been less than unity for year $t_0 - j$, then sales grew more quickly between $t_0 - j$ and t_0 than gross fixed assets, and there is evidence that capital assets were underutilized in $t_0 - j$; otherwise the greater than proportionate expansion in sales would not have been possible.

The capacity variable used here is not, of course, an infallible measure of capital utilization. It was used in the earlier study mainly because no better measure seemed available. A similar situation pertains in the present study. Unfortunately, the peak S/K ratios in the 1951–1954 period almost always occur in 1951 so there is almost certainly a strong bias toward finding higher C with I correlations in that year than the other years included in this study. Accordingly, alternative formulations of the acceleration principle, represented by the absolute sales and the first difference in sales variables, have always been tested interchangeably with C in the present study to provide a check on the extent of bias introduced by this clustering of the R_{Ii}'s.

First difference variables, like change in sales, also represent an effort to remove characteristics specific to an individual firm. The convention for identifying first difference variables has been to append a prime mark after the letter notation.

Both the first difference and normalized variables probably will reflect transient or short-run influences present in the cross-section samples. Thus, the inclusion of both an absolute sales level and a capacity measure as explanatory variables in a cross-section investment study should provide an opportunity to measure the relative extent of long-run and short-run sales influences on investment. Assuming that the prior grouping of the sample with respect to capital intensity has resulted in reasonably homogeneous strata, the sales variable should reflect the long-run influence of a relatively high within industry sales position on investment; the fact that the sales variable tends to be autocorrelated in cross-section samples (i.e., high sales firms in an industry tend to remain so and vice versa) reinforces this interpretation. By contrast, the capacity variable, normalized in terms of each individual firm's own experience, should measure the influence of transient deviations around the long-run position. Obviously, a first difference variable should function similarly to the normalized variable. To the extent, moreover, that expectations are geared more to long-run than to short-run developments, the absolute variable should be a better measure of expectations. Also inclusion of both short-run and long-run influences in the same model reduces the chances of "regression fallacy bias" influencing the results.

A somewhat more complete statement of the accounting characteristics of the variables can be obtained from Chapter 4 of the earlier investment study. This is particularly true of the ten variables that are common to the two studies: investment (I), sales (S), profits (P), depreciation expense (D), change in sales (S'), net quick liquidity stock (L), gross fixed assets (K), cash dividend payments (V), depreciation reserves (A), and capacity utilization (C). Furthermore, four other variables listed in Table III–1 — the net stock of money and near money (M), accounts payable (U), the total of

TABLE III–1

Variable Code: Cross-Section Analyses

t	the time period, so that as a subscript it denotes the year to which a particular flow variable refers and the end-of-year value for stock values; if no time subscript is given, the current year, t, is to be understood.
I	investment in new and used plant and equipment.
S	sales.
P	net profit (net income to surplus).
D	depreciation expense.
S'	$S_t - S_{t-1}$ = the current change in sales.
L	stock of net quick liquidity defined as current assets less inventory and current liabilities.
A	depreciation reserves taken as an approximate measure of the age of the capital stock.
M	net stock of money and near money, i.e., cash plus marketable securities less short-term notes payable to banks.
U	accounts payable.
L'	the change in working capital; specifically the first difference of current assets (including inventories) less current liabilities.
K	gross fixed assets.
V	total cash dividends.
T	$P + D$ = cash throw-off.
Y	total current inventories.
Y'	$Y_t - Y_{t-1}$ = the change in current inventories.
R_{Y_i}	the minimum ratio between end-of-year inventory stock and that same year's sales attained by the ith firm during the years 1951–1954.

current inventories (Y), and the change in working capital (L')[12] — are essentially variations of the liquidity stock measure and the comments made on net quick liquidity stock in the earlier study apply to these new variables as well. Similarly, the five cash throw-off variables $(T, T - V, T - V - L', T - V - N,$ and $P - V)$ are merely additive combinations of the original variables. Accordingly, their accounting properties also can be deduced from the accounting properties of the underlying variables.

The only accounting values involved in the present study and not discussed in the earlier study are contained in the last six variables

[12] It should be noted that L' is not net of changes in inventories whereas the variable L itself is net of inventories. While there is this difference in the definition of the two variables, it was felt that they were sufficiently alike that it would have been more misleading to give them separate designations than to retain the same basic alphabetic code for both.

TABLE III–1 (continued)

R_{Ri}	the minimum ratio between end-of-year accounts receivable and the same year's sales attained by the ith firm during the years 1951–1954.
R_{Ii}	the minimum ratio between end-of-year gross fixed assets and the same year's sales attained by the ith firm during the years 1951–1954.
C_i	$R_{Ii} \cdot S_i$ = an approximate measure of needed capacity for the ith firm; C and S always pertain to the same time periods and have the same time subscripts.
N_i	$R_{Yi}S_i' + R_{Ri}S_i' - (U_{(t-1)i} - U_{ti})$ = estimated net new cash needed for working capital purposes by the ith firm.
$T - V$	cash throw-off less cash dividend payments.
$T - V - L'$	cash throw-off less cash dividends and the *actual* change in working capital.
$T - V - N$	cash throw-off less cash dividends and the net *estimated cash needed* for working capital purposes.
$P - V$	net profits less cash dividends.
B	long-term debt.
W	net worth.
X	$B + W$ = book value of invested capital.
Z	$\dfrac{B}{B + W}$ = ratio of long-term debt to book invested capital.
F	preferred stock.
Z_a	$\dfrac{B + F - L}{B + W} = Z_a$ adjusted for preferred stock and liquid asset holdings.

in Table III–1, relating to various measures of debt and net worth. In these six variables, three new accounting concepts are involved: long-term debt, net worth, and preferred stock. Long-term debt is simply the sum of mortgage, bond, and term loans for a period greater than one year; therefore, almost all types of debt recorded on the liability side of the balance sheet are included except accrued payables and loans with less than a one-year term, that is, debts recorded as current liabilities. The net worth variables follow conventional accounting descriptions; total net worth is the sum of common stock and capital surplus, preferred stock, and earned surplus. The preferred stock value is simply the recorded paid-up value of preferred stock carried on the balance sheet.

It must be emphasized that the variables listed in Table III–1 are not all the variables employed at some point in the present study. Several other variables (for the most part combinations of the same accounting values employed in defining the variables recorded in Table III–1) were tested in the preliminary analyses of the present study. A description of these other variables is presented in subsequent chapters.

In short, the variables described in Table III–1 are essentially the more important or commonly mentioned cross-section variables. While the notation developed in Table III–1 will be followed throughout subsequent chapters, an attempt will be made to present brief verbal descriptions of the various variables as well as their alphabetic code designations wherever they are used. The need to refer back to Table III–1 has thus been minimized but not eliminated.

The time-series variables are listed in Table III–2. This set is considerably smaller than that employed in the cross-section study, reflecting the fact that most of the preliminary sorting or elimination of different investment hypotheses was performed as part of the cross-section analyses. There are, of course, some variables, like the interest rate and stock price variables, that were considered

TABLE III–2

Variable Code: Time-Series Analyses

I	expenditures for new plant and equipment by manufacturing firms.
C^M	an index of capacity utilization as measured by the ratio of the Federal Reserve Board's production index and the McGraw-Hill capacity series.
C^P	an alternative capacity utilization series measuring the ratio between the value of the Federal Reserve Board's production index for year t and the previous peak value for the series.
FA'	the change in gross fixed assets from period $t-1$ to period t.
$(T - V)$	liquidity flow — the sum of depreciation expense and profits less dividends paid out.
$(T - V)^*$	variable $T - V$ adjusted for working capital needs.
r	quarterly average of Moody's AAA industrial bond rate.
sp	quarterly average of Standard and Poor's index of 425 industrial stocks.
S'	change in sales from period $t-1$ to t.
$\left.\begin{array}{l}Q_1 \\ Q_2 \\ Q_3 \\ Q_4\end{array}\right\}$	Seasonal dummy variables (given the value 1 for the proper season and zero for all other seasons).
$t - 1$	used as a subscript to designate the quarter to which an observation pertains; $t - 0$ or t indicates the present period, $t - 1$ designates the immediately preceding quarter, $t - 2$ indicates a two-quarter lag, etc.

primarily time-series or "time-effect" variables and these were only analyzed as part of the time-series analyses.

III. *Summary*

It is worth emphasizing that the cross-section samples used in the present study have essentially the same basic characteristics as the samples used in the 1946–1950 investment study. For example, the coverage of total investment is almost identically the same, being well over half for most of the industry groups.[13] Similarly, the size distribution of firms in the present sample is essentially the same as in the earlier sample [14] except that there has been a slight reduction, approximately three to four percentage points, in the relative representation of smaller firms (those between zero and $4.9 million of gross fixed assets), a result attributable mainly to the general growth of the economy over time.

Similarly, as a sample of the entire universe of manufacturing firms the cross-section sample used in the present study would be biased in the same important respects as the earlier sample: (1) only registered corporations are included; (2) no representation is given to certain important but less capital intensive industries in the manufacturing sector; (3) few very small firms are to be found in the sample; [15] (4) no firms involved in major mergers in the 1951–1954 period are included; (5) firms which leased most of their equipment have been excluded; and (6) firms which rent rather than sell their products are excluded.[16] With the exception of the fourth of these characteristics, the 1951–1954 sample shares the same biases as the

[13] Details on sample coverage will be found in Table 3, p. 45, of the Meyer and Kuh study.

[14] Details will be found in Table 4, p. 47, of the Meyer and Kuh study.

[15] The large firm bias results from the fact that several small firms had to be excluded because they failed to report needed information, particularly gross fixed assets, depreciation reserves, and depreciation expense. Failure to report any one of these figures usually coincided with failure to report the other two. Gross fixed assets was an indispensable variable for the present studies because it was taken as the best measure of size and often used as a deflator for other variables. A full explanation of the reasons for using this variable as a deflator are given in the Meyer and Kuh investment study, pp. 59, 83–84.

[16] These exclusions are almost self-explanatory but a more complete account of the underlying rational will be found in Meyer and Kuh, p. 40.

1946–1950 sample. However, unlike the 1946–1950 sample, the present sample does not exclude rapidly expanding firms.

It is more difficult to specify any obvious biases in the time-series sample since this sample, by necessity, represents more an acceptance of what is available than any conscious choice or selection from alternatives. There simply are not too many alternative sources of good time-series data on investment. In fact, it could be argued that the only reasonably good investment series available is the Securities and Exchange Commission — Office of Business Economics sample used in this study, a sample which dates back only to 1948 for practical purposes. A vivid impression of the importance of this sample can be obtained by perusing the National Income Accounts and noting the heavy reliance placed on this series for obtaining the producer durables component of Gross National Product.

Obviously, neither the cross-section or time-series samples used here is a random, probability sample in the strict sense. They are, however, important and interesting samples for studying business behavior. The results reported later should be evaluated mainly on their own merits and considered interesting to the extent that the universes they represent are also interesting. Because of these sampling characteristics, the probability tests reported must be interpreted cautiously and with circumspection. While not rigorous, these tests do provide a certain objective basis for making at least limited comparisons among the different results and between the results reported here and in other studies.

Chapter **IV** | *Cyclical Patterns, 1946 to 1958*

I. *Introduction*

The central focus of the accelerator-residual funds theory is on cyclical changes in the relationship of investment to its determinants. When existing productive facilities are fully utilized, a capacity utilization variable is hypothesized to have the closest relationship. Contrarily, the residual funds variable is assumed to provide the best explanation when over-all profits and liquidity stock are deficient or declining and capacity is below full utilization levels. Obviously, in order to test empirically for the existence of these essentially nonlinear relationships a determination first must be made of the underlying business conditions during the periods under analysis. For this study these periods are 1951 to 1954 inclusive, as represented by a cross-section sample of individual manufacturing firms for each year, and 1949 through 1958, as contained in a time series composed of quarterly data on all manufacturing and a number of component industries.

A natural first stage in ascertaining the course of the business cycle is, of course, to determine over-all economic performance as measured by gross national product and conventional national income figures. Accordingly, an evaluation of such figures occupies

49

Section II of this chapter. However, because capacity utilization, profit, and liquidity stock characteristics, which are the dominant considerations in determining the nonlinearities in the accelerator-residual funds theory, could deviate from the aggregate performance of the entire economy, more detailed surveys are presented in Sections III and IV respectively of (a) liquidity flow and stock positions of manufacturing corporations and (b) the pattern of capacity utilization in manufacturing. Finally, because of the special importance of the years 1951 to 1954 in this study (being the years from which the individual firm cross-section observations are drawn), additional detail on the particular performance of profits and capacity utilization in these industries is provided in Section V. Finally, a brief summary is to be found in Section VI.

II. *Economic Aggregates and the Over-all Performance of the Postwar U.S. Economy*

From the end of World War II until 1958 the United States economy can be said to have gone through three major business cycles. By most historical standards these cycles were mild in extent but they were nevertheless still pronounced enough to be characterized as true cyclical fluctuations.

The first postwar cycle began with a surge of consumer expenditures and prosperity. Starting slowly in the second half of 1945, it gathered momentum and reached an upper turning point sometime in the second half of 1948. Thereafter came the so-called inventory recession of 1949, which was more or less terminated by early 1950.

The second major cycle can be said to have its origins in the middle of 1950 when the early stages of the Korean War boom began. This boom continued on through most of 1951 and 1952, slowed down a bit in late 1952, and slid off very slowly into the extremely mild recession of early 1954. This, in turn, was quickly abated with recovery already well under way by the fourth quarter of 1954.

The third postwar cyclical upswing started with the business investment and automobile boom of 1955. Activity continued on a more or less high but flat plateau throughout 1955 and into the third quarter of 1956. The recessionary stage of this third cycle began to set in sometime during or shortly after the middle of 1957.

These cyclical patterns are aptly illustrated by the movements in the seasonally adjusted quarterly totals of Gross National Product in constant dollars shown in Table IV–1. As can be seen, GNP reached local peaks in the fourth quarter of 1948, the second quarter of 1953, and the third quarter of 1957, the quarters probably best representing the peaks of these three major postwar cycles. The troughs of these cycles, by contrast, can be noted by the local minimums in GNP observable in the second quarter of 1949, the second quarter of 1954, and the first quarter of 1958.

Also tabulated in Table IV–1 are figures on gross private domestic investment and producers' durable equipment expenditures. Producers' durable equipment, like GNP, peaks in the fourth quarter of 1948. That, however, is about the extent of the cyclical synchronization between the turning points of the producers' durable series and those for GNP. The peaks and troughs in producers' durables tend to come one to two quarters *later* than those in GNP in 1949, 1953, and 1954 while in the 1956–1957 upswing the peak durable equipment outlay notably *leads* the peak in aggregate economic activity.

Much has been said about the unique characteristics of each of these cyclical swings. In fact, every separate prosperity and recession period in the first decade and one-half after the end of World War II appears to have its own distinctive and highly intriguing aspects. There is, for example, the fact that the first postwar prosperity surge was interrupted in the middle of 1947 by at least a minor disinvestment in inventories. So strong were the forces of expansion during this period, however, that this inventory pause had no pronounced influence on the over-all performance of the economy.

Similarly, a number of interesting discussions have been generated on the question of exactly what caused the first postwar downturn, that of 1949. As is obvious from the figures in Table IV–1, inventory disinvestment certainly played a role. Still, the quarter recording the highest level of nonfarm inventory disinvestment was the fourth quarter of 1949 when recovery was already well under way. Indeed, when one looks at the underlying figures, it is tempt-

TABLE IV-1

Gross National Product or Expenditure, Seasonally Adjusted Quarterly Totals at Annual Rates, in Millions of Constant Dollars, 1947–1958

	GNP	Personal Consumption Expenditures	Consumer Durable Expenditures	Gross Private Domestic Investment	New Construction	Producers' Durable Equipment	Change in Business Inventories	Gov't Purchases of Goods and Services
1947								
I	278.4	192.5	21.8	40.6	18.4	21.5	.6	36.8
II	280.4	196.1	23.1	39.3	18.3	21.6	−.5	36.3
III	282.9	196.9	23.5	39.2	20.2	21.6	−2.5	38.0
IV	287.2	197.0	24.7	46.4	22.3	22.1	2.0	37.6
year	282.3	195.6	23.3	41.5	19.9	21.7	−.1	37.2
1948								
I	286.4	198.1	24.0	47.4	22.0	22.8	2.7	37.9
II	293.3	199.0	24.8	50.7	23.1	22.6	4.9	42.0
III	295.6	199.4	25.2	51.3	23.0	22.5	5.8	43.5
IV	297.3	200.6	24.3	49.5	22.2	23.3	4.1	45.3
year	293.1	199.3	24.6	49.8	22.7	22.8	4.4	42.1
1949								
I	291.5	199.9	23.7	41.9	21.3	21.0	−.4	46.3
II	290.3	203.6	26.0	35.8	21.4	20.4	−6.0	47.4
III	295.6	204.8	27.1	39.8	22.5	19.3	−2.0	48.2
IV	293.0	209.0	28.5	36.4	23.9	18.5	−6.0	46.8
year	292.7	204.3	26.3	38.5	22.3	19.8	−3.6	47.2
1950								
I	302.7	210.7	29.0	46.2	25.3	18.2	2.7	44.6
II	312.0	214.2	29.8	53.8	27.3	21.1	5.4	43.5
III	325.6	225.6	37.3	56.5	28.3	23.0	5.2	44.2
IV	331.6	217.0	32.2	66.3	28.0	22.8	15.5	48.3
year	318.1	216.8	32.1	55.9	27.4	21.3	7.2	45.1

TABLE IV-1 (continued)

	GNP	Personal Consumption Expenditures	Consumer Durable Expenditures	Gross Private Domestic Investment	New Construction	Producers' Durable Equipment	Change in Business Inventories	Gov't Purchases of Goods and Services
1951								
I	334.0	222.3	33.0	59.1	27.6	21.5	10.0	52.5
II	340.0	214.5	27.8	62.7	26.2	22.0	14.5	61.1
III	346.3	217.5	28.1	57.7	25.6	22.3	9.8	67.6
IV	346.9	219.8	27.7	51.9	25.3	22.2	4.5	71.6
year	341.8	218.5	29.2	57.7	26.0	22.0	9.7	63.3
1952								
I	349.6	220.0	27.0	52.7	25.7	22.5	4.6	73.4
II	349.3	222.7	28.4	46.0	25.8	22.9	−2.7	77.7
III	352.6	223.8	27.0	49.5	25.7	20.0	3.8	79.5
IV	362.3	230.2	31.6	53.2	26.5	21.8	4.9	80.0
year	353.5	224.2	28.5	50.4	26.0	21.8	2.6	77.7
1953								
I	368.9	234.0	33.0	52.8	27.1	23.1	2.6	83.0
II	373.2	236.2	33.5	53.0	27.6	22.2	3.2	85.1
III	370.2	236.0	33.7	51.0	27.6	22.6	.7	84.4
IV	363.9	234.1	32.1	45.4	27.8	22.2	−4.6	84.9
year	369.0	235.1	33.1	50.6	27.6	22.5	.5	84.3
1954								
I	360.4	233.4	31.2	46.9	27.9	21.5	−2.5	80.1
II	359.5	236.4	32.2	48.9	30.2	20.7	−2.9	75.2
III	362.1	239.0	32.4	48.9	30.2	20.7	−2.0	73.6
IV	370.1	243.2	33.9	52.2	31.5	19.9	.8	72.2
year	363.1	238.0	32.4	48.9	29.7	20.8	−1.6	75.3

TABLE IV-1 (continued)

	GNP	Personal Consumption Expenditures	Consumer Durable Expenditures	Gross Private Domestic Investment	New Construction	Producers' Durable Equipment	Change in Business Inventories	Gov't Purchases of Goods and Services
1955								
I	382.2	248.7	37.9	58.5	33.5	20.3	4.7	73.4
II	389.5	253.7	39.0	62.3	34.0	21.7	6.5	73.1
III	397.5	259.9	41.5	63.9	34.2	23.7	6.0	72.6
IV	401.1	261.8	39.9	65.2	33.7	24.4	7.1	73.5
year	392.7	256.0	39.6	62.5	33.9	22.5	6.1	73.2
1956								
I	398.8	263.2	38.9	62.8	32.7	24.3	5.8	71.8
II	398.9	263.7	38.0	61.5	32.6	24.7	4.1	71.5
III	400.2	263.4	37.1	61.4	32.3	25.2	3.9	72.1
IV	405.5	266.9	38.2	61.3	31.8	25.5	4.0	73.5
1957								
I	409.6	268.9	38.9	59.8	31.9	25.4	2.5	75.8
II	410.0	270.4	38.5	59.3	31.7	24.8	2.8	76.0
III	411.0	273.4	39.0	58.9	31.7	24.9	2.3	74.8
IV	403.8	272.1	37.7	54.1	31.6	23.6	−1.0	75.4
1958								
I	393.0	268.9	34.9	46.8	31.0	20.4	−4.6	77.0
II	395.2	270.9	34.7	45.8	30.2	19.1	−3.4	78.6
III	402.9	274.4	35.1	48.1	30.6	18.8	−1.3	80.2
IV	413.6	278.7	37.5	54.7	32.1	19.5	3.1	81.2

Sources: 1947–1955, *U.S. Income and Output*, pp. 124–125.
1956–1958, Statistical Supplement to *Survey of Current Business*, 1961, p. 4.

ing to describe the 1949 downturn as having its source in a durable goods recession since reasonably sharp declines took place in both consumer durables and new construction expenditures in the third and fourth quarters of 1948 and almost all forms of durable outlays turned down in the first quarter of 1949.

There is less room for speculation about the Korean War boom, lasting from the middle of 1951 to the middle of 1953. By almost any standards it was a spectacular surge in activity accompanied by a quite conventional inflation in which aggregate demand ran well ahead of aggregate productive capacity. During this remarkable boom GNP measured in *real* terms rose by almost 20% and prices by approximately 15%. Furthermore, the increase in activity was shared by almost all sectors of the economy, though producers' durable equipment expenditure during this period did *not* rise by anywhere near the same relative amounts as did business inventory investments or personal consumption expenditures. Specifically, producers' durable expenditures were at virtually the same level at the peak of the boom in the first half of 1953 as it was in the recessionary first half of 1950. By contrast, consumption expenditures rose 10% during that same period, especially if the "war scare buying" that characterized the third quarter of 1950 is discounted.

The most distinctive characteristic of the recession of 1953–1954, the deflationary stage in the second cycle, is its mildness. The absolute decline in GNP was only $10 billion, representing a very modest 2.5% to 3% of activity. Furthermore, the downturn more or less ran its course in only four quarters, thus making it remarkably short-lived as well as slight in total impact. Unquestionably, one of the main factors contributing to the mildness of this recession was the excellent performance of construction which actually continued to rise throughout the 1953–1954 recession. The causes of the 1953–1954 downturn seem to lie in a combination of events: reduced federal government spending, a decline in private investment, and considerable inventory disinvestment.

The turn toward prosperity in 1955 was marked by sharp rises in expenditures on both producers' and consumers' durables, with automobiles receiving particular emphasis. By any standards, the economy was experiencing a full fledged investment boom in producers' durable equipment expenditures by the fourth quarter of 1955. Perhaps the most remarkable aspect of the 1955–1957 expansion was the rapidity of the rise in 1955 and then the stability, at a remarkably high level, that ensued throughout 1956 and into the middle of 1957. It could be argued, though, that the economy did experience a sort of last, final fling during the third and fourth quarters of 1956 when GNP rose from a level of $400 to $407 billion (at annual rates and in constant dollars). This new level of $407 billion was maintained through the next three quarters, the decline finally coming in late 1957.

The decline in 1957 is usually attributed to a combination of reduced government expenditures and inventory disinvestment by business. The decline in government outlays, moreover, is almost entirely federal in origin. Federal government expenditures declined by $1.6 billion between the second quarter of 1957 and the fourth quarter while state and local governments continued to increase their expenditures. Another notable aspect of the recession of 1958 was the degree to which the federal government was willing to use its fiscal powers as a corrective. It was during this period that a peacetime record federal deficit of $12.5 billion was attained and, as can be seen from Table IV–1, the annual rate of total government expenditure rose by about $7 billion between the third quarter of 1957 and the end of 1958.

In sum, each of the three cycles seems to have its own distinctive causes and features. A major impetus to the first expansion obviously was provided by pent-up demands for all types of consumer goods. The origin of the second upturn apparently lay in the general expansion of the money supply and the accompanying increase in effective demand generated by the "guns and butter" economic strategy that was followed during the Korean War. The third and last surge is clearly associated with the 1955 boom in automobile sales and with the very substantial increase in business demands for producers' durable equipment.

Similarly, a different central causative force seems to have been at work in each of the three recessions. In the first there was a drop in consumers' and producers' expenditures on durables followed by business inventory disinvestment. In the second recession inventory disinvestment seems to have been the principal adverse factor, though a considerable decline is also observable in business purchases of producers' durables. In the third decline a drop occurred in expenditures on producers' durables and in consumer expenditures on durables. These declines in durables were then eventually followed by some inventory disinvestment, thus giving the 1958 recession very much the same outward appearance as that of 1949.

III. *Manufacturing Liquidity and Financial Patterns: 1947–1958* [1]

In discussing business liquidity it is necessary to differentiate first between stocks and flows and secondly between trend and cycle. While these effects obviously are not totally independent, the major developments are best delineated by considering each separately. The analysis is further facilitated by considering the data in *relative* terms since stocks and flows in manufacturing funds are best interpreted in relationship to other stock and flow measures of manufacturing activity. Relative or ratio figures also automatically tend to eliminate most price effects, and price changes were quite pronounced during the postwar period under study. In addition, ratio figures, besides seeming to be sensible, long have been sanctified by banking and brokerage house custom as a simple means of relating financial ability to financial requirements.

The trends and cyclical behavior in three of the more relevant liquidity stock ratios during the period 1947 through 1958 are shown in Figure IV–1. A rather sharp decline trendwise in the relative holdings of liquidity stocks by manufacturing corporations occurred during the period. Manufacturing corporations in aggregate apparently revised downward what they considered to be required holdings of liquidity stocks relative to sales and current liabilities. Moreover, some increased willingness to finance accounts receivable and inventories through the use of short-term credit seems to have taken place, as indicated by the separation between the current assets to current liabilities and the cash plus government to total current liabilities ratios that occurred during

---

[1] This section is adapted from Kuh and Meyer, "Investment, Liquidity, and Monetary Policy." Some of the material presented there was, in turn, adapted from the work done as part of this study.

the years 1951 through 1956. (Accounts receivable and inventories are, of course, the principal difference between current assets and cash plus governments.) Finally, and perhaps most importantly, the ratio of quick liquidity (cash plus governments) to sales declined more or less systematically over the entire period.

FIGURE IV–1

Manufacturing Quick Ratio, Current Ratio, and Quick Assets to Sales Ratio, 1947–1958

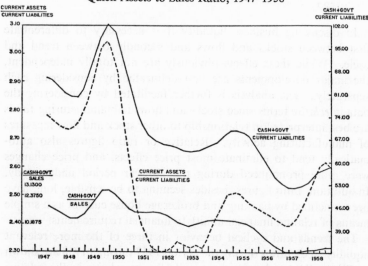

The cyclical behavior of the current asset ratios was also highly suggestive. Above all, relative holdings of liquidity tended to increase during recessions. Stocks of liquidity seemed to be highly plentiful in early revival periods and then were systematically worked off as the cyclical upturn proceeded. Thus, an increase in relative liquidity was observable during late 1949, the second half of 1953, the first part of 1954, the last half of 1957 and the first part of 1958, all periods of business decline. On the other hand, the cyclical upswings of 1950 through 1953 and 1954 through early 1957 were periods during which relative liquidity stocks declined. (Such a decline also occurred, incidentally, during the business improvement of 1959, which is not shown on the chart.) In sum, relative measures of liquidity stock have trended downward for the past decade, have shown notable increases during recessions and early upswings of the business cycle, and have declined during the latter part of business upswings.

These conclusions are based, however, on an impressionistic reading of the charts and highly aggregative data. As something of a check, linear least squares regressions also were fitted to the SEC–FTC data for individual (2 digit SIC) manufacturing industries to determine "normal" or average relationships between business liquidity and different classes of assets and levels of operation during the years 1947 to 1958. Discrepancies of actual levels from these average relationships for any one period provide a very rough index of financial stringency, availability, or need in a period.

Money and marketable securities (quick assets) were taken to be linear functions of sales, the level of federal tax accruals, short-term bank debt, and the change in sales. Generally, two explanatory variables, sales and the level of federal tax accruals, by themselves accounted for about 90% of the variation in quick assets during the 1947 to 1958 period. On the other hand, short-term bank debt proved to have a weak relationship with quick assets; furthermore, it was consistently negative, suggesting that short-term bank borrowing is caused by scarcity of cash rather than being a reason for holding cash, despite the ostensibly widespread practice of compensating balances being tied to bank loans. Similarly, the change in sales variable had a generally negligible and negative influence on quick asset levels.

Whether or not all the underlying assumptions of the model are reasonable, and they probably are not, the functions do provide some crude information about the "established relationships" between different interdependent financial and operating measures. Furthermore, percentage discrepancies between the values predicted by the equations and actual values of quick assets should indicate periods when financial patterns deviated sharply from the norm. The percentage discrepancies listed in Table IV–2 for five quarters are considered to be of particular interest because they correspond to quarters either very early or very late in cyclical recovery phases.

These data lend useful detail and generally confirmatory substance to the earlier discussion. Particularly noteworthy is the way

TABLE IV-2

Estimated Percentage Excess or Deficiency of Cash and Marketable Securities for Selected Quarters by Industry, 1950-1957 *

Industry	Early Recovery Cycle Stage			Late Recovery Cycle Stage	
	2nd Quarter 1950	3rd Quarter 1955	4th Quarter 1958	2nd Quarter 1952	2nd Quarter 1957
Iron and Steel	6.6%	1.8%	11.6%	11.5%	−17.6%
Nonferrous Metal	3.7	1.9	−14.4	−14.6	−23.4
Electrical Machinery	−7.8	5.8	.2	9.5	−12.4
Other Machinery	1.6	6.5	−6.3	6.2	−6.4
Motor Vehicles	9.0	22.5	−25.1	−11.1	−23.2
Other Transportation	−2.2	2.2	15.6	2.2	−1.6
Stone, Clay, and Glass	6.8	−1.0	.7	6.0	−2.3
Food	4.3	2.2	−1.1	6.5	−3.9
Textiles	−4.2	−2.7	11.9	3.8	1.1
Paper	4.7	2.1	−.5	8.9	−9.1
Chemicals	1.1	5.0	−9.4	8.6	−8.3
Rubber	14.5	−5.7	−16.1	11.2	−14.9
Petroleum and Coal	1.8	−5.6	14.0	−.1	−1.1

* These percentages were computed by using the formula $\dfrac{M - \hat{M}}{M}$ where M = actual money and marketable securities; $\hat{M}$ = an estimate of M obtained from the linear least squares function $\hat{M} = f(S,G,B,S')$, where S = sales, G = federal income tax liabilities, B = short term bank borrowing, and S' = change in sales.

in which the second quarters of 1950 and 1957 seem to have been contrasting extremes in business liquidity. In the middle of 1950, just before the Korean boom began, quick assets exceeded "normal levels" in most industries, while the reverse was true in the middle of 1957 when the 1955–1957 investment boom was coming to a close. On the other hand, the second quarter of 1952, coming late in the Korean boom, contrasts sharply with the second quarter of

FIGURE IV-2
Manufacturing Net Profit Margin and Dividend
Payout, 1947–1958

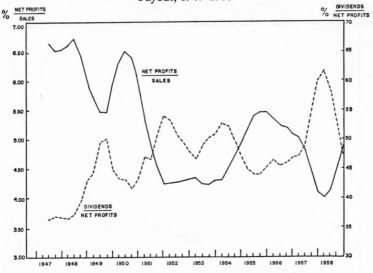

1957, also a late boom period. Clearly, business liquidity was relatively much greater at the end of the earlier upswing, indicating the extent of the liquidity legacy left by the Korean War boom.

A primary source of funds *flowing* into business firms is, of course, profits. Furthermore, the availability of retained earnings from profits depends crucially on the level of the dividend payout. The net profit to sales and the dividend payout ratios are shown in Figure IV-2. These two series exhibit somewhat opposing trend patterns. The profit margin has manifested a downward drift while the dividend payout ratio has, if anything, moved upward. Since

1951, though, both series have been remarkably devoid of trend elements, the profit margin ratio moving cyclically around the reasonably stable central tendency of approximately 5% and the dividend payout ratio doing the same around a 50% mean.

Consequences flowing from a decline in the profit margin accompanied by a slight increase in the dividend payout ratio are depicted

FIGURE IV-3

Manufacturing Total Internal Finance, Net Retained Earnings, and Depreciation: Four-Quarter Moving Totals, 1947–1958
(billions of dollars)

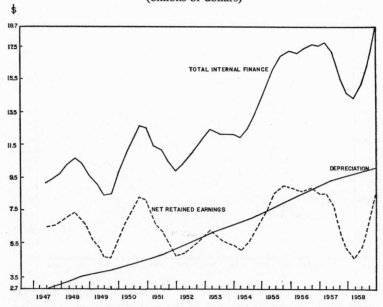

in Figure IV-3, which presents data on manufacturers' net retained earnings, depreciation expense, and total internal finance. Specifically, the net retained earnings figure, *even in its raw form without price correction or being taken in ratio to other series*, remains remarkably stable throughout the period. By contrast, the depreciation and total internal finance series (also in their original form without price correction or being relative to other series) increased steadily throughout the postwar period. Moreover, since net retained earnings plus depreciation essentially equals total internal finance available from operations, it is quite clear that all the growth in internal finance during the period is attributable to the rise in depreciation expenses. Even more direct evidence on this point is shown in Figure IV–4, which plots the ratio of manufacturing depreciation charges to total internal finance.

FIGURE IV–4

Ratio of Depreciation to Internal Finance in
Manufacturing, 1947–1958

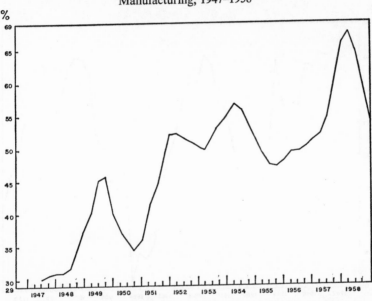

The flow of funds available from internal sources also displays an interesting cyclical pattern, in many ways very much like that for the relative liquidity stock measures. Specifically, net retained earnings seem to rise early in business cycle recoveries, or even at the end of recessions, and then decline somewhat as the cyclical recovery moves forward. For example, sharp upward increases in net retained earnings occurred during the first three quarters of 1950 and the end of 1954 and the early part of 1955, periods of early cyclical recovery. Since investment programs also increase during cyclical upswings and current asset stock positions are depleted the longer the cyclical upswing continues, it seems highly likely that the flow of funds from internal sources becomes less plentiful relative to requirements the longer the cyclical upturn persists. Scarcity of internal cash relative to requirements in the late phases of the upswing is also evidenced, at least to a rough degree of ap-

FIGURE IV-5

Manufacturing Ratio of External Cash Finance to
Total Finance, 1947–1958

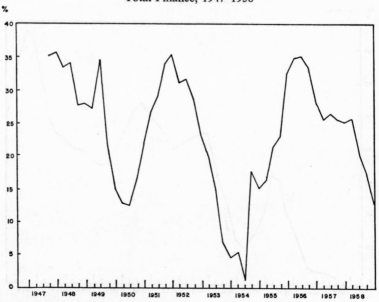

proximation, by an increase in the use of external financing at such times, as illustrated by the data charted in Figure IV-5. Specifically, external finance becomes a relatively less important component of total manufacturing finance during recessions, particularly toward the end of recessions. Similarly, an increase in the relative use of external finance tends to come somewhat later than the improvement in net retained earnings during the periods of cyclical revival.

These various trends in manufacturing finance are summarized

FIGURE IV-6
Manufacturing Total Finance, 1947–1958
(billions of dollars)

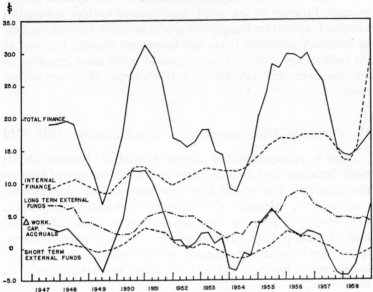

in Figure IV-6. First, the total finance series indicates over-all requirements. Second, the gap between the total finance figure and the internal finance figure, charted immediately below the total finance series in Figure IV-6, is a good measure of the pressure or the lack of pressure for the use of external sources. (This pressure might be slightly better represented by the gap between the sum of the internal finance series and the change in trade accrual series which more or less automatically follows cyclical patterns.) If attention is focused on the long-term and short-term external fund series in Figure IV-6, it is clear that the use of both external sources tends to rise toward the middle or the end of the cyclical upturn. Furthermore, and not unexpectedly, short-term external debts seem to be retired during recession. Finally, Figure IV-6 also displays the generally heavy reliance of the manufacturing sector on internal funds.

In sum, manufacturers' utilization of external funds displays marked cyclical variability: external funds seem needed mainly in the later stages of the cyclical upswing and relatively little in the early stages of an upswing and downswing. This cyclical pattern suggests, in terms of the supply and demand analysis outlined in Chapter I, either that there is fair synchronization between the flow of internally generated funds and investment demand for most of the cycle or that external funds appear so much more expensive to manufacturers than internal funds that external funds are seldom used.

IV. *Pattern of Manufacturing Capacity Utilization, 1947–1950*

There is perhaps nothing economists studying business investment decisions need quite so badly as a good measure of productive capacity. The lack of a good capacity measure derives from many sources. Above all, though, dollar measures of capital stock, hard enough to come by themselves, are very difficult to convert into physical productivity equivalents. Among other problems, technology is constantly changing so that a dollar spent on capital is continually buying a different amount of productive capability. In addition, products and their qualities continually undergo change so that an incontrovertible measure of output is also difficult to establish. Less directly, altered technologies and changes in expectations about product obsolescence can change the durability built into the capital stock, thus modifying the relationship between the stock of capital and the flow of its services. Similarly, managements and labor learn as they use new machines, so that productivity changes with the age of the capital stock. In the same vein, "down time" for repairs and maintenance usually has a cycle over the life of equipment, being high at first, declining rapidly, and then rising again with age.[2] Furthermore, work rules, overtime payments, and similar labor-management bargains can influence the productive capability of a given capital stock. Finally, there is the old and always difficult accounting problem of using depreciation allowances to convert a gross monetary stock of capital into a

---

[2] Note that this altered pattern of productive usefulness will not be approximated by any currently employed depreciation or capital consumption adjustments.

meaningful measure of net capital stock, one of the most complex and difficult problems in the whole range of economic measurement.[3] In short, the expected flow of services from a given dollar value of capital stock is a complex function of many things, most of which are difficult to measure.

The McGraw-Hill Economics Department, recognizing these difficulties with monetary measures of capital stock, has attempted to improve capacity measurements by asking businessmen directly about their capacity utilization.[4] Essentially two types of questions have been asked. First, how much increase in productive capacity occurred in a given year? Second, how much of capacity was being used at a specific point in time? [5] From the answers to these questions capacity indexes have been constructed that, to at least a first approximation, reflect many of the intangibles that are not measured by any available dollar stock of capital figure. Needless to say, though, the direct questionnaire approach has its own special problems, although on balance these problems are probably no worse or less than those encountered in the monetary stock approach.

One researcher, Frank deLeeuw, of the staff of the Board of Governors of the Federal Reserve, in a highly interesting and suggestive study, "The Demand for Capital by Manufacturers," [6] has integrated these different measures into a still different capacity

---

[3] A most pertinent quotation on these difficulties is contained in U.S. Office of Business Economics, *U.S. Income and Output: A Supplement to the Survey of Current Business* (1958), p. 95: "The revisions in capital consumption analysis were wholly statistical. This is an area of national income research where much new development work is needed so as to derive more meaningful measures of the volume of capital used up in production than are afforded by book depreciation charges."

[4] For background information on the McGraw-Hill Surveys, see Dexter M. Keezer, Robert P. Ulin, Douglas Greenwald, and Margaret Matulis, "Observations on the Predictive Quality of McGraw-Hill Surveys of Business' Plans for New Plants and Equipment," in Universities — National Bureau of Economic Research, *The Quality and Economic Significance of Anticipations Data*, Special Conference Series, No. 10 (Princeton: Princeton University Press, 1960).

[5] The answer, of course, when expressed in percentage terms needs only be divided into a measure of output to construct a measure of productive capability.

[6] Paper presented at the December 1960 meeting of the Econometric Society, St. Louis, Missouri. While this book was in press, parts of this paper were published as "The Concept of Capacity," *Journal of the American Statistical Association*, Vol. 57, No. 300 (December 1962), pp. 826–839, and "The Demand for

index for manufacturing. Basically, deLeeuw uses the "how much of capacity was being used" question to define his trend. To derive cyclical variations he "splits the difference" (by averaging) between two other indexes, one based on the monetary value of the capital stock and the second on the question: "How much did capacity increase?" The net result is, not unexpectedly, to end up with an index that is itself very close to a simple average of the monetary capital stock and direct questionnaire indexes.

Still another possible measure of capacity utilization over time is at least implicitly suggested by the previous peak performance comparative capacity measure described in the last chapter and used in the Meyer-Kuh cross-section study. In this approach, some current measure of output would be compared to its own previous peak value. Such an index shares most of the disadvantages of the monetary stock index, though not necessarily to the same degree. The main virtue of such an approach compared to the monetary stock technique is that, like the direct questionnaire indexes, the definition of the base is continually updated over time in an expanding economy. One of the more obvious formulations of such a comparative peak index would be the ratio of the Federal Reserve Board Manufacturing Production Index's current value to the previous peak value for that same series.

For purposes of comparison and evaluation, examples of these different concepts employed as capacity utilization measures are shown in Table IV-3. In the first column is the four-quarter moving average of the comparative peak index using the FRB production index as the measure of output. In the second column is the four-quarter moving average of the index obtained by using the FRB production index as the measure of output and the McGraw-Hill capacity index based on the question of "How much did capacity increase?" In column 3 is the four-quarter moving average of an

---

Capital Goods by Manufacturers," *Econometrica*, Vol. 30, No. 3 (July 1962), pp. 407–423. Also while in press, two excellent discussions of these capacity measures appeared: A. M. Phillips, "An Appraisal of Measures of Capacity," and C. L. Schultze, "Uses of Capacity Measures for Short-Run Economic Analysis," both in *American Economic Review*, Vol. 53, No. 2 (May 1963), pp. 275–307.

TABLE IV-3
Manufacturing Capacity Utilization Indexes, 1949–1958
(Four-Quarter Moving Averages) *

Year & Quarter		Previous Peak Performance Comparative Production Index	McGraw-Hill Capacity Index	Capital Stock Based Index	deLeeuw † Index
1949	III	.94	.71	.86	.78
	IV	.94	.71	.86	.77
1950	I	.98	.72	.89	.80
	II	1.01	.75	.93	.86
	III	1.03	.78	.97	.92
	IV	1.04	.80	1.01	.93
1951	I	1.03	.81	1.03	.94
	II	1.00	.80	1.03	.93
	III	.99	.79	1.02	.89
	IV	.99	.77	1.00	.88
1952	I	.99	.76	.98	.89
	II	1.00	.76	.98	.88
	III	1.03	.77	.99	.89
	IV	1.03	.78	1.01	.95
1953	I	1.04	.80	1.04	.96
	II	1.03	.80	1.04	.96
	III	.99	.78	1.02	.94
	IV	.96	.75	.99	.87
1954	I	.93	.72	.96	.83
	II	.92	.70	.94	.83
	III	.91	.69	.94	.82
	IV	.93	.70	.95	.84
1955	I	.96	.71	.98	.87
	II	.99	.72	1.00	.90
	III	1.01	.73	1.03	.91
	IV	1.01	.74	1.03	.92
1956	I	1.01	.73	1.02	.90
	II	1.00	.72	1.02	.89
	III	.99	.71	1.01	.87
	IV	.99	.71	1.01	.89
1957	I	.99	.70	1.01	.88
	II	.99	.70	1.00	.86
	III	.97	.68	.97	.85
	IV	.94	.65	.94	.80
1958	I	.91	.62	.91	.74
	II	.89	.60	.88	.73
	III	.91	.60	.88	.77
	IV	.92	.61	.91	.79

* All four-quarter moving averages are centered on the *beginning* of each specified quarter.

† A. M. Phillips, "An Appraisal of Measures of Capacity," *American Economic Review*, Vol. 53, No. 2 (May 1963), p. 285. This series has not been averaged.

index formed by the ratio of the FRB index divided by the Department of Commerce estimates of the real net capital stock in manufacturing. In column 4 are presented some representative figures obtained by the "deLeeuw compromise." Only the patterns of covariation in these different series should be compared since their absolute values differ arbitrarily due to the use of different base years in their construction. The comparative peak index, moreover, has a sliding base by definition.

The different capacity utilization indexes follow more or less the same pattern. Peaks are recorded either in the last quarter of 1950 or the first of 1951, the first of 1953, and the fourth of 1955. Troughs occur in the first quarters of 1952, the third of 1954, and the second of 1958. Moreover, none of the indexes achieves the same heights in the final peak, the fourth of 1955, as in the previous peak in early 1953. The capital stock based index falls barely short of the previous peak while the McGraw-Hill index is markedly lower and the current to previous peak and deLeeuw indexes are in between. This marked departure between the McGraw-Hill and the capital stock capacity indexes observable in 1955, 1956, and 1957 may be attributable to the fact that the capital stock capacity index underestimates the capacity available because of an overestimate of the physical depreciation of the capital stock during that period. This overestimation of physical depreciation would not be surprising, given the complexity and difficulty of converting recorded accounting depreciation figures into physical equivalents, during a period like the 1950's when depreciation accounting procedures were undergoing fairly rapid change.

One special problem is brought forth by a comparison of the capacity utilization figures with the liquidity data presented in the preceding section. Specifically, there is at least a minor conflict between the availability of plentiful liquidity and high capacity utilization, the two underlying specifications required for acceleration effects to dominate residual funds in the accelerator-residual funds hypothesis. Periods near the end of cyclical upswings often are difficult to classify, and particularly difficult is the period from the second quarter of 1956 through the middle of 1957 (especially if the capital stock based utilization index is considered more valid than the McGraw-Hill index).

V. *Some Special Data on the Years 1951 Through 1954*

The 1951–1954 period plays a special role in the empirical analyses that follow because it is for this period that detailed cross-section samples have been collected. As already noted, 1951 was in general a year of high activity and rapid expansion associated with the bread and butter economic strategy of the Korean emergency; 1952 was a period of slackened expansion but still high-level business activity; 1953 was a year of some retrenchment and by the end of the year of mild recession; and 1954 was a year in which a brief and mild recession ended and some upturn was observable.

It is entirely possible, of course, that while the over-all economy behaved in a certain fashion, specific industries could have quite contrary experiences. Since the cross-section analyses were performed on an industry-by-industry basis, the possibility of specific industries deviating sharply from the over-all pattern is one of substantial importance in interpreting the cross-section results. Therefore, an industry-by-industry report on the behavior of capacity utilization, retained earnings, profits, and liquid assets during the period 1951–1954 is presented in Tables IV–4, IV–5, IV–6 and IV–7.

From these tables it is evident that the broad picture presented by the analysis of the aggregates is more or less confirmed in the detailed figures on the performance of the individual industries. As can be seen from Tables IV–4 and IV–5, which present industry averages for each year for the deflated capacity utilization and profit variables, 1951 was a year of extremely high-level activity in United States manufacturing industries. The capacity utilization ratio was over unity, hypothetical full utilization, for almost every industry in the study, and average profits were very high in 1951, indeed remarkably high in several industries.

On the other hand, the 1951 performance was not quite so exceptional in terms of two other average ratios, average retained earnings plus depreciation expense deflated by gross fixed assets as reported in Table IV–6 and average net quick assets deflated by gross fixed assets as reported in Table IV–7. In 1952, 1953, and 1954 reduced profits were offset to a marked degree by increased depreciation expenses so that the average retained earnings plus depreciation expense to gross fixed asset ratios did not drop as

TABLE IV-4

Average Capacity Utilization Rates
by Industry, 1951-1954
(Full utilization = 1.000)

Industry	1951	1952	1953	1954
Pulp and Paper	1.176	.939	.927	.884
Light Chemicals	1.082	.961	.896	.861
Heavy Chemicals	1.069	.914	.906	.836
Petroleum	1.106	1.017	.988	.912
Rubber	1.109	.962	.951	.788
Heavy Steel	1.171	.908	.922	.659
Fabricated Metal Products	1.036	.988	.936	.790
Special Industrial Machinery	.932	.948	.972	.887
General Industrial Machinery	1.051	1.039	.941	.801
Machine Tools	.878	1.008	1.004	.779
Heavy Equipment, Engines, and Turbines	1.087	1.009	.889	.719
Air Conditioning, Heating, and Similar Equipment	.975	.947	1.005	.961
Household Durables	.905	.991	1.023	.748
Light Electrical Machinery	1.029	.900	.903	.758
Heavy Electrical Machinery	1.127	.933	.924	.767
Electronics	.956	.995	1.056	.903
Auto Fabricators	.966	.890	.980	.769
Auto Parts and Accessories	1.052	.931	.929	.716
Basic Textiles	1.056	.941	.812	.700
Other Textiles	1.009	.920	.834	.787

dramatically after 1951 as the profit to gross fixed asset ratios. Similarly, the average net quick asset to gross fixed ratios were actually higher for most industries at the beginning of 1952 than at the beginning of 1951. In fact, for 10 out of the 20 industries the quick asset ratio peaked at the beginning of 1952, a hardly surprising result given the high level of fund inflow during 1951.

While profits took rather surprising and substantial drops from 1951 to 1952 and 1953, capacity utilization remained quite high in these years. For almost all industries, the 1953 figures are more or less like those for 1952, utilization going up in a few and down in a few others. There was, moreover, some slight tendency for gross retained earnings, as measured by retained earnings plus depreciation expense, to improve slightly between 1952 and 1953, while the quick asset position deteriorated slightly for a majority of the industries between the beginning of 1952 and the beginning of 1953.

TABLE IV–5

Average Profit to Gross Fixed Asset Ratios
by Industry, 1951–1954

Industry	1951	1952	1953	1954
Pulp and Paper	.16	.11	.11	.11
Light Chemicals	.23	.16	.15	.15
Heavy Chemicals	.13	.10	.09	.09
Petroleum	.11	.08	.08	.07
Rubber	.17	.12	.12	.09
Heavy Steel	.19	.13	.13	.09
Fabricated Metal Products	.28	.22	.29	.16
Special Industrial Machinery	.26	.20	.18	.21
General Industrial Machinery	.35	.31	.28	.27
Machine Tools	.23	.26	.24	.21
Heavy Equipment, Engines, and Turbines	.45	.41	.35	.32
Air Conditioning, Heating, and Similar Equipment	.37	.36	.31	.32
Household Durables	.25	.23	.18	.18
Light Electrical Machinery	.27	.15	.18	.11
Heavy Electrical Machinery	.35	.25	.21	.17
Electronics	.46	.36	.34	.34
Auto Fabricators	.20	.20	.20	.16
Auto Parts and Accessories	.25	.19	.18	.12
Basic Textiles	.15	.09	.05	.01
Other Textiles	.09	.07	.06	.02

One of the more notable aspects of the 1952 data is how little effect the steel strike of that year seems to have had.

The 1953–1954 recession is clearly reflected in all the 1954 figures. Substantially lower capacity utilization and profit figures are recorded for 1954 than for any of the other years in the sample. Similarly, the average retained earnings plus depreciation expense ratio declined for 11 of the 20 industries in 1954. However, it is highly suggestive of the sharp increase in depreciation expenses over the period that the average retained gross earnings ratio improved in 9 of the 20 industries in 1954 while the net profit ratio improved in only 2 of the 20. Thus, in terms of the gross availability of internal financing, 1954 was not a markedly inferior year to 1953. Similarly, the tendency for business holdings of liquid assets to increase during recessions shows up in the net quick asset ratios which actually increased in 12 out of 20 industries between the beginning of 1953 and the beginning of 1954. In terms, therefore, of

TABLE IV-6

Average Retained Earnings Plus Depreciation Expense
to Gross Fixed Asset Ratios by Industry, 1951–1954

Industry	1951	1952	1953	1954
Pulp and Paper	.158	.110	.112	.107
Light Chemicals	.136	.090	.096	.107
Heavy Chemicals	.114	.081	.092	.097
Petroleum	.125	.104	.108	.103
Rubber	.148	.111	.122	.100
Heavy Steel	.158	.110	.126	.082
Fabricated Metal Products	.205	.160	.248	.125
Special Industrial Machinery	.179	.143	.136	.153
General Industrial Machinery	.214	.172	.162	.329
Machine Tools	.162	.211	.211	.163
Heavy Equipment, Engines, and Turbines	.404	.387	.345	.390
Air Conditioning, Heating, and Similar Equipment	.324	.312	.264	.378
Household Durables	.173	.132	.132	.131
Light Electrical Machinery	.227	.133	.182	.135
Heavy Electrical Machinery	.252	.185	.155	.131
Electronics	.335	.250	.259	.440
Auto Fabricators	.156	.162	.183	.149
Auto Parts and Accessories	.199	.157	.161	.194
Basic Textiles	.109	.074	.046	.010
Other Textiles	.081	.072	.067	.067

both the flow of available internal funds and the stock of liquid
assets, business was in a moderately and surprisingly affluent position during the mildly recessionary year of 1954.

VI. *Summary*

While the period from the end of World War II to the end of 1958
was not one of sharp turns and dramatic traumas in the business
cycle, it was at least a period of some variety. Specifically, three
complete cycles are observable during these years, and each of the
three upturns and each of the three downturns seems to have some
distinguishing characteristics of its own. Shifts in consumer expenditures, inventory accumulation, and producers' purchases of
durable equipment can all be discerned as initiating factors in both
declines and upswings. Even more importantly from the standpoint of this study, these different cyclical phases were marked by

TABLE IV-7

Average Net Quick Asset * to Gross Fixed
Asset Ratios by Industry, 1951–1954

Industry	1951	1952	1953	1954
Pulp and Paper	.187	.313	.250	.233
Light Chemicals	.392	.398	.357	.391
Heavy Chemicals	.269	.312	.255	.280
Petroleum	.124	.128	.118	.102
Rubber	.252	.305	.198	.213
Heavy Steel	.300	.415	.235	.271
Fabricated Metal Products	.367	.445	.279	.298
Special Industrial Machinery	.349	.250	.208	.182
General Industrial Machinery	.595	.679	.647	.664
Machine Tools	.389	.341	.442	.525
Heavy Equipment, Engines, and Turbines	.356	.214	.271	.301
Air Conditioning, Heating, and Similar Equipment	.336	.257	.315	.232
Household Durables	.714	.481	.522	.365
Light Electrical Machinery	.543	.349	.396	.377
Heavy Electrical Machinery	.397	.524	.434	.358
Electronics	1.033	.167	.390	.123
Auto Fabricators	.346	−.012	.124	.195
Auto Parts and Accessories	.388	.423	.339	.422
Basic Textiles	.149	.136	.129	.155
Other Textiles	.232	.166	.198	.220

* Net quick assets are defined as cash plus marketable securities less notes payable to banks. The ratios pertain to the beginning of each year.

considerable differences in the liquidity and capacity utilization positions of manufacturing firms. Therefore, the period presents a sufficient variety of experience to test to at least some degree the bifurcated or nonlinear behavior patterns suggested by the accelerator-residual funds hypothesis.

| Chapter **V** | *Investment Decisions, 1951–1954:*
A Preliminary Cross-Section Analysis |

I. *Procedures and General Principles*

The choice of variables and the specification of hypotheses obviously can be crucial in conditioning the entire character of any empirical study. Strangely, though, in economics this aspect of empirical work is often reported only in the most cursory fashion.

The choice of variables sometimes may be considered self-evident. For example, if one particular hypothesis is to be tested, the variables may seem, at least at first glance, to be closely specified by the nature of the theory. Unfortunately, most economic theories are seldom formulated so as to be uniquely specifiable in terms of observable quantities. The empirical investigator usually must choose from a number of more or less imperfect empirical approximations to the variables conceived by the theorist. Furthermore, some theorists are often less than specific about the appropriateness in their models of time lags, nonlinearities, and variable transformations such as logarithms or first differences.

The empiricist, moreover, is interested in a more difficult problem as a rule than simply confirming the plausibility or implausibility of a given theory. A number of different theories may have been propounded as explanations of the same or closely related phenomena. Not uncommonly these theories conflict with one another. The empirical investigator will be interested in at least narrowing the range of admissible theories, that is, in rejecting some theories as in direct conflict with the available evidence. In practice, much or indeed most of this sorting will take the form of rejecting particular variables because they have no observable influence in specified relationships.

The existence of these conflicts in the theory behooves the investigator to test the implications of questionable or contested theories whenever possible. In keeping with this principle, the closeness of the relationships between various candidate variables and other variables usually is compared by most empiricists before making a final decision to include any variable in a more formal empirical model, that is, to accept one particular formulation as a maintained hypothesis. To make these needed preliminary comparisons, simple correlation coefficients often are used and will be so used in this study. However, relying on simple correlations for the performance of this function raises the possibility that significant relationships may be overlooked because they are obscured by offsetting intercorrelations with other variables. Some "strategic" intercorrelations are accordingly reported in the preliminary analyses of this chapter.

Separating more promising from less promising variables can be greatly facilitated by initially grouping the different "candidate" variables into reasonably similar clusters. For this purpose, existing theory can be used to define broad groups of roughly interchangeable or equivalent variables, and comparisons within these clusters usually will constitute a sufficient basis for preliminary selection of variables. In the present study the pertinent clusters will be defined as: (1) capacity utilization, profit, and sales variables; (2) measures of internally generated funds or cash throw-off; (3) measures of debt, equity position, and financial risk; (4) current assets and related measures of the stock of liquidity; (5) first difference formulations of different cash flow and liquid asset variables; and (6) capital asset and other lagged investment variables.

II. *Capacity, Profit, and Sales Variables*

In the accelerator-residual funds hypothesis, relationship of capacity and profit variables to investment depends on general business conditions. The capacity variable should provide the best explanation of investment when capacity is fully utilized and the profit variable the best when over-all profits and liquidity stock are declining. As outlined in the preceding chapter, business conditions during the years 1951–1954 can be broadly pictured as follows: 1951 was a year of exceptional expansion and buoyancy in economic activity; 1952 and, to a lesser extent, 1953 were good, sound years for manufacturing business; and 1954 was mildly but not seriously depressed. According to the residual funds hypothesis, therefore, capacity or acceleration variables should provide a good explanation of investment during 1951 and a poor explanation during 1954, while the 1952–1953 results should be of mixed character. Furthermore, cash flows, profits and depreciation expense should be more closely related to investment during 1954 than during 1951; similarly, the 1953 performance of these variables should be better than that for 1952. To the extent, moreover, that profits are a measure of market power, the relationship between profits and investment might even be negative during 1951.

A comparison of the simple correlations between the capacity, profit, lagged profit, and sales variables generally sustains these expectations. In Table V–1 the variable of these four that has the highest simple correlation with investment is recorded for each industry-year. The number in parentheses beside each letter is the correlation between the recorded best-performance variable and investment (to the nearest two decimal places).

The capacity variable clearly records the closest relationships with investment during the boom year of 1951 and the sales variable the second best. Profit variables clearly dominate the results for the years 1953 and 1954, though not as completely as the capacity variable dominates the 1951 results. Moreover, the dominance of the profit variables in the later years increases somewhat if the sales variable is suppressed, as shown in Table V–2. Profit variables perform "second best" to two of the four sales variables reported in the 1953 column of Table V–1 and to five out of six of the sales variables reported for 1954. Thus, ignoring the sales variable, 13 out of 20 industries record a higher simple correlation between profits and investment than between capacity and investment during 1953; the equivalent figure for 1954 is 16 out of 20. Furthermore,

TABLE V-1

Capacity, Profit, and Sales Comparisons Based on Simple
Correlations with Investment by Industry, 1951–1954 †

Industry	1951	1952	1953	1954
Pulp and Paper	$S(.31)$	$S(.21)$	$C(.38)$	$C(.31)$
Light Chemicals	$C(.58)$	$P_{t-1}(.36)$	$C(.41)$	$P(.51)$
Heavy Chemicals	$C(.31)$	$C(.28)$	$P_{t-1}*(.03)$	$P(.20)$
Petroleum	$P(.40)$	$S(.70)$	$P(.41)$	$P(.61)$
Rubber	$C(.81)$	$P\&P_{t-1}(.15)$	$P_{t-1}\&P(.30)$	$C\&P_{t-1}(.53)$
Heavy Steel	$C(.39)$	$P_{t-1}(.49)$	$P_{t-1}(.18)$	$S*(.20)$
Fabricated Metal Products	$S(.27)$	$S(.65)$	$P(.25)$	$S*(.27)$
Special Industrial Machinery	$S(.53)$	$C(.37)$	$C(.36)$	$P*(.49)$
General Industrial Machinery	$C(.15)$	$P_{t-1}*(.05)$	$C*(.02)$	$C*(.05)$
Machine Tools	$C(.44)$	$C(.61)$	$S(.43)$	$S(.41)$
Heavy Equipment, Engines, and Turbines	$C\&S(.60)$	$S(.39)$	$S(.33)$	$P\&P_{t-1}(.75)$
Air Conditioning, Heating, and Similar Equipment	$C(.64)$	$S*(.27)$	$S*(.50)$	$C*(.41)$
Household Durables	$S(.37)$	$S(.61)$	$S(.27)$	$S*(.39)$
Light Electrical Machinery	$S(.55)$	$P_{t-1}*(.49)$	$P_{t-1}*(.58)$	$S(.36)$
Heavy Electrical Machinery	$C(.77)$	$P_{t-1}(.11)$	$C*(.09)$	$P_{t-1}(.55)$
Electronics	$C(.73)$	$C(.40)$	$P(.88)$	$P(.64)$
Auto Fabricators	$C(.82)$	$P(.30)$	$C(.57)$	$C(.21)$
Auto Parts and Accessories	$C(.45)$	$C(.28)$	$P(.50)$	$P(.63)$
Basic Textiles	$C(.51)$	$P_{t-1}\&P(.19)$	$P_{t-1}(.45)$	$S(.67)$
Other Textiles	$C(.69)$	$P(.39)$	$P_{t-1}(.40)$	$P_{t-1}*(.12)$

† The variable reported in code form for each industry-year in this table is
the variable that had the highest simple correlation with investment of the following four variables: current profits (P); lagged profits (P_{t-1}); capacity (C);
and sales (S).

* For these industry-years the results are closely bunched for several variables,
either making it impossible to specify one variable as more important or making
the reported variable only slightly more important than others.

most, though certainly not all, of the recorded correlations are
reasonably substantial.

It is somewhat disquieting that the relative performance of the
capacity and sales variables for different industries does not always
conform during these years to what would be predicted on the basis
of the profit and capacity average values recorded in Tables IV–5
and IV–4; the household durable and electronic industries in 1953
are particularly adverse examples. These may be due, of course,
to intercorrelations; in a complete model, performance and prediction may be in closer agreement. The results for 1952 are some-

what heterogeneous and also not completely in conformance with expectations. The profit variable rather surprisingly does best in 11 of 20 industries.

Another unexpected feature of Table V–2 is the seemingly better performance of lagged than unlagged profits. In the 1946–1950 investment study the only three industries that yielded markedly

TABLE V–2

A Comparison of Capacity and Profit Simple Correlations with Investment by Industry, 1951–1954

Industry	1951	1952	1953	1954
Pulp and Paper	P	P	C	C
Light Chemicals	C	P_{t-1}	C	P
Heavy Chemicals	C	C	P_{t-1}	P
Petroleum	P	P	P	P
Rubber	C	P	P_{t-1}	$C\&P_{t-1}$
Heavy Steel	C	P_{t-1}	P_{t-1}	P_{t-1}
Fabricated Metal Products	P	P	P	P
Special Industrial Machinery	P	C	C	P
General Industrial Machinery	C	P_{t-1}	C	C
Machine Tools	C	C	$P_{t-1}\&C$	P_{t-1}
Heavy Equipment, Engines, and Turbines	C	C	C	P_{t-1}
Air Conditioning, Heating, and Similar Equipment	C	C	C	C
Household Durables	P	C	P_{t-1}	P
Light Electrical Machinery	P	P_{t-1}	P_{t-1}	$P_{t-1}\&C$
Heavy Electrical Machinery	C	P_{t-1}	C	P_{t-1}
Electronics	C	C	P_{t-1}	P
Auto Fabricators	C	P	C	C
Auto Parts and Accessories	C	C	P	P
Basic Textiles	C	P_{t-1}	P_{t-1}	P_{t-1}
Other Textiles	C	P	P_{t-1}	P_{t-1}

better explanations of investment with lagged than with unlagged profits were pulp and paper, petroleum, and fabricated metal products. In the present case, a close scrutiny of the simple correlations suggests that in nine industries lagged profits is a better variable than current profits. These industries are: pulp and paper, rubber, heavy steel, household durables, light electrical machinery, heavy electrical machinery, auto parts and accessories, basic textiles, and other textiles. Somewhat disturbing is the fact that only one industry, pulp and paper, belongs to both the 1946–1950 and 1951–1954 groups.

Otherwise the data have a strong tendency toward autocorrelation. As shown in Table V–3, the correlations between lagged and unlagged profits are quite high. In many cases the "intercorrelations" between the two profit variables are higher than the corresponding correlations between profits and the proposed dependent variable, investment. Under such "collinear" circum-

TABLE V–3

Correlations Between Lagged and Unlagged Profits by Industry, 1952–1954 *

Industry	1952	1953	1954
Pulp and Paper	.76	.87	.67
Light Chemicals	.84	.80	.89
Heavy Chemicals	.83	.77	.73
Petroleum	.73	.88	.80
Rubber	.88	.92	.76
Heavy Steel	.83	.95	.87
Fabricated Metal Products	.83	.18	.32
Special Industrial Machinery	.93	.84	.89
General Industrial Machinery	.95	.99	.98
Machine Tools	.66	.88	.66
Heavy Equipment, Engines, and Turbines	.99	.99	.99
Air Conditioning, Heating, and Similar Equipment	.99	.98	.99
Household Durables	.81	.89	.96
Light Electrical Machinery	.21	.44	.63
Heavy Electrical Machinery	.95	.96	.87
Electronics	.97	.93	.36
Auto Fabricators	.13	.78	.72
Auto Parts and Accessories	.85	.95	.73
Basic Textiles	.71	.78	.83
Other Textiles	.84	.87	.93

* Because of a desire to economize on the computational procedures, the 1951 results were not obtained.

stances, there is almost always a danger of the regression estimates being the arbitrary, perhaps random, result of a few extreme observations. These high intercorrelations also point to another conclusion (that might have been deduced from the inconsistent industry pattern in the performance of the profit variables as explanations of investment): lagged and unlagged profits are so highly correlated that in most instances it makes little difference which is chosen as an explanatory variable. There is also a tendency for the current rather than the lagged variable to be superior when the intercorrelation is relatively low; in three of the five cases for which the intercorrelation is below .5, current profits has a higher simple correlation with investment than lagged profits. The two contrary cases are both in the light electrical machinery industry; consequently, only in this industry would the case for the use of lagged profits appear incontrovertible.

Seriously harmful collinearity may also arise between the sales and profit variables. These variables were so closely interrelated in the 1946–1950 study that they were never included in the same model. Since the early postwar period, however, a number of developments have occurred that might have reduced this close relationship. As a matter of empirical fact, greatly reduced intercorrelations between profits and sales are observable for the 1951–1954 period compared with 1946–1950. The 1951–1954 sales-profit correlations are presented in Table V–4; they should be compared

TABLE V–4

Simple Correlations Between Profits and Sales by Industry, 1952–1954

Industry	1951	1952	1953	1954
Pulp and Paper	.45	.34	.51	.41
Light Chemicals	.17	.03	.13	.23
Heavy Chemicals	.34	.42	.50	.53
Petroleum	.10	−.13	−.08	−.05
Rubber	.42	.12	.04	.15
Heavy Steel	.87	.86	.89	.84
Fabricated Metal Products	.78	.76	.16	.87
Special Industrial Machinery	.77	.63	.78	.70
General Industrial Machinery	.85	.88	.83	.87
Machine Tools	.50	.62	.62	.41
Heavy Equipment, Engines, and Turbines	.27	.17	.23	.56
Air Conditioning, Heating, and Similar Equipment	.27	.28	.27	.21
Household Durables	.81	.80	.73	.93
Light Electrical Machinery	.78	.34	.78	.39
Heavy Electrical Machinery	.85	.76	.75	.65
Electronics	.96	.90	.95	.78
Auto Fabricators	.38	.33	.21	.65
Auto Parts and Accessories	.50	.38	.24	.53
Basic Textiles	.48	.70	.77	.47
Other Textiles	.38	.34	.19	·20

with intercorrelations for the earlier period that were generally in the range of .8 or greater. The 1951–1954 correlations, though high, are not prohibitively high in all industries. In particular, an opportunity would seem to exist for testing in the same model the relative effect of profits and sales on investment in several industries. However, the heavy steel, fabricated metal products, special industrial machinery, household durables, and the three electrical industries would still appear to have dangerously high sales with profit intercorrelations.

III. *Cash Throw-Off Variables*

Several different definitions might be given to cash throw-off or, more exactly, residual funds available for physical investment purposes. At one extreme would be the simple sum of profits and depreciation expense; at the other would be profits plus depreciation expense less all possible claims on cash except investment outlays, a variable, for example, like $T - N - V$. Five different liquidity flow variables have been tested as part of this study: profits plus depreciation expense or cash throw-off, T; cash throw-off less dividends, $T - V$; cash throw-off less both dividends and working capital needs, $T - L' - V$; cash throw-off less all possible claims as previously defined in Chapter III, Table III–1, $T - N - V$; and profits less dividends, $P - V$. The performance of each of these variables in explaining investment has been compared not only each with the other but also with profits and depreciation expense. A summary of these comparisons is contained in Table V–5. As before, the variables reported in the table are the ones recording the highest simple correlation with investment for each industry-year; the number in parentheses after each letter is the corresponding highest correlation rounded to two decimal places.

The two dominant cash throw-off variables are obviously D, depreciation expense, and $T - L' - V$, internally available cash left after meeting current asset and dividend "demands" on funds. Furthermore, depreciation expense is clearly the better of these two, lending sustenance to the earlier finding that depreciation expense seems to have an influence on investment differentiable from other types of internal liquidity flows. The superior performance of the

TABLE V-5

Cash Throw-Off Comparisons Based on Simple Correlations
with Investment by Industry, 1951–1954 †

Industry	1951	1952	1953	1954
Pulp and Paper	D(.41)	D(.55)	T-V(.41)	T(.32)
Light Chemicals	D(.63)	D(.62)	T-V(.39)	P(.51)
Heavy Chemicals	D(.57)	D(.16)	T-L'-V(.46)	D*(.49)
Petroleum	T*(.55)	T-L'-V*(.66)	T*(.59)	P*(.61)
Rubber	T-L'-V*(.66)	T-V*(.23)	D(.53)	D(.64)
Heavy Steel	*(.37–.48)	D(.65)	T-L'-V(.81)	T-L'-V(.39)
Fabricated Metal Products	D(.32)	D(.32)	T-L'-V(.39)	T-N-V(.29)
Special Industrial Machinery	T(.36)	D(.40)	T-L'-V(.49)	T(.54)
General Industrial Machinery	P-V*(.12)	T-N*-V(.22)	T-L'-V*(.24)	T-L'-V*(.06)
Machine Tools	D(.47)	D(.62)	T-L'-V(.45)	T-V(.44)
Heavy Equipment, Engines, and Turbines	D(.45)	D(.56)	D(.60)	*(.70–.74)
Air Conditioning, Heating, and Similar Equipment	D(.39)	D(.44)	D(.52)	D(.33)
Household Durables	T-N-V(.50)	P-V(.17)	T-L'-V(.56)	T-L'-V(.50) & P-V
Light Electrical Machinery	T-L'-V*(.66)	D*(.36)	D(.70)	D(.73)
Heavy Electrical Machinery	D(.44)	T-L'-V(.61)	D(.38)	D(.74)
Electronics	T-V(.20)	T-N-V(.62)	D&T(.85–.86)	*(.64–.70)
Auto Fabricators	T-L'-V(.40)	T-N-V(.48)	D(.66)	D(.40)
Auto Parts and Accessories	P-V(.32)	D*(.28)	P(.50)	*(.52–.59)
Basic Textiles	D(.36)	P-V(.21)	T-L'-V(.62)	*(.24–.27)
Other Textiles	*(.09–.15)	T&D(.44–.45)	T(.34)	D(.12)

† Variables compared: T, D, T-V, T-L'-V, T-N-V, P-V, P.

* For these industry-years the results are closely bunched for several variables, either making it impossible to specify one variable as more important or making the reported variable only slightly more important than others.

depreciation expense variable might be attributed to differences in equipment durability of different firms but this seems unlikely with stratified industry samples like those used here. In the years 1951 through 1954, moreover, depreciation expense was more a measure of available funds and less a measure of capital replacement needs than in the 1946–1950 period (when the capital need relationship was probably slight enough),[1] because of accelerated amortization granted during the Korean emergency.[2]

The simple profit variable does very poorly compared with the more refined measures of cash throw-off. Profit is the variable of closest relationship with investment in only three of the eighty industry-years of experience reported in Table V–5. Furthermore, the picture is little altered if the dominant depreciation expense variable is eliminated from consideration; as shown in Table V–6, in only one case — auto fabricators for 1951 — does the profit variable perform second best to depreciation expense. Indeed, the main effect of suppressing the depreciation expense variable is to lay greater stress on the second best performance of $T - L' - V$, cash throw-off after current asset and dividend demands have been met.[3] Even profits adjusted for dividend payments, $P - V$, appears

---

[1] A test of this relationship will be found in Meyer and Kuh, *The Investment Decision*, Chapter 7.

[2] Since depreciation expense figures were accepted as they were shown in reports to stockholders, some accelerated amortization may not be entered as depreciation expense in the present sample to the extent that particular firms chose to report "accelerated depreciation" only to the Internal Revenue Service and not to stockholders. Using the stockholder report figure, however it may have been constituted, can be justified on the grounds that this figure reflects individual management's "true attitudes" on what the correct depreciation figure should be and that decisions were based on this figure even if it differs from the figure used for tax purposes. Of course, when depreciation expense is added to profits to form a cash throw-off measure, these distinctions are immaterial since what is not reported in one of these two figures must be recorded in the other.

[3] It would be tempting, because of depreciation expenses' seemingly special influence on investment, to include depreciation expense as a separate variable in a regression model along with an adjusted cash throw-off variable like $T - L' - V$. Unfortunately, something of a double counting or contradiction in hypotheses is involved if both depreciation expense and a cash throw-off variable are included in the same model. Since cash throw-off equals profits plus depreciation expenses ($T = P + D$), including both depreciation expense and cash throw-off simultaneously in the same model would amount to assigning two different weights to the influence of depreciation expense on investment. These considerations lead to the almost inescapable conclusion that two different cash flow models should be tested. The first would include profits (or profits less dividends) and depreciation expense separately, but because of possible collinearity, would not include a sales variable. The second model would include sales and cash throw-off net of current asset and dividend needs but not depreciation expense. The first model would have the advantage of measuring the apparently important independent influence of depreciation expense on investment while the second offers an opportunity to separate, at least partially, financial and expectational influences on investment.

more often in Table V–6 than the simple profit variable, P.[4] These results support the residual funds hypothesis that current profits influence investment *in the short run* mainly as a source of internally available funds and not as a measure of expectations.

TABLE V–6

Cash Throw-Off Comparisons Exclusive of Depreciation Expense Based on Simple Correlations with Investment by Industry, 1951–1954 †

Industry	1951	1952	1953	1954
Pulp and Paper	*T-V*	*T-V*	*T-V*	*T*
Light Chemicals	*T-V*	*T-L'-V*	*T-V**	*P*
Heavy Chemicals	*T-V*	*T-V*	*T-L'-V*	*T-V*
Petroleum	*T*	*T-L'-V*	*T*	*P*
Rubber	*T-L'-V*	*T-V*	*T*	*T*
Heavy Steel	*T-V*	*T-L'-V*	*T-L'-V*	*T-L'-V*
Fabricated Metal Products	*	*	*T-L'-V*	*T-N-V*
Special Industrial Machinery	*T*	*T-V*	*T-L'-V*	*T**
General Industrial Machinery	*P-V&T-V*	*T-N-V**	*T-L'-V*	*T-L'-V*
Machine Tools	*T-V*	*T-L'-V**	*T-L'-V*	*
Heavy Equipment, Engines, and Turbines	*	*	*	*
Air Conditioning, Heating, and Similar Equipment	*T-L'-V*	*	*	*
Household Durables	*T-N-V*	*P-V*	*T-L'-V*	*T-L'-V*
Light Electrical Machinery	*T-L'-V*	*T-L'-V*	*T*	*
Heavy Electrical Machinery	*T-V*	*T-L'-V*	*T-L'-V*	*T*
Electronics	*P-V**	*T-N-V*	*	*
Auto Fabricators	*P**	*T-N-V**	*	*T-L'-V*
Auto Parts and Accessories	*P-V&T-V*	*T-V**	*P*	*
Basic Textiles	*T-N-V*	*P-V*	*T-L'-V*	*
Other Textiles	*	*T**	*T*	*

† Variables compared: *T, T-V, T-L'-V, T-N-V, P-V, P*.

* For these industry-years the results are closely bunched for several variables, either making it impossible to specify one variable as more important or making the reported variable only slightly more important than others.

As a variable to be included in any final multivariable regression model, an adjusted cash throw-off or residual funds measure has another important advantage over profits. As might be expected, the intercorrelation between the adjusted variables and sales is con-

---

[4] These two variables are, however, so closely interrelated (almost always the correlation is .75 or larger and often greater than .90) that they cannot be effectively differentiated.

siderably lower than between profits and sales. These intercorrelations are low enough, in fact, that certain fund flow variables might be used in the same multi-variable model as a sales variable, thus permitting a more efficacious test to be made of the relative roles of financial and expectational influences on investment. In particular, the correlations between sales and the most promising of the cash throw-off variables, $T - L' - V$, reported in Table V-7, actu-

TABLE V-7

Simple Correlations Between Sales and Free Retained Funds
by Industry, 1951–1954

Industry	1951	1952	1953	1954
Pulp and Paper	−.12	.19	.24	−.03
Light Chemicals	−.05	−.14	.38	−.31
Heavy Chemicals	.16	−.03	−.26	−.27
Petroleum	−.45	.66	.41	−.19
Rubber	.18	−.38	.49	−.14
Heavy Steel	.37	.25	.06	.33
Fabricated Metal Products	−.06	−.06	.08	−.40
Special Industrial Machinery	.40	−.79	.15	.29
General Industrial Machinery	.24	−.29	−.07	.61
Machine Tools	−.16	−.11	.39	.01
Heavy Equipment, Engines, and Turbines	.16	.15	.18	.53
Air Conditioning, Heating, and Similar Equipment	.07	.20	.35	.01
Household Durables	.19	.16	.27	.22
Light Electrical Machinery	.20	.32	.62	−.12
Heavy Electrical Machinery	.26	.06	−.31	−.27
Electronics	.70	.55	.38	−.10
Auto Fabricators	.04	−.22	.14	−.46
Auto Parts and Accessories	−.03	.32	−.26	.42
Basic Textiles	.37	.10	.22	−.59
Other Textiles	−.34	.14	.35	.55

ally appear more than small enough to permit including both in the same model. The correlation between these two variables is almost invariably lower than the corresponding sales-profit correlation reported in Table V-4, and (with the possible exception of the electronics industry for the year 1951) there would appear to be no serious danger of harmful collinearity being created by including both variables in the same regression model.

IV. *Debt-Equity Variables*

Hypotheses long have been advanced that individual firms' investment rates will be influenced by the composition of their long-term debt and equity accounts. Basically these hypotheses reflect a rational and plausible desire to establish financial and money market influences on business investment decisions. The mechanism usually assumed is that as debt increases relative to equity, investment declines because outside financing becomes more difficult to obtain or, at least, more expensive. In one of its better formal presentations this proposition has been called the "principle of increasing risk." Not unsurprisingly, the obvious point has been made that the validity of the principle of increasing risk may be greatly mitigated by equity shares becoming more attractive when their leverage is increased by a plentiful supply of debt; it is, in fact, conceivable that an increase in the price of equity shares, caused by a firm's obtaining additional debt financing, might make outside money more rather than less available. Of course, for this offset to be operative, there can be no strong managerial prejudice against equity financing. Since such prejudices seem to exist among large American manufacturing firms, the principle of increasing risk *a priori* would seem to be an operative possibility. Furthermore, there must be some limit beyond which any favorable effects of additional leverage cease to operate.

The available evidence on the principle of increasing risk is not, however, strongly corroborative. In the 1946–1950 investment study the relationships between various debt-equity ratios and investment were so weak in a number of test cases that no debt-equity variables were included in the final models. The tests, however, were limited in number and extent. A more comprehensive and systematic evaluation therefore was undertaken as part of this study. Again, the evidence was overwhelmingly negative.

Six different formulations of debt-equity variables were tested: (1) long-term debt lagged, or in notational form, B_{t-1}; (2) long-term debt unlagged, B_t; (3) net worth lagged, W_{t-1}; (4) the ratio of current long-term debt to the current book value of invested capital, Z_t; (5) the ratio of lagged long-term debt to the lagged book value of invested capital, Z_{t-1}; and (6) the ratio of lagged long-term debt plus preferred stock less net quick liquidity to the lagged book value of invested capital, $Z_{a(t-1)}$. The simple correlations between these variables and investment are shown in Table V–8. The debt-equity variable having the highest simple correlation with investment that is also of the "correct sign" is reported in each case; since correctness is defined by the predictions that would be made by the increasing risk hypothesis, a negative correlation with investment would be expected of all the variables except net worth. When all the signs are incorrect according to the increasing risk hypothesis (i.e., all the simple correlations are positive except that between net worth and investment), the term "NCS" has been entered in the table. As before, the value in parentheses after each variable code is the value of the correlation between the reported variable and investment.

The results presented in Table V–8 provide little empirical sustenance for the principle of increasing risk. In 12 of the 80 industry-years none of the correlations have signs in agreement with the increasing risk principle. Of the remaining 68 cases, only 31 of the reported correlations are greater than .20; furthermore only 13 are greater than .30. The same point is made even more forceably if the signs of all six variables' simple correlations with investment are inspected. Since there are six variables and 80 industry-years, the total number of correlations to be considered is 480. Of these 480, only 194 have signs that agree with those expected under the increasing risk principle. If a cross-section relationship does exist therefore between debt-equity variables and investment, the evidence suggests that in the range of observable evidence the "leverage effect" probably outweighs increasing risk. A positive relationship between debt and investment is, of course, also consistent with the earlier finding that debt is likely to be unwanted or not available except in growth situations. Therefore, to the extent that firms with different growth prospects are represented *within* an industry sample, a positive debt-investment relationship on the cross section might be expected.

Debt-equity ratios would seem to be, moreover, examples *par excellance* of variables that will be under managerial control and that might be expected to vary *among firms* in response to different policy orientations. As such, these variables probably are best

TABLE V-8

Comparison of Measures of Debt and Financial "Risk" Simple Correlations
with Investment by Industry, 1951–1954 †

Industry	1951	1952	1953	1954
Pulp and Paper	$W(.31)$	$W(.12)$	NCS	$W(.06)$
Light Chemicals	$Z_a(-.11)$	NCS	$Z_a(-.12)$	$Z_a(-.32)$
Heavy Chemicals	$W(.10)$	$Z_a(-.06)$	NCS	NCS
Petroleum	$W(.37)$	$W(.32)$	$W(.24)$	$W(.37)$
Rubber	$W(.23)$	$Z_a(-.17)$	$Z_a(-.11)$	$Z_a(-.10)$
Heavy Steel	$W(.07)$	$W(.17)$	$Z_a(-.06)$	$Z(-.19)$
Fabricated Metal Products	$W(.10)$	NCS	$Z_{t-1}(-.57)$	$Z(-.31)$
Special Industrial Machinery	$W(.46)$	$W(.13)$	$Z_{t-1}(-.03)$	$W(.46)$
General Industrial Machinery	$Z(-.22)$	$B_{t-1}\&Z(-.21)$	$Z\&Z_{t-1}(-.21)$	$Z\&Z_{t-1}(-.16)$
Machine Tools	$W(.12)$	$W(.02)$	$W(.08)$	NCS
Heavy Equipment, Engines, and Turbines	$W(.29)$	NCS	NCS	$W(.27)$
Air Conditioning, Heating, and Similar Equipment	$Z(-.34)$	$Z(-.29)$	$W(.24)$	$Z_a(-.06)$
Household Durables	$Z(-.26)$	$W(.04)$	$B(-.22)$	$W(.23)$
Light Electrical Machinery	$Z_a(-.06)$	$W(.15)$	$W(.23)$	NCS
Heavy Electrical Machinery	$W(.49)$	$W(.18)$	$W(.08)$	$W(.42)$
Electronics	NCS	$W(.26)$	$W(.83)$	$B(-.24)$
Auto Fabricators	$Z_{t-1}(-.14)$	$B_{t-1}\&Z(-.05)$	$Z_a(-.20)$	$Z_a(-.20)$
Auto Parts and Accessories	$W(.09)$	$W(.20)$	$W(.43)$	$W(.42)$
Basic Textiles	$Z(-.28)$	$B_{t-1}(-.18)$	NCS	$W(.39)$
Other Textiles	$Z(-.27)$	$Z_{t-1}(-.03)$	$B_{t-1}\&Z(-.16)$	NCS

NCS = No "a-priori correct" sign for any of the correlation results.

† Variables compared: B_t, B_{t-1}, W_{t-1}, Z_t, Z_{t-1}, and $Z_{a(t-1)}$. (The $t-1$ subscript has been omitted from W and Z_a since it is not needed to differentiate these variables from other variables.)

analyzed in cross-section data as dependent variables in a regression analysis in which investment is one of the explanatory variables. This should be particularly true for the relatively small range of variation in debt-equity ratios encountered in the present sample. If there is an empirical case for the principle of increasing risk when using cross-section data, it is probably at the extreme of substantial over-involvement in debt; at some level of indebtedness relative to invested equity, lenders must, it seems, become hesitant to offer a firm more funds except under stringent and expensive conditions. The strong aversion of most large United States manufacturing firms to debt of all types precludes the observation of many of these extremes in the sample used in this study. For a sample of small, very new firms this might not be true.

V. *Liquidity Stock Variables*

One of the more persistent hypotheses about investment behavior is that the rate of investment will increase with an increase in the stock of liquid assets held by those making investment decisions. Liquid assets have been used, for example, as explanatory variables in such widely different investment models as an aggregate investment function for the entire United States economy [5] and a microfunction explaining investment in consumer durables by individual households.[6] With the exception of consumer durable expenditures right after World War II, there seems to be little empirical evidence of any substantial relationship between liquid assets and investment. The findings of the 1946–1950 study of business investment behavior were particularly negative; in that study the net quick liquidity stock (L) was as often as not negatively related to investment and the over-all average of the observed simple and partial correlations was essentially zero.

These negative findings about the influence of the *stock* of liquidity on investment contrast sharply with those for the *flow* of

[5] See Lawrence Robert Klein and A. S. Goldberger, *An Econometric Model of the United States, 1929–1952* (Amsterdam: North-Holland Publishing Co., 1955).

[6] James Tobin and Harold W. Watts, *Consumer Expenditures and the Capital Account*, Cowles Foundation Paper No. 165, New Haven: Cowles Foundation, 1961.

liquidity. Indeed, so sharp is the contrast that the negative findings might be suspected and attributed to improper definition of what is the crucially important liquidity stock in business decisions. To test for this possibility 17 different liquidity stock variables were employed in the preliminary analyses of the present study; [7] even ignoring lagged values of what were otherwise identical variables, 9 different liquidity stock concepts were used.[8] These were: (1) lagged and current inventory values; (2) the difference between lagged (and unlagged) inventory and current inventory needs as estimated by multiplying the minimum ratio between inventory and sales attained by the particular firm in the 1951–1954 period by current sales; (3) lagged and unlagged cash plus marketable securities less notes payable to bank; (4) the difference between lagged (and unlagged) available cash plus marketable securities less notes payable to banks and currently required cash plus marketable securities less notes payable to banks estimated by the minimum ratio of cash plus marketable securities less notes payable to banks to sales attained by the particular firm in the 1951–1954 period multiplied by current sales; (5) lagged and unlagged cash plus marketable securities plus accounts receivable; (6) the difference between lagged and unlagged accounts receivable and required accounts receivable as measured by the minimum ratio of accounts receivable to sales attained by the particular firm during the 1951–1954 period multiplied by current sales; (7) the difference between lagged (and unlagged) cash plus marketable securities plus accounts receivable as defined by multiplying the minimum ratio between cash plus marketable securities plus accounts receivable to sales attained by the particular firm in the 1951–1954 period by current sales; (8) net quick liquidity, i.e., current assets less inventories and current liabilities; and (9) lagged and unlagged accounts receivable. It should be noted that variables (2), (4), (6), and (7) have been normalized to eliminate individual firm differences, the technique used being conceptually identical to that previously employed in defining the capacity variable.

[7] It was feasible to test the relationship between this rather long list of different liquidity stock variables and investment because the calculations could be inexpensively appended to exploratory investigations being undertaken as part of a study of corporation liquidity preference functions.

[8] In addition, there were two first difference liquidity stock variables tested. These are discussed in the next section with other first difference variables.

The only liquidity measure in this rather long list that seemed remotely related with investment was what might be called the net quick monetary stock, *M*. The simple correlations between this variable and investment are presented in Table V–9. They are not impressively large correlations. Even for this "best" of the liquidity stock variables, 53 out of 80 of the simple correlations with investment are between plus and minus .20.

TABLE V–9

Simple Correlations Between Net Quick Monetary Stock and Investment by Industry, 1951–1954

Industry	1951	1952	1953	1954
Pulp and Paper	.49	.07	.18	.08
Light Chemicals	−.29	.10	.01	.17
Heavy Chemicals	−.17	−.13	.23	.13
Petroleum	.32	.13	.33	.40
Rubber	.10	.27	−.11	−.20
Heavy Steel	.33	.55	−.05	.19
Fabricated Metal Products	−.15	.27	.13	−.18
Special Industrial Machinery	−.13	−.05	−.12	.35
General Industrial Machinery	−.07	.06	−.02	−.03
Machine Tools	−.03	−.20	.03	−.03
Heavy Equipment, Engines, and Turbines	.08	−.09	.38	.63
Air Conditioning, Heating, and Similar Equipment	.06	.14	−.15	.11
Household Durables	.04	.03	−.13	.32
Light Electrical Machinery	.11	.14	.38	−.13
Heavy Electrical Machinery	.25	.39	−.20	.17
Electronics	.04	.51	.59	.32
Auto Fabricators	.54	.41	.42	.24
Auto Parts and Accessories	.08	.16	.18	.59
Basic Textiles	−.08	.08	.08	−.08
Other Textiles	−.38	.26	−.14	−.32

The probable explanation of these low correlations is that the level of current assets held by different firms is likely to be determined by basic differences in policy orientation. As long as the stock of liquidity is near the desired policy level, the absolute value is unlikely to have much influence on investment expenditures. Most firms in a cross-section sample will be near their target goals, except under exceptional circumstances, as just after a war or during extremely tight monetary conditions. Somewhat more positive results reported in the next section on the relationship between investment and the *change* in liquidity stock of individual firms lend some further credence to this view. Nevertheless, it is striking how poorly the "normalized" liquidity stock variables perform.

VI. *First Difference Variables*

The possibility exists that even if the absolute values of certain variables do not have a mechanistic, causal relationship with investment, year-to-year changes in these variables will. As already pointed out, first differencing is one possible way of normalizing different firm observations so as to abstract from differences in long-term policy target levels represented by the absolute value of the variables. Four different first difference variables were tested as part of the preliminary analyses of this study. These were the change in profits, the change in sales, the change in cash plus marketable securities less notes payable to banks, and the change in inventories. None of these four first difference variables proved to have particularly high simple correlations with investment. The inventory and profit first differences recorded particularly low simple correlations with investment. The poor performance of the inventory variable was not unexpected. That of the profit variable, however, was surprising; furthermore, the change in profit simple correlations with investment were as often negative as positive.

One explanation of the negative correlations between profit change and investment would be that the firms experiencing the largest absolute changes in profits were the firms that also had the highest profit levels throughout the period. That is, the firms with the largest negative changes in profits from 1951 on were still the firms with the highest absolute profit levels; since a positive relationship between total profits and investment might be expected, the negative relationship between the change in profits and investment follows. If the percentage change in profits had been used instead of the absolute change in profits, different results might have been obtained.

Another possible explanation of the low negative correlations between profit change and investment would be a lagged reaction coefficient effect. The change in profit variable tested in the present study, it must be remembered, is the current change, pertaining to the same year as the investment variable. Thus current declines in profits might have been preceded by positive changes in profits that induced the present high level of investment outlays. The best available evidence indicates, however, that investment in most, though hardly all, manufacturing industries responds to profit changes with only a six- to twelve-month lag. Since the present study is based on annual data, much of this lag effect should have been encompassed.

The essentially zero character of the profit change with investment results might also be attributable to the offsetting action of two other influences: on the one hand, investment should decline when profits decline because of dampened expectations and reduced availability of internal financing; on the other hand, desire to improve position, by cutting costs or improving product through enlarged investment expenditures, might be incited by a declining profit position. The appeal of this market share "explanation" of an inverse relationship between investment and profit changes is seriously lessened, however, by the presence of mostly positive correlations between changes in sales and investment; these correlations are reported in Table V–10. Indeed, the contrast in the change in sales and change in profits results is one of many bits of evidence on the substantial reduction in the correlation between the sales and profit variables in the cross-section samples of the 1951–1954 period as contrasted with that of 1946–1950.

The change in sales simple correlations, as might be expected, displays approximately the same pattern of relationships with investment as the capacity variable. Where the capacity variable records a relatively high correlation (see Table V–2), so does the change in sales variable as a rule. A check of the intercorrelations between change in sales and capacity utilization confirms the point. Unlike the 1946–1950 period, these correlations are sufficiently high to make inclusion of both variables in the same regression equation doubtful on collinearity grounds. The change in sales simple correlations with investment would seem high enough, moreover, to justify the testing of a separate accelerator model using change in sales as the main explanatory variable rather than capacity utilization. The danger of the capacity variable sometimes

TABLE V–10

Simple Correlations Between Current Change in Sales
and Investment by Industry, 1951–1954

Industry	1951	1952	1953	1954
Pulp and Paper	.16	.18	.24	.43
Light Chemicals	.27	.25	.34	.09
Heavy Chemicals	.10	.22	−.07	.26
Petroleum	.03	−.16	.37	−.21
Rubber	.34	−.10	.40	.50
Heavy Steel	.08	−.42	.10	.00
Fabricated Metal Products	.09	.09	−.04	−.21
Special Industrial Machinery	.55	.33	.17	−.09
General Industrial Machinery	.05	−.14	.10	.03
Machine Tools	.29	.38	.18	.21
Heavy Equipment, Engines, and Turbines	.34	.32	.28	−.01
Air Conditioning, Heating, and Similar Equipment	.62	.07	.49	.60
Household Durables	.21	.36	.33	.35
Light Electrical Machinery	.34	.19	−.36	.14
Heavy Electrical Machinery	.34	−.13	.05	.24
Electronics	.14	−.20	.81	.15
Auto Fabricators	.16	−.14	.46	.25
Auto Parts and Accessories	.46	.05	−.18	.34
Basic Textiles	−.43	−.21	.03	.06
Other Textiles	−.03	.30	.64	.44

giving rise to misleadingly large correlations with investment, for reasons explained in Chapter III, reinforces this point.

The most intriguing of the first difference results are between the change in liquidity stock and investment. As shown in Table V–11, the simple correlations are mainly negative in sign and, in many cases, reasonably substantial. Apparently, investment was often financed by reductions in liquidity stock. This could be explicable either because liquid assets were built up to a point in excess of desired stocks prior to a planned investment program or because liquid assets in excess of desired levels were commonly in supply during the 1951–1954 period and firms used these funds to maintain investment programs that might otherwise have been reduced to keep outlays within internally available financial limits.[9]

[9] These observations are confirmed by some field studies reported by Robert F. Vandell in his unpublished thesis submitted to the Harvard Graduate School of Business Administration in partial fulfillment of the requirements for the D.C.S. degree.

TABLE V-11

Simple Correlations Between Investment and the Change in Cash Plus
Marketable Securities Less Notes Payable to Banks by Industry, 1951–1954 *

Industry	1952	1953	1954
Pulp and Paper	−.38	−.15	.05
Light Chemicals	−.55	−.34	−.31
Heavy Chemicals	−.06	−.46	−.59
Petroleum	.01	−.04	.18
Rubber	−.11	−.12	−.60
Heavy Steel	−.86	−.03	−.24
Fabricated Metal Products	−.52	−.22	.05
Special Industrial Machinery	−.11	−.28	.06
General Industrial Machinery	−.34	−.06	−.46
Machine Tools	−.19	−.24	−.21
Heavy Equipment, Engines, and Turbines	−.05	−.16	−.27
Air Conditioning, Heating, and Similar Equipment	−.49	−.50	−.46
Household Durables	.07	.28	.12
Light Electrical Machinery	.09	−.54	.37
Heavy Electrical Machinery	−.51	−.17	−.05
Electronics	−.33	−.40	−.52
Auto Fabricators	−.40	−.20	−.21
Auto Parts and Accessories	−.37	.02	−.35
Basic Textiles	.07	−.57	.38
Other Textiles	−.52	−.33	−.47

* The 1951 results are not available.

At any rate, a comparison with the results reported in Table V–9
indicates that the first difference liquidity stock variable has a much
closer relationship with investment than any absolute form of the
variable. Accordingly, individual firm normalization, as achieved
by first differencing, seems to have been beneficial, and if any money
stock variable were to be included in a regression type investment
model, a first difference variable would seem the most promising.

Use of such a variable in a regression model poses some difficult
identification questions, however. Explicitly, is the reduction in
liquidity a cause or effect of increased investment? A defensible
case might be made on either side of this issue. It would seem best
therefore to confine attention to the correlation relationships between changes in the liquidity stock and investment and to lag the
change in liquidity stock if it is used as an explanatory variable for
investment in a regression model. Similar remarks apply to the

$T - L' - V$ variable, reported on previously, though with considerably less force.

VII. *Capital Stock and Prior Investment Variables*

A number of interesting hypotheses exist about the relationship of various capital stock or prior investment measures to current investment outlays. There is, for example, the well-known theory that investment should increase, everything else being equal, with the age of the capital stock since the older the existing equipment, the greater are the possibilities of cost reduction and product improvement being effectuated by new investment. In the 1946–1950 cross-section sample, however, an inverse relationship seemed to exist between investment and age of capital stock; this was attributed to a "senility effect" that made the age of capital stock (as measured by the ratio of depreciation reserves to gross fixed assets) on a cross-section sample more a measure of senile managerial attitudes than of the marginal efficiency of new investment outlays. The senility effect clearly suggests that an element of continuity exists in investment planning.

Continuity in investment expenditures also has been recently hypothesized on somewhat different, very modern grounds. Recent developments in automation and continuous process manufacturing operations have been held by some to make investment outlays so large in scope that planning must be executed over extremely long time horizons. This, in turn, necessitates stabilization of investment outlays and the elimination of opportunities to adjust investment to short-run fluctuations in profits, sales, or other performance variables. In short, investment in continuous process, automated industries should have greater continuity and less relationship to current performance than in nonautomated, discrete "batch" industries.

Still another capital stock to investment relationship of great interest is that between the size of capital stock taken as a measure of firm size and the rate of investment. The major concern is whether small or large firms are growing at quicker internal (as contrasted with external growth through merger) rates.

To test these various hypotheses three different capital stock-prior investment variables' simple correlations with current investment were obtained. These three variables were: lagged investment, I_{t-1}; the reciprocal of lagged gross fixed assets, $1/K_{t-1}$; and the sum of investment over the 1951–1954 period deflated by gross fixed assets in 1950,[10] I_{51-54}/K_{50}.

The reciprocal of gross fixed assets was employed rather than gross fixed assets itself in order to check the appropriateness of gross fixed assets as a deflator. A necessary, though not sufficient, condition for deflation not to create misleadingly high (or "spurious") correlations between deflated variables is that the regression coefficient associated with the reciprocal of the deflator be zero in a multiple regression equation which includes all the relevant variables. The chances of obtaining the needed zero regression coefficient can be roughly evaluated by observing the size of the simple correlation between the dependent variable (in this case investment) and the deflator's reciprocal.

The simple correlations between the reciprocal of gross fixed assets and investment, as shown in Table V–12, are not overly large in most cases. Only the petroleum, household durables, and auto fabrication industries apparently record simple correlations that might lead to substantial regression coefficients for the reciprocal of lagged gross fixed assets in a multivariable model.

The simple correlations between the reciprocal of gross fixed assets and investment also lend at least some sustenance to the view that large firms have a more rapid internal expansion rate than small firms. The preponderance of the correlations have negative signs, and in only one industry, petroleum, would there appear to have been any substantial growth advantage with the small firms in the 1951–1954 period. This contrasts with the results obtained in the 1946–1950 study.[11] Some significance might also be at-

[10] The proxy age variable employed in the earlier study, depreciation reserves deflated by gross fixed assets (or the percentage of gross fixed assets written off the books), was not employed in the present study. The grant of accelerated depreciation privileges to defense industries during the Korean emergency tended to obscure the relationship between this variable and the actual age of a firm's capital stock during the period under study. Therefore, the relative growth variable, I_{51-54}/K_{50}, was used instead. The relative growth variable, however, has several disadvantages as compared with the original age variable if this could have been obtained without the obfuscation of accelerated amortization.

[11] Meyer and Kuh, Chapter 10.

TABLE V-12

Simple Correlations Between the Reciprocal of Lagged Gross Fixed Assets
and Investment by Industry, 1951–1954

Industry	1951	1952	1953	1954
Pulp and Paper	.25	.30	−.10	.15
Light Chemicals	.09	−.17	−.17	−.30
Heavy Chemicals	−.11	−.08	.03	−.26
Petroleum	.16	.52	.26	−.37
Rubber	−.26	−.39	−.27	−.21
Heavy Steel	−.06	−.09	−.10	.11
Fabricated Metal Products	.01	.01	−.12	−.24
Special Industrial Machinery	.27	−.15	.11	.31
General Industrial Machinery	−.12	−.13	−.21	−.11
Machine Tools	.13	−.14	−.34	.08
Heavy Equipment, Engines, and Turbines	−.06	−.36	−.42	−.22
Air Conditioning, Heating, and Similar Equipment	−.08	−.02	.02	.33
Household Durables	−.33	−.26	.23	−.55
Light Electrical Machinery	−.11	.11	.04	.37
Heavy Electrical Machinery	−.24	−.30	−.40	−.12
Electronics	−.37	−.48	−.03	.09
Auto Fabricators	−.43	−.50	−.45	−.38
Auto Parts and Accessories	−.01	−.20	−.43	−.36
Basic Textiles	.03	−.11	−.05	.24
Other Textiles	−.26	.34	−.09	−.29

tached to the 1951 results being slightly less negative than for the other years. A common view, sustained in the earlier study, is that there is no aid to small business quite as effective as general prosperity; as already noted, 1951 was clearly the most prosperous of the four years analyzed here.

The results for 1951 are, though, no exception to the general pattern in the simple correlations between lagged and current investment, reported in Table V-13. Lagged investment records a fairly systematic and highly positive correlation with investment during every year. It is quite clear that there is considerable continuity in individual firms' investment patterns. Such findings are, of course, quite consistent with a host of hypotheses concerning gestation lags and the lumpiness of investment expenditures as outlined earlier. The exact interpretation that one wishes to attach to these continuity effects remains, however, very much a matter of choice.

TABLE V–13

Simple Correlations Between Lagged and Current Investment
by Industry, 1951–1954

Industry	1951	1952	1953	1954
Pulp and Paper	.51	.59	.20	.27
Light Chemicals	.60	.62	−.05	.07
Heavy Chemicals	.54	.26	.29	.23
Petroleum	.69	.61	.17	.35
Rubber	.11	.11	.67	.37
Heavy Steel	.91	.87	.77	.24
Fabricated Metal Products	.60	.53	.24	.41
Special Industrial Machinery	.58	.54	.27	.46
General Industrial Machinery	.92	.99	.97	.98
Machine Tools	.69	.62	.53	.38
Heavy Equipment, Engines, and Turbines	.84	.72	.54	.54
Air Conditioning, Heating, and Similar Equipment	.73	.49	.69	.31
Household Durables	.58	.34	.11	.37
Light Electrical Machinery	.87	.21	.41	.33
Heavy Electrical Machinery	.82	.63	.29	.38
Electronics	.90	.83	.65	.25
Auto Fabricators	.84	.81	.89	.81
Auto Parts and Accessories	.71	.32	.21	.39
Basic Textiles	.86	−.16	.47	.54
Other Textiles	.92	−.02	.27	.49

Just as a design is not discernible in the year-to-year simple correlations between current and lagged investment, there is no strong pattern in the industry-by-industry results. In particular, the three industries in the sample that might be most strongly characterized as automated and continuous process in nature — pulp and paper, heavy chemicals, and petroleum — record relatively low correlations between current and lagged investment. However, these three industries, as shown in Table V–13, also record relatively low relationships between investment and the current output or performance variables. The lack of any substantial relationship between the lagged and unlagged investment variables in these three industries would seem, though, to cast doubt on the "stabilized investment under automation" hypothesis.

Although investment may not be strongly stabilized by considerations of automation, there are, as already noted, other grounds for persistence in investment levels. In this vein, the simple correlations between investment and the "over-all growth" measure, I_{51-54}/K_{50}, provide additional evidence that individual firm investment levels tend to perpetuate themselves. As shown in Table V–14, large positive values characterize the correlations between these two variables.

TABLE V–14

Simple Correlations Between Investment and Internal Growth
by Industry, 1951–1954

Industry	1951	1952	1953	1954
Pulp and Paper	.41	.46	.18	.33
Light Chemicals	.80	.81	.27	.59
Heavy Chemicals	.63	.84	.55	.38
Petroleum	.91	.57	.21	.31
Rubber	.86	.37	.51	.55
Heavy Steel	.89	.58	.66	.78
Fabricated Metal Products	.45	.66	.27	.16
Special Industrial Machinery	.73	.30	.54	.51
General Industrial Machinery	.99	.99	.98	.99
Machine Tools	.67	.85	.69	.46
Heavy Equipment, Engines, and Turbines	.77	.73	.82	.49
Air Conditioning, Heating, and Similar Equipment	.88	.72	.78	.64
Household Durables	.54	.90	.34	.68
Light Electrical Machinery	.86	.00	.18	.21
Heavy Electrical Machinery	.90	.79	.50	.38
Electronics	.83	.93	.78	.49
Auto Fabricators	.88	.96	.87	.84
Auto Parts and Accessories	.78	.66	.63	.54
Basic Textiles	.48	.63	.41	.31
Other Textiles	.60	.64	.74	.62

VIII. *Summary*

The preliminary analyses reported in this chapter, mainly conducted by comparing simple correlations between investment and other proposed variables for a cross-section sample of manufacturing firms during the 1951–1954 period, have yielded results largely consistent with the earlier 1946–1950 findings. In particular, these preliminary results accord with expectations based on the "accelerator-residual funds theory of investment." Thus the closest simple correlations with investment were recorded for the capacity utilization and change in sales variables under prosperous conditions, while the profit or related cash throw-off variables displayed a closer relationship with investment in less buoyant periods.

Even more significantly from the standpoint of the residual funds hypothesis, the correlations between investment and various refinements of the cash throw-off concept were almost invariably higher than between investment and simple profits. The most promising of these modified cash throw-off variables was profits plus depreciation expense less cash needed for dividend payments and increased working capital. The modified cash throw-off variables also had the substantial advantage over profits of not being highly correlated with the sales variable.

The simple correlations between investment and various asset composition or stock variables were very low and sometimes had signs contrary to *a priori* expectations. This was particularly true of various liquidity stock and debt to net worth ratio variables that were tested. Again, these results agreed with those obtained for the 1946–1950 period.

		Investment Decisions, 1951–1954:
Chapter	**VI**	*A Cross-Section Evaluation of*
		Alternative Models

I. *Models, Hypotheses, and Their Limitations*

The preliminary analyses reported in the last chapter indicated that the accelerator-residual funds theory supplies a potentially useful framework for the further study of short-run investment decisions by large manufacturing corporations in the 1951–1954 period. However, only about seven of the many variables subjected to preliminary analysis seemingly held enough promise for inclusion in formal models. These seven variables, with their notations, were: (1) capacity utilization, C; (2) profits less dividend payments, $P - V$; (3) depreciation expense, D; (4) change in sales between last year and the current year, S'; (5) cash available from current operations after meeting dividend and working capital needs, $T - L' - V$; (6) current sales, S; and (7) lagged investment, I_{t-1}.

The preliminary analyses also provided helpful information on how to fit these seven variables into appropriate models. For example, rather high intercorrelations were discovered between capacity and changes in sales and between the retained earnings variable, $P - V$, and sales, thus suggesting the possibility of harmful collinearity if combinations of these variables were included in the same model. More specifically, inclusion of the sales variable with

104

the residual funds variable, $T - L' - V$, probably would not be harmful, while it would be harmful to include sales with the simple residual funds variable, $P - V$. Also, including change-in-sales and capacity in the same model seemed inappropriate. In a somewhat different but related vein, conceptual reasons were advanced in the preceding chapter for not including a "residual cash throw-off" variable (i.e., $T - L' - V$) and depreciation expense in one model, since doing so would amount to including depreciation expense twice.

These and similar considerations greatly narrow the number of feasible possibilities. Only about four different basic combinations of the seven variables would seem appropriate. In general notational form, the four feasible models are:

$$Model\ I: \quad I = f(C, P - V, D, I_{t-1});$$
$$Model\ II: \quad I = f(S', P - V, D, I_{t-1});$$
$$Model\ III: \quad I = f(C, T - L' - V, S, I_{t-1});$$
$$Model\ IV: \quad I = f(S', T - L' - V, S, I_{t-1}).$$

These four models also implicitly include the capital stock as a variable since it has been used throughout as a deflator.

The odd numbered models, I and III, embody capacity-acceleration concepts while the even numbered, II and IV, are simple acceleration models. The first two models hypothesize a special role for depreciation expense while the last two models emphasize, instead, the contrasting influences that liquid funds and sales expectation might have on investment. Furthermore, in light of the distributed lag or reaction coefficient interpretations discussed in Chapter II, these four basic models can be interpreted as two different "target level" formulations of residual funds hypotheses and three different distributed lag or reaction coefficient formulations of accelerator-capital stock adjustment models. In these interpretations special attention focuses on the role of lagged investment as an explanatory variable. The two residual fund models could be written:

$$Model\ R\text{-}1: \quad I_t = f(P - V, D, I_{t-1});$$
$$Model\ R\text{-}2: \quad I_t = f(T - L' - V, I_{t-1});$$

and the accelerator-capital stock models would be:

$$Model\ A\text{-}1:\ I_t = f(S, I_{t-1});$$
$$Model\ A\text{-}2:\ I_t = f(S', I_{t-1});$$
$$Model\ A\text{-}3:\ I_t = f(C, I_{t-1}).$$

An interesting question is whether it is appropriate to extend these basic models to include measures of other influences on investment besides those directly involved in the underlying hypotheses. The question is posed in its most difficult form where a measure of one of the other potential influences (for example, expectations) coincides with one of the residual funds or accelerator measures just listed in the abbreviated models. A particularly important example of such a situation arises with the sales variable since this variable might be hypothesized to influence investments for reasons other than as a measure of output-generated demands for greater capacity. For instance, if the level of sales is hypothesized to influence investment by, say, influencing expectations, it might be legitimately argued that sales should be included as an additional variable in the second and third versions, A-2 and A-3, of the accelerator models. Equally forceful arguments could be made for including a measure of profits or of internal fund flows as additional variables in the accelerator-capacity models. Conversely, sales or capacity utilization might be deemed legitimate additional variables to be included in the residual fund models. These arguments suggest that the basic four variable models, I through IV, are legitimate formulations for statistical testing even if one of the more specific models, *R-1*, *R-2*, *A-1*, *A-2*, or *A-3*, are considered to be of central theoretical importance.

The analyses that follow therefore focus primarily on the explanatory power, or the lack thereof, of the basic four variable models, I–IV. However, extended or augmented versions of these models are also analyzed. Specifically, two additional variables were included in every model *after* the basic four explanatory variables' parameters had been estimated. These two variables were a change in net-quick money, M', and the reciprocal of gross fixed assets, I/K_{t-1}.

The reciprocal of gross fixed assets, $1/K_{t-1}$, was included mainly for technical statistical reasons, that is, to check on the possibility that deflating the other variables by gross fixed assets could have led to a major distortion in the correlation results. This variable also has some interest beyond the purely statistical. Specifically, it provides a method of evaluating alternative formulations of the distributed lag or delayed adjustment models and of testing for the effects of firm size on investment.

Change in net-quick money was included as an additional variable strictly because the partial correlations between this variable and investment have an intrinsic interest of their own. As noted in the last chapter, it would be difficult to justify the change in net-quick money variable as an explanatory variable in a regression model in which investment is the dependent variable. At a minimum, there would be some question whether changes in net-quick money stocks were a cause of or caused by investment expenditures. Accordingly, only partial correlations between the changes in net-quick money and investment are reported. One simple and direct way to interpret these partial correlations would be to view them as a form of "residual analysis" directed to the question of determining if firms that experience sharp changes in their net-quick money position were also firms that had exceptionally large positive deviations of their actual investment from the investment that would have been predicted by the basic models.

As will shortly become obvious, the explanatory power of the basic models is not of a quality that would lead one to put any very strong confidence in any of the estimates of their regression coefficients. The variables observed or obtained from business reports often are not direct, unequivocal functions of other observed variables but, instead, are subject to control, in this case managerial control, and are modified according to choices of policy objectives, choices which can vary widely between the different firms included in the samples. Under such circumstances, the usual causality and nonstochastic assumptions about the independent variables in the regression model are questionable. Of course, if only the fixity of the independent variables were in question, a regression application still might be salvaged if the relative variance of the different variables were known or could be estimated. However, the results still would not have behavioral content without a causality assumption, and existing empirical knowledge and theories of the firm are often insufficient to sustain one causal interpretation over others. Therefore, statistical interdependence analyses, correlation being the simplest of the type, may often be preferable. Indeed, the data obtained from cross-section samples are often so "behaviorally heterogeneous" that the best that might be expected is to obtain information that could be used to sort out different contending causality assumptions by use of interdependence analyses.

The statistical problems created by the presence of "behavioral heterogeneity" in cross-section data are, in fact, quite considerable. Underlying regression applications is the belief that all, or nearly all, the data being analyzed are generated by more or less the same functional relationship. For example, in a regression model the relationship between the dependent and independent variables should be approximately the same (within, say, statistical error on a covariance test) for all the behavioral units observed; if this is not true, any behavioral implications derived from the procedure are questionable because nonhomogeneous elements are being aggregated. Considerations of this kind strongly suggest that simple or even complex regression models also will not be suitable for analyzing cross-section samples, particularly of business data. For this and other reasons, correlation analyses often have been relied upon for econometric studies of cross-section data.

While a correlation analysis will circumvent the dependence difficulty, it will not provide a fully satisfactory analysis of heterogeneous data. At best, the correlations usually furnish only a rough measure of the extent and relative balance of conflicting behavioral patterns present in the data. For example, a low correlation might be taken to indicate no really dominant behavioral pattern existing for the group under analysis, while a high correlation could be considered as evidence to the contrary.

Some individual firm differences that create sample heterogeneity might be eliminated by "normalization" of the observations, that is, by performing a transformation that eliminates the constant differences between observations. One example of such a "normalization" is the measure of capacity utilization employed in this study. By defining the target utilization of capacity as a minimum ratio between capital stock and sales achieved by the individual firm in a specified period, different concepts of productive capacity held by firms in the same industry are eliminated to some extent. Other simple methods of normalizing cross-section data are to include lagged values of a dependent variable as an independent variable in the regression function (as is done in models tested here) and to make the dependent variable a first difference between this year's and last year's values. However, very real limits exist on what can be done to adapt these data to the specifications of a statistical regression model. Therefore, while both partial regression and partial correlation results are reported in subsequent sections of this chapter, the reports are tendered with considerable reservation, particularly as to whether these results are directly adaptable to estimating structural relationships between investment and the hypothesized explanatory variables. In short, the emphasis is mainly upon the potential usefulness of these results in reducing the number of different contending hypotheses about investment behavior as a *preliminary* step to developing better models for explaining and forecasting investment relationships for more aggregative data. It would be extremely dangerous to construe in any very literal sense the regression estimates that follow as representing true structural parameters.

II. *Partial and Multiple Correlation Results: The Four Basic Models*

As a first step toward evaluating the empirical results, consideration will be given to the question of which of the four basic models, I through IV, provides the best general or over-all explanation of investment behavior. One simple, though by no means universally satisfactory, measure of over-all performance of a regression model is the coefficient of multiple correlation or, alternatively, the coefficient of multiple determination (which is the coefficient of multiple correlation squared and provides a direct and simple measure of the extent to which the explanatory variables taken as a group explain the variation in the dependent variable, the coefficient of multiple determination being the percentage of total variation of the dependent variable explained by the regression equation).

The coefficients of multiple determination for each industry, year, and model are shown in Table VI–1. On the whole, the coefficients

TABLE VI-1

Coefficients of Multiple Determination by Industry, 1951–1954
(Four Explanatory Variables in Each Model)

Industry	1951				1952			
	Model I	Model II	Model III	Model IV	Model I	Model II	Model III	Model IV
Pulp and Paper	.41	.41	.42	.42	.47	.47	.35	.35
Light Chemicals	.67	.67	.54	.58	.48	.48	.50	.50
Heavy Chemicals	.50	.53	.36	.39	.17	.12	.21	.14
Petroleum	.57	.58	.50	.49	.43	.42	.75	.76
Rubber	.75	.38	.84	.62	.12	.08	.11	.05
Heavy Steel	.86	.86	.85	.84	.76	.79	.84	.85
Fabricated Metal Products	.50	.43	.68	.50	.46	.21	.67	.24
Special Industrial Machinery	.43	.59	.51	.58	.42	.38	.36	.35
General Industrial Machinery	.87	.87	.85	.85	.99	.99	.99	.98
Machine Tools	.52	.54	.55	.60	.60	.52	.72	.69
Heavy Equip., Engines, and Turbines	.84	.88	.87	.90	.61	.63	.61	.59
Air Conditioning, Heating, etc.	.70	.66	.68	.61	.36	.34	.27	.27
Household Durables	.62	.61	.64	.54	.57	.53	.66	.56
Light Electrical Machinery	.83	.82	.83	.85	.30	.16	.40	.21
Heavy Electrical Machinery	.86	.81	.83	.85	.50	.55	.62	.62
Electronics	.77	.38	.90	.80	.81	.83	.75	.79
Auto Fabricators	.89	.81	.88	.83	.71	.72	.79	.80
Auto Parts and Accessories	.58	.59	.55	.61	.18	.17	.14	.13
Basic Textiles	.86	.77	.85	.87	.11	.10	.17	.19
Other Textiles	.86	.86	.91	.88	.25	.26	.09	.14

TABLE VI-1 (continued)

Industry	1953				1954			
	Model I	Model II	Model III	Model IV	Model I	Model II	Model III	Model IV
Pulp and Paper	.29	.20	.31	.20	.18	.24	.22	.25
Light Chemicals	.22	.18	.21	.18	.32	.37	.07	.05
Heavy Chemicals	.16	.13	.29	.34	.28	.27	.26	.31
Petroleum	.22	.28	.25	.33	.47	.46	.28	.30
Rubber	.59	.64	.53	.60	.56	.56	.46	.50
Heavy Steel	.63	.64	.76	.75	.14	.09	.22	.23
Fabricated Metal Products	.14	.11	.26	.20	.26	.28	.30	.40
Special Industrial Machinery	.17	.09	.40	.33	.44	.46	.27	.30
General Industrial Machinery	.95	.95	.97	.97	.97	.96	.97	.97
Machine Tools	.31	.31	.51	.54	.38	.33	.48	.38
Heavy Equip., Engines, and Turbines	.51	.53	.41	.44	.79	.80	.80	.80
Air Conditioning, Heating, etc.	.57	.51	.61	.58	.34	.46	.32	.47
Household Durables	.08		.37	.44	.50	.54	.64	.57
Light Electrical Machinery	.50	.54	.23	.35	.61	.58	.31	.30
Heavy Electrical Machinery	.27	.23	.29	.18	.59	.60	.50	.48
Electronics	.83	.92	.89	.93	.73	.69	.93	.91
Auto Fabricators	.90	.91	.82	.85	.81	.74	.75	.71
Auto Parts and Accessories	.17	.18	.11	.15	.43	.52	.45	.46
Basic Textiles	.25	.25	.55	.54	.49	.35	.70	.69
Other Textiles	.32	.43	.37	.44	.39	.39	.59	.42

of multiple determination are neither notoriously high nor notoriously low, especially if account is taken of the fact that the results are based on cross-section samples for which the number of "true" degrees of freedom is probably much closer to the number of actual observations than is the case with time-series samples. Indeed, a noticeable characteristic of most cross-section analyses in economics has been low correlation — possible evidence, also, of the behavioral heterogeneity mentioned previously.

Since Models I and III differ from II and IV respectively, only in the type of acceleration concepts used (Models I and III being of a capacity type while Models II and IV are change-in-sales models), it seems, generally speaking, that one acceleration concept does as well as the other in terms of over-all explanatory power as measured by the multiple correlation coefficients. If any valid distinctions can be made, the capacity models apparently record a slightly better performance in 1951 while the simple acceleration models do better during the later years, 1953 and 1954. Because of the high concentration of minimum values for the capital stock to sales ratio in 1951, however, there is a danger that the superior performance of the capacity models in 1951 may be attributable to "spurious" influences.

A more pertinent and interesting result that emerges from a comparison of the coefficients of multiple determination is that Models III and IV tend, on the whole, to provide better explanations of investment behavior than Models I and II. The major difference between these two sets of models is that I and II take account of expectational and fund flow influences on investment through the variables net profits after dividends, $P - V$, and depreciation expense, D, while III and IV take account of these effects through the sales variable, S, and the net cash available after meeting dividend and working capital needs, $T - L' - V$. The larger multiple correlations for Models III and IV indicate that depreciation expense may not have as strong and special an influence on investment as suggested by the simple correlation comparisons reported in the last chapter. Such a conclusion also is sustained by a detailed examination of the actual partial correlations between investment and depreciation expense. Specifically, inclusion of the lagged investment variable tends to diminish the importance of depreciation expense as shown in Table VI-2 where the partial correlations between investment and depreciation expense both before and after inclusion of the lagged investment variables are presented. With the partial exception of the 1951 results, there is a pronounced tendency for the depreciation expense correlation with investment to drop markedly after the introduction of lagged investment. Furthermore, the general correlation of the depreciation expense variable with investment seems to be markedly lower in the last three years of the study than in the first, the depreciation expense variable apparently being mainly a measure of the same influences on investment as the lagged investment variable in the years 1952, 1953, and, to a lesser extent, 1954.

One plausible explanation of this pattern is that from 1952 on accelerated amortization privileges granted during the Korean emergency began to show themselves in the reported depreciation expense figures. If, as seems likely, those receiving the accelerated amortization also invested more rapidly than others during the Korean War years 1951 to 1953, a tendency will exist for the depreciation expense figures to be related from 1952 on with heavier investment in the immediately preceding years. In 1951, on the other hand, this "continuity effect" induced by accelerated amortization had not yet taken hold. Furthermore, after 1952, while depreciation expense remains a measure of available liquid funds, it must have been increasingly recognized as only a very crude approximation to any sort of investment replacement needs.

Taken together, all these considerations strongly suggest that with some exception for the year 1951, Models III and IV are probably more useful empirically than Models I and II. Empirical grounds for preferring Models III and IV are strongly complemented, moreover, by important conceptual considerations favoring these models. As noted in the last chapter, the net cash available from current operations after meeting dividend and current working capital needs is clearly a purer measure of available funds than any strictly profit-oriented measure (which profits after dividends as used in Models I and II would be) since profit variables also will be gauges of expectations. Similarly, the sales variable might be justified as a better measure of expectations than any profit figure, particularly if the latter is adjusted for "prior financial

TABLE VI-2

Partial Correlations Between Investment and Depreciation Expense Before and After Introducing Lagged Investment as an Explanatory Variable by Industry, 1951–1954 * (Model I)

Industry	1951	1952	1953	1954
Pulp and Paper	.32	.55	.32	.18
	.32	.42	.14	.09
Light Chemicals	.48	.61	.01	.41
	.58	.40	.06	.43
Heavy Chemicals	.48	.15	.25	.44
	.51	−.01	.29	.41
Petroleum	.48	.39	.39	−.10
	.41	.25	.36	−.35
Rubber	.26	.16	.52	.62
	.11	.09	.39	.48
Heavy Steel	.31	.61	.45	.22
	.19	.07	.24	.15
Fabricated Metal Products	.33	.03	.09	.19
	.34	.07	.10	.06
Special Industrial Machinery	.21	.42	.13	.37
	.16	.33	.01	.36
General Industrial Machinery	−.14	−.30	−.32	−.17
	.41	−.43	−.37	−.14
Machine Tools	.31	.41	.17	.38
	.20	.11	−.15	.22
Heavy Equip., Engines, and Turbines	.32	.51	.68	.22
	−.43	.27	.45	−.46
Air Conditioning, Heating, etc.	.63	.52	.53	.25
	.59	.32	.11	.10
Household Durables	−.14	−.18	.06	−.12
	−.20	.28	.04	−.28
Light Electrical Machinery	.54	.30	.63	.72
	.22	.17	.59	.68
Heavy Electrical Machinery	.65	−.08	.35	.72
	.51	−.32	.29	.66
Electronics	−.01	.37	.75	.72
	.42	−.22	.32	.67
Auto Fabricators	.16	.39	.72	.58
	−.27	.01	.62	−.21
Auto Parts and Accessories	−.01	.19	−.06	.44
	.12	.18	−.15	.45
Basic Textiles	.19	−.10	−.15	−.16
	−.37	−.09	−.08	−.26
Other Textiles	.15	.47	.33	−.11
	−.13	.47	.18	−.19

* The upper correlation is "before," the lower "after" introducing lagged investment.

claims." It is also more in keeping with conventional economic theory to hypothesize that depreciation expense does not have any influence on investment decisions differentiable from that of other funds generated by current operations. In addition, Models III and IV present a better opportunity to compare the relative importance of financial flow and expectational effects than is possible with the other alternatives.[1] The net cash available from current operations, $T - L' - V$, unlike any simple profit variable, is not highly correlated with sales. A comparison, therefore, of the partial correlations between investment and sales and between investment and the free retained funds variable, $T - L' - V$, should provide at least a crude test of the relative importance of these different influences on investment decisions. The partial correlations for making these comparisons are presented in Tables VI–3 and VI–4.[2] Sharp differences are observable in the relative performance of the two variables in different years. In particular, the sales variable clearly records a closer correlation with investment in 1951 than the retained funds variable while the situation is just reversed for the years 1953 and 1954 — 1952 results being about equally unimpressive for both variables. The time pattern of these results thus agrees with that hypothesized by the accelerator-residual funds theory.

It is also instructive to compare the partial correlations between investment and sales and investment and change in sales with the partial correlations between investment and free retained funds. The pertinency of such comparisons is that sales and change in sales might be construed as reasonably direct indicators of expectations and accelerator effects. The partial correlations between investment and sales and investment and change in sales are shown in Tables VI–4 and VI–5. Both sets of results display approximately the same year-to-year pattern, although change in sales has a closer relationship with investment in the years 1953 and 1954 than the

[1] In this important respect the models are also superior to any tested in the earlier Meyer-Kuh study of investment behavior.

[2] Both Model III and IV results have been presented for the $T - L' - V$ variable to provide evidence that it does not make much difference which model's results are reported for any specific variable; subsequently, in order to save space, only Model III results will be presented with, of course, the major exception of the change-in-sales variable which appears only in Model IV.

TABLE VI-3

Partial Correlations Between Investment and Free Retained Funds by Industry, 1951–1954

Industry	Model III				Model IV			
	1951	1952	1953	1954	1951	1952	1953	1954
Pulp and Paper	.31	-.10	.32	-.18	.32	-.08	.32	-.09
Light Chemicals	-.28	.30	.14	.06	-.43	.31	.21	.08
Heavy Chemicals	-.27	-.09	.38	.44	-.16	-.04	.46	.46
Petroleum	.14	.46	.47	-.02	.16	.49	.44	.09
Rubber	.64	-.15	-.11	.24	.75	-.11	.01	.40
Heavy Steel	-.18	.60	.62	.32	-.30	.59	.60	.30
Fabricated Metal Products	-.61	-.45	.45	.24	-.27	-.28	.37	.25
Special Industrial Machinery	-.25	.06	.51	-.06	-.15	-.03	.49	.02
General Industrial Machinery	.03	.40	.59	.46	.03	.34	.61	.34
Machine Tools	.33	.36	.45	.48	.34	.52	.47	.41
Heavy Equip., Engines, and Turbines	.19	-.30	.37	.67	.27	-.27	.42	.63
Air Conditioning, Heating, etc.	-.19	.17	-.14	-.08	.11	.17	-.11	.09
Household Durables	.00	.01	.57	.59	.03	-.47	.61	.33
Light Electrical Machinery	.43	.37	.07	-.33	.51	.29	.09	-.31
Heavy Electrical Machinery	.23	.50	.35	.00	.17	.43	.32	.03
Electronics	-.81	.36	.68	.94	-.82	.02	.11	.93
Auto Fabricators	.14	.51	.31	-.05	.45	.57	.29	-.11
Auto Parts and Accessories	.22	.04	-.24	.54	.21	-.04	-.14	.56
Basic Textiles	-.42	-.28	.64	-.13	-.25	-.35	.63	-.03
Other Textiles	.20	-.26	.21	-.18	.10	-.13	.22	-.32

sales variable. In both cases the partial correlations with investment are lower than those between investment and free retained
funds in 1953 and 1954. This again lends substance to the view
that under recessionary business conditions, when capacity is not
fully utilized, the availability of funds tends to be relatively more
influential in the investment decision. Considerable variation is
observable, however, in the results for the different industries;
for example, residual funds perform very well in 1954 in the auto-
motive and nonelectrical machinery sectors but poorly in textiles

TABLE VI–4

Partial Correlations Between Investment and Sales by Industry, 1951–1954
(Model III)

Industry	1951	1952	1953	1954
Pulp and Paper	.35	.05	−.19	.14
Light Chemicals	.08	−.33	−.06	.12
Heavy Chemicals	.01	−.23	−.22	.05
Petroleum	.07	.46	−.07	−.42
Rubber	.00	.08	.14	.10
Heavy Steel	.08	−.10	.03	.10
Fabricated Metal Products	.47	−.57	−.08	.18
Special Industrial Machinery	.42	−.03	.09	.28
General Industrial Machinery	.06	.07	−.21	−.31
Machine Tools	−.03	.53	.25	.07
Heavy Equip., Engines, and Turbines	.74	.26	.09	.48
Air Conditioning, Heating, etc.	.53	.05	.35	.01
Household Durables	.49	.50	.02	.03
Light Electrical Machinery	.41	.02	.16	.23
Heavy Electrical Machinery	.52	−.44	.11	.56
Electronics	.73	.04	.82	.79
Auto Fabricators	.21	−.38	−.39	−.44
Auto Parts and Accessories	−.03	.03	−.05	−·22
Basic Textiles	.21	.09	.16	.65
Other Textiles	.65	.22	−.38	.58

and electrical machinery. It would be dangerous, moreover, to
conclude that there are no expectational influences at work on
short-run investment planning in 1953 and 1954. For at least
three industries, rubber, air conditioning, and other textiles, the
relationships between expectational variables and investment ap-

pear to be at least as strong as those between free retained funds and investment throughout the sample period.

Change in sales and sales are, of course, hybrid variables since they measure both acceleration and expectational influences upon investment. It is therefore interesting to compare the results for the two variables with each other. An interesting aspect of such comparisons, as a juxtaposition of Tables VI–4 and VI–5 indicates, is how much better the absolute sales variable does than the change

TABLE VI–5

Partial Correlations Between Investment and Change
in Sales by Industry, 1951–1954
(Model IV)

Industry	1951	1952	1953	1954
Pulp and Paper	−.02	.07	.34	.31
Light Chemicals	.47	−.06	.31	.04
Heavy Chemicals	.28	.22	.27	.42
Petroleum	−.05	−.36	.35	−.20
Rubber	.13	−.17	.50	.51
Heavy Steel	−.16	−.28	.17	.16
Fabricated Metal Products	−.36	.41	.13	−.41
Special Industrial Machinery	.41	.27	.07	−.19
General Industrial Machinery	.07	.54	−.13	.46
Machine Tools	.41	−.19	−.28	.02
Heavy Equip., Engines, and Turbines	−.22	.05	−.21	.63
Air Conditioning, Heating, etc.	.54	−.02	−.04	.61
Household Durables	.08	.39	.41	.26
Light Electrical Machinery	−.27	−.02	−.44	.19
Heavy Electrical Machinery	.13	−.15	.03	.11
Electronics	.23	−.51	.70	.33
Auto Fabricators	−.39	.31	.47	.28
Auto Parts and Accessories	.46	−.11	−.20	.26
Basic Textiles	−.58	.13	−.23	.05
Other Textiles	−.18	.24	.61	.19

in sales variable as an explanation of investment during the very inflationary year of 1951. The superior performance of the sales variable in 1951 is all the more remarkable because the sales results, as reported in Table VI–4, pertain to Model III which also includes the capacity variable, while the change-in-sales results, reported in Table VI–5, are for Model IV which does not include the capacity variable. Even more pertinently, a close inspection of the Model IV results indicates that the relative importance of the change-in-sales variable is almost always reduced by introducing the absolute sales variable. At least to some extent, this explains why the change-in-sales variable does not live up to the empirical promise displayed in the simple correlations used in the preliminary analyses reported in the last chapter. In fact, the change-in-sales variable does not record a markedly closer relationship with investment than does the absolute sales variable even in 1951 when, by hypothesis, capacity and acceleration influences should dominate.

The partial correlations between investment and capacity utilization are reported in Table VI-6. While the closeness of fit between the capacity variable and investment is clearly greatest in 1951, and greater in that year than for any other variable included in the basic models, the margin of superiority over the absolute sales variable

TABLE VI-6

Partial Correlations Between Investment and
Capacity Utilization by Industry, 1951–1954
(Model III)

Industry	1951	1952	1953	1954
Pulp and Paper	.05	.02	.49	.25
Light Chemicals	.40	−.03	.36	.13
Heavy Chemicals	.20	.36	.03	.33
Petroleum	.08	−.06	.11	−.07
Rubber	.77	−.30	.35	.44
Heavy Steel	.32	−.18	.24	.12
Fabricated Metal Products	−.66	.80	.29	.15
Special Industrial Machinery	.17	.30	.33	−.04
General Industrial Machinery	−.01	.64	.04	.59
Machine Tools	.29	.34	−.14	.43
Heavy Equip., Engines, and Turbines	.49	.21	.01	−.11
Air Conditioning, Heating, etc.	.63	−.06	.29	.44
Household Durables	.47	.58	.24	.46
Light Electrical Machinery	.03	.49	−.22	.22
Heavy Electrical Machinery	.34	.18	.36	.21
Electronics	.73	−.30	−.48	.51
Auto Fabricators	.63	.25	.25	.44
Auto Parts and Accessories	.26	.16	.01	.21
Basic Textiles	.64	.02	−.26	−.16
Other Textiles	−.53	−.07	.54	−.56

is not overwhelmingly great.   In fact, in 9 of the 20 industries included in the study the sales variable actually records a higher partial correlation with investment in 1951 than the capacity variable.   If allowance is also made for the possibility of a spurious correlation between capacity and investment in 1951 because so many of the peak utilization figures occur in that year, the performance of the sales variable might be considered superior to that of the capacity variable in 1951.   At any rate, whichever measure of acceleration effects is used, sales, change-in-sales, or capacity utilization, these variables uniformly do better in 1951 than the residual funds variable, $T - L' - V$, lending further corroboration to the basic nonlinearity hypothesized in the accelerator-residual funds hypothesis.

The fourth variable included in all the basic statistical models,

TABLE VI–7

Partial Correlations Between Current Investment
and Lagged Investment by Industry, 1951–1954
(Model III)

Industry	1951	1952	1953	1954
Pulp and Paper	.48	.57	.24	.32
Light Chemicals	.54	.47	.02	.07
Heavy Chemicals	.45	.21	.17	.26
Petroleum	.61	.61	.10	.41
Rubber	.67	.18	.70	.35
Heavy Steel	.89	.76	.55	.28
Fabricated Metal Products	.77	.21	.18	.41
Special Industrial Machinery	.55	.46	.24	.39
General Industrial Machinery	.92	.99	.98	.99
Machine Tools	.63	.62	.57	.34
Heavy Equip., Engines, and Turbines	.77	.67	.58	.60
Air Conditioning, Heating, etc.	.44	.40	.64	.39
Household Durables	.74	.55	.06	.67
Light Electrical Machinery	.75	.31	.39	.31
Heavy Electrical Machinery	.77	.58	.43	.56
Electronics	.52	.81	.88	.65
Auto Fabricators	.62	.77	.70	.82
Auto Parts and Accessories	.65	.25	.23	.34
Basic Textiles	.86	−.16	.37	.61
Other Textiles	.91	.08	.45	.73

lagged investment, has consistently high partial correlations with investment, as shown in Table VI–7. While over-all these partial correlations are relatively high compared with results obtained for the other variables, a distinction must be made for this variable between the interdependency as measured by correlation coefficients and the dependency relationship as reflected in the regression parameters. As shown in Table VI–12, the partial regression coefficients between investment and lagged investment tend to be slightly lower in 1951 than in the three other years, particularly 1952.

It is quite clear, moreover, that the lagged investment variable's partial correlations with current investment, strong in all years, are relatively strongest in 1951 and 1952. In 1952, in fact, lagged investment is the only one of the variables in the basic models to record consistently high partial correlations with current investment. As already noted, that is definitely not true of 1951 when the capacity and sales variables are usually well correlated with current investment. These contrasts between the 1951 and 1952 results are more dramatically highlighted by the partial regression results reported in Table VI–12. In essence, none of the conventional explanatory variables for investment, such as sales, capacity, change in sales or liquidity flow, seem to work well in 1952. One possible explanation might be that somewhat different firms recorded high investment rates in 1951 than in 1952. For example, one hypothesis might be that small firms invested relatively more than large firms in the extremely prosperous year of 1951 and less in the less buoyant year of 1952.

III. *Partial Correlation Results: The Extended Models*

Some evidence on the legitimacy of this small firm – large firm hypothesis is at least suggested by the pattern of relationships between current investment and the inverse of the capital stock, one of the two additional variables whose correlations with investment were checked by including them in the extended (more than four variable) versions of the underlying models. The partial correlations between this "auxiliary variable" and investment must be interpreted, however, with great caution. For one thing, considerable intercorrelation or multicollinearity was observable when more than four variables were included in the analysis at one time. Furthermore, the regression constant in the extended models with the inverse capital stock included are probably more pertinent measures of the influence of capital stock itself than the partial correlation between this inverse variable and investment.[3] The partial correlations between investment and the inverse of capital stock, for what they are worth, are shown in Table VI–8. As can be seen from the table, there is no particular tendency for the 1951 partial correlations to be more or less positive than those for the other years; therefore these partial correlations lend very little empirical sustenance to any hypothesis that small firms were investing relatively more in 1951 than large firms.

TABLE VI–8

Partial Correlations Between Investment and
the Inverse of the Capital Stock by Industry, 1951–1954
(Augmented Model III)

Industry	1951	1952	1953	1954
Pulp and Paper	−.05	.40	−.03	−.07
Light Chemicals	.52	−.37	.04	−.29
Heavy Chemicals	.14	.12	.14	−.27
Petroleum	−.19	−.36	.20	−.28
Rubber	−.26	−.38	−.01	−.14
Heavy Steel	.12	−.25	−.01	.00
Fabricated Metal Products	.11		−.30	−.57
Special Industrial Machinery	−.51	−.39	.03	.07
General Industrial Machinery	−.48	−.10	.07	.36
Machine Tools	.03	.04	−.26	.02
Heavy Equip., Engines, and Turbines	−.31	−.40	−.21	−.10
Air Conditioning, Heating, etc.	−.32	.04	−.12	.20
Household Durables	−.24	.32	.35	−.62
Light Electrical Machinery	−.29	.36	−.12	.46
Heavy Electrical Machinery	−.45	−.12	−.20	.11
Electronics	−.29	−.46	.24	−.55
Auto Fabricators	.10	−.14	.04	−.04
Auto Parts and Accessories	−.03	−.13	−.51	−.40
Basic Textiles	−.06	−.02	−.35	.54
Other Textiles	.30	.21	.32	−.80

[3] For an explanation of this point see Edwin Kuh and John R. Meyer, "Correlation and Regression Estimates When the Data Are Ratios," *Econometrica*, Vol. 23, No. 4 (October 1955), pp. 400–416.

On the other hand, the signs of the regression constants when the inverse of capital stock is included are somewhat favorable to the hypothesis that small firms were more active investors in 1951 than large firms. This sign pattern is shown in Table VI-9. Given

TABLE VI-9

Sign Pattern of Constants in Regression Models
with Inverse of Capital Stock Included by Industry, 1951–1954
(Augmented Model III)

Industry	1951	1952	1953	1954
Pulp and Paper	+	+	−	−
Light Chemicals	−	+	−	+
Heavy Chemicals	−	−	+	−
Petroleum	+	−	+	+
Rubber	−	+	−	−
Heavy Steel	−	+	−	+
Fabricated Metal Products	−	+	+	−
Special Industrial Machinery	+	+	−	+
General Industrial Machinery	−	−	−	−
Machine Tools	−	−	+	−
Heavy Equip., Engines, and Turbines	−	−	+	−
Air Conditioning, Heating, etc.	−	+	−	−
Household Durables	−	−	+	−
Light Electrical Machinery	+	−	+	−
Heavy Electrical Machinery	+	+	−	−
Electronics	−	+	+	−
Auto Fabricators	−	−	−	−
Auto Parts and Accessories	−	+	+	+
Basic Textiles	+	+	+	+
Other Textiles	−	+	−	+

the fact that gross fixed assets was used as the deflator throughout these models, it could be hypothesized that the constant in the regression equation including the inverse of gross fixed assets would have been the regression coefficient associated with gross fixed assets if that variable had been directly included in the model.[4] Under such circumstances, furthermore, a positive regression coefficient would indicate a positive relationship between size and investment, and a negative coefficient would indicate a negative relationship. Accordingly, the fact that negative constants are

[4] *Ibid.*

somewhat more preponderant in 1951, particularly as compared with 1952 and 1953, at least suggests the possibility that small firms were relatively more active investors in 1951 than large firms, again as compared with the years of 1952 and 1953.

The other variable, change in net quick liquidity, included in the extended versions of the models also displayed some rather interesting interyear differences in its relationships with investment. As shown in Table VI–10, for this variable as for the lagged invest-

TABLE VI–10

Partial Correlations Between Investment and Change
in Net Quick Liquidity by Industry, 1952–1954
(Augmented Model III)

Industry	1952	1953	1954
Pulp and Paper	−.40	−.18	−.14
Light Chemicals	−.33	−.48	−.26
Heavy Chemicals	.10	.02	−.54
Petroleum	.08	.29	.67
Rubber	−.01	.14	−.57
Heavy Steel	−.42	.12	.00
Fabricated Metal Products	.03	−.37	.13
Special Industrial Machinery	−.33	−.27	−.04
General Industrial Machinery	.39	.22	.00
Machine Tools	−.50	−.17	−.36
Heavy Equip., Engines, and Turbines	−.42	−.28	−.07
Air Conditioning, Heating, etc.	−.70	−.78	−.60
Household Durables	−.04	.30	−.36
Light Electrical Machinery	−.51	−.45	.53
Heavy Electrical Machinery	−.55	.16	−.17
Electronics	−.09	−.04	.83
Auto Fabricators	−.76	−.23	−.74
Auto Parts and Accessories	−.47	−.04	.00
Basic Textiles	−.14	−.28	−.31
Other Textiles	−.53	−.71	−.05

ment variable 1952 is clearly a very different year from the other years in the sample. (For technical reasons, namely, because of the manner in which the data were set up for computer processing, it was impossible to obtain results readily for this variable for the year 1951.) While there is no discernible pattern in the partial correlations between change in net quick liquidity and investment for the years 1953 and 1954, there is a very pronounced tendency for negative correlations between these two variables to appear in 1952.

The year 1952 is, in sum, a year of sharply differentiated behavior from that observable in the other years. First, lagged investment tends to be more closely related to current investment in that year. Second, there is some slight suggestion, as shown by the signs in Table VI-9, that large firms invested relatively more in 1952 than small firms. Third, firms that were willing or able to reduce liquidity substantially in 1952 seemed to be relatively larger spenders on investment than those who would not or could not. The pattern of behavior suggested by these findings clearly does not coincide with that hypothesized by any of the standard interpretations employed here for a residual funds-accelerator model or, for that matter, with almost any model of investment previously suggested in the literature.

A somewhat different model apparently is needed. One possible alternative might be a liquidity stock-lagged adjustment model in which years just after an extremely sharp upsurge in business activity were such that carryover effects dominated investment behavior. Specifically, in such years, firms that are well supplied with stocks of liquidity and have already undertaken or begun rather large-scale investment projects will continue on with their investment projects and, furthermore, will establish the dominant investment patterns.

The applicability of such a model could be very restricted. The year 1952 was not only a year of exceptional results in this investment study but was also a year marked by extremely unusual economic circumstances. First of all, there was some interruption of investment programs occasioned by the steel strike of 1952. Second, a considerable proportion of the investment in 1952 in manufacturing was probably related to programs initiated in late 1950 and 1951 as part of the Korean mobilization program. Third, this mobilization program also resulted in a number of restrictions being placed upon investment activities of nondefense industries late in 1951 and throughout most of 1952. While the extent of these special circumstances could easily be overestimated, there is no question that they did impart to 1952 investment patterns a number of special characteristics that would not be encountered under normal peacetime conditions.

IV. *An Evaluation of Alternative Investment Models*

With this additional model admitted to consideration, the number of permissible interpretations of the basic models is enlarged from the original five reported in Section I — two residual fund models, *R-1* and *R-2*, and three accelerator models, *A-1*, *A-2*, and *A-3* — to six. The preceding analysis also strongly suggests, however, that at least two of the original five models are not strongly corroborated by the empirical evidence obtained from the cross-section analyses, the two unsatisfactory models being the first residual funds model, *R-1* (which incorporates a separate depreciation expense variable) and the second accelerator model, *A-2* (which employs a change in sales concept). If these two models are excluded, four models remain of intrinsic or special interest: (1) the straightforward residual funds model, *R-2*, which does not incorporate depreciation separately; (2) an absolute sales variable formulation of the acceleration concept, *A-1*, which incorporates some expectational effects as well; (3) a capacity formulation of the acceleration concept, model *A-3*; and (4) the new liquidity stock-lagged adjustment model just enunciated.

Evaluation of the relative empirical qualities of these four models can be obtained from the partial correlation results just reported. Specifically, taking account of both the correlation properties *and* the agreement between the *a priori* expectation about the sign of the relationship between particular explanatory variables and the dependent variable, investment, a *judgment* can be made as to which of the four remaining models provides the best explanation of investment for all the 80 industry-years of experience embodied in the cross-section samples. The results of such an analysis are reported in Table VI–11; these results conveniently summarize much of the preceding discussion.

The capacity and absolute sales models clearly dominate the 1951 results. Similarly, the liquidity stock-lagged adjustment model is most prominent in 1952. The residual funds model dominates the 1953 results and to a lesser extent those for 1954 as well. The asterisks shown in Table VI–11 designate industry-years in which the average capacity utilization of the industry exceeded unity, these being the years when the highest correlations might be expected according to the residual funds-acceleration hypothesis between acceleration variables and investment. On the whole, this additional information does not prove particularly rewarding as an explanation of the "exceptional cases" in the years 1952, 1953, and 1954. Specifically, four industries recorded average capacity utilization rates greater than unity in 1953 (machine tools, air conditioning, household durables, and electronics), and in none of these four industries does an acceleration variable dominate: indeed, in three of the four industries a residual funds model performs best.

TABLE VI–11

A Performance Comparison of Capacity (*C*), Residual Fund (*R*),
Sales (*S*) and Liquidity Stock-Lagged Adjustment (*L*)
Models by Industry, 1951–1954

Industry	1951	1952	1953	1954
Pulp and Paper	R or S	L or S	R or C	C
Light Chemicals	C^*	$L + R$	C'	?
Heavy Chemicals	C^*	C	R	R
Petroleum	?*	R^*	R	?
Rubber	C^*	L?	C'	$C + L$
Heavy Steel	C^*	$R + L$	R	R
Fabricated Metal Products	S^*	C'	R	R
Special Industrial Machinery	S	L	R	S
General Industrial Machinery	?*	C'^*	R	$R + C'$
Machine Tools	C'	S^*	R^*	$R + C$
Heavy Equip., Engines, and Turbines	S or C^*	L^*	R	R
Air Conditioning, Heating, etc.	C' or S	L	L^*	L
Household Durables	C	C' or S	R^*	$R + L$
Light Electrical Machinery	R^*	$R + C$	L	C
Heavy Electrical Machinery	C^*	R	?	$S + L$
Electronics	C or S	$R + L$	R^*	$R + S$
Auto Fabricators	C or S	R	L	L
Auto Parts and Accessories	C'^*	L		R
Basic Textiles	C^*	?	$R + L$	$S + L$
Other Textiles	S^*	L	L	S

NOTES: 1. *C'* indicates *S'* also provides a good explanation in same industry-year.
2. * indicates cases where $\overline{C} > 1.0$ for the industry-year.
3. Question marks indicate doubtful "identifications."

V. *Regression Parameters and Results*

These identifications of useful or best models are illustrated further by the tabulation of "significant" regression coefficients, shown in Table VI–12. For purposes of this tabulation a significant regression coefficient was defined as one that had a *t* ratio (the regression coefficient divided by its standard error) greater than *unity* and with the "correct" *a priori* sign. Significance, therefore, has been defined approximately as meeting a 15% to 25% confidence level on a one tail test, the exact level depending on the degrees of freedom involved.

Included in the table are results for the four variables which on the basis of the preceding partial correlation analyses proved to be the most significant or interesting: capacity, residual funds, absolute sales, and lagged investment. The capacity and residual funds results are taken from Model III while the sales results are taken from Model IV; this choice was rather arbitrary and was dictated mainly by the fact that there was somewhat less collinearity between the sales and change-in-sales variable than between the sales and capacity variable. However, in almost no case would it make any great difference if the results had been taken for any one of the variables on the alternative model; specifically, with the exception of the lagged investment variable for which results are reported for both Models III and IV, the significant regression parameters obtainable from one model differed by less than 15% from those obtainable from the alternative model in almost all cases. Indeed, the coefficients obtainable from the two different models very rarely differed by more than one point in the third decimal place.

For reasons alluded to earlier, neither the significance tests nor the regression coefficients themselves should be interpreted too literally. Questions could be raised about the legitimacy of several of the underlying assumptions required for a strict normal regression model application; e.g., randomness of the underlying sampling procedure, the "behavioral homogeneity" of the individual observation units, and the normality of the conditional distributions.

It does seem legitimate, though, to consider these regression results as at least suggestive evidence. First, as they almost must by

TABLE VI–12

"Significant" Regression Coefficient Estimates by Industry, 1951–1954 *

Industry	1951			
	Variables			
	C (Model III)	$T-L'-V$ (Model III)	S (Model IV)	I_{t-1} (Model III or IV)
Pulp and Paper		.21 (.11)	.04 (.02)	.23 (.07)
Light Chemicals	.36 (.21)			.36 (.14)
Heavy Chemicals	.10 (.09)			.37 (.14)
Petroleum				.30 (.08)
Rubber	.64 (.18)	.37 (.15)		.43 (.16)
Heavy Steel	.06 (.03)		.01 (.01)	.37 (.03)
Fabricated Metal Products			.03 (.01)	.82 (.16)
Special Industrial Machinery				.32 (.12)
General Industrial Machinery				1.20 (.14)
Machine Tools	.10 (.08)	.09 (.06)		.36 (.10)
Heavy Equip., Engines, and Turbines	.16 (.08)		.04 (.017)	.39 (.08)
Air Conditioning, Heating, etc.	.23 (.08)		.02 (.01)	.16 (.11)
Household Durables	.18 (.10)		.01 (.007)	.59 (.16)
Light Electrical Machinery		.15 (.08)	.02 (.01)	.43 (.09)
Heavy Electrical Machinery	.19 (.15)		.02 (.015)	.58 (.13)
Electronics	.23 (.11)			.16 (.13)
Auto Fabricators	.34 (.12)		.02 (.02)	.44 (.18)
Auto Parts and Accessories	.13 (.11)			.44 (.13)
Basic Textiles	.46 (.18)		.04 (.018)	.80 (.15)
Other Textiles			.04 (.03)	1.06 (.15)

* Applicable standard errors are shown in parentheses beneath the regression coefficients.

TABLE VI-12 (continued)

| Industry | 1952 Variables | | | |
	C (Model III)	P+DE−V (Model III)	S (Model IV)	I$_{t-1}$ (Model III or IV)
Pulp and Paper			.019	.47
			(.010)	(.12)
Light Chemicals		.27		.40
		(.23)		(.19)
Heavy Chemicals	.78			1.10
	(.37)			(.75)
Petroleum		.46	.031	.78
		(.18)	(.010)	(.20)
Rubber				
Heavy Steel		.69		1.22
		(.15)		(.16)
Fabricated Metal Products				.62
				(.25)
Special Industrial Machinery	.14			.64
	(.10)			(.29)
General Industrial Machinery	.54	.11		1.09
	(.17)	(.07)		(.03)
Machine Tools	.21	.15	.032	.75
	(.13)	(.10)	(.010)	(.22)
Heavy Equip., Engines, and Turbines				.52
				(.15)
Air Conditioning, Heating, etc.				.71
				(.43)
Household Durables	.55			1.05 .58
	(.22)			(.46)(.44)
Light Electrical Machinery	.11	.10		.13
	(.05)	(.06)		(.10)
Heavy Electrical Machinery		.27		.62
		(.13)		(.23)
Electronics				1.07
				(.39)
Auto Fabricators		.19		.70 .82
		(.10)		(.18)(.15)
Auto Parts and Accessories				.22 .31
				(.22)(.22)
Basic Textiles				
Other Textiles				

TABLE VI–12 (continued)

Industry	1953 Variables			
	C (Model III)	T−L′−V (Model III)	S (Model IV)	I_{t-1} (Model III or IV)
Pulp and Paper	.40 (.13)	.48 (.25)		
Light Chemicals	.18 (.12)			
Heavy Chemicals		.19 (.09)		
Petroleum		.78 (.29)		
Rubber		.10 (.09)		.70 .59 (.24)(.19)
Heavy Steel	.15 (.10)	.18 (.04)		.45 (.11)
Fabricated Metal Products	.16 (.12)	.05 (.02)		
Special Industrial Machinery	.19 (.13)	.32 (.13)		.30 (.28)
General Industrial Machinery		.43 (.16)		.97 (.05)
Machine Tools		.22 (.10)	.012 (.008)	.40 (.14)
Heavy Equip., Engines, and Turbines		.04 (.03)		.84 (.32)
Air Conditioning, Heating, etc.	.16 (.14)		.016 (.011)	.66 (.21)
Household Durables		.25 (.11)		
Light Electrical Machinery			.013 (.010)	.82 .47 (.48)(.47)
Heavy Electrical Machinery	.26 (.17)	.10 (.07)		.48 .26 (.27)(.24)
Electronics		.15 (.08)		1.54 1.20 (.41)(.37)
Auto Fabricators		.96 (.92)		1.06 (.35)
Auto Parts and Accessories				.40 (.34)
Basic Textiles		.72 (.27)		.30 .37 (.24)(.23)
Other Textiles	.16 (.08)			.45 (.28)

TABLE VI-12 (continued)

| Industry | 1954 Variables | | | |
	C (Model III)	$T-L'-V$ (Model III)	S (Model IV)	I_{t-1} (Model III or IV)
Pulp and Paper	.20			.51 .43
	(.13)			(.27)(.27)
Light Chemicals				
Heavy Chemicals	.11	.21		.29
	(.06)	(.08)		(.20)
Petroleum				.37
				(.16)
Rubber	.34	.60 †	.036	1.00
	(.23)	(.42)	(.025)	(.89)
Heavy Steel		.19	.008	.18
		(.09)	(.007)	(.10)
Fabricated Metal Products		.12	.022	.63
		(.12)	(.010)	(.33)
Special Industrial Machinery			.003	.31
			(.003)	(.17)
General Industrial Machinery	.49	.31		1.20
	(.18)	(.16)		(.05)
Machine Tools	.20	.36	.015	.47 .34
	(.10)	(.15)	(.011)	(.30)(.32)
Heavy Equip., Engines, and Turbines		.08	.016	.56
		(.02)	(.011)	(.20)
Air Conditioning, Heating, etc.	.42			.54
	(.23)			(.34)
Household Durables	.15	.25		.63
	(.08)	(.10)		(.20)
Light Electrical Machinery			.009	.22
			(.007)	(.17)
Heavy Electrical Machinery			.021	.46
			(.007)	(.18)
Electronics	.21	.13†	.010	.44 .27
	(.17)	(.02)	(.004)	(.25)(.20)
Auto Fabricators	.13			.89
	(.08)			(.20)
Auto Parts and Accessories		.27		.30 .22
		(.11)		(.21)(.21)
Basic Textiles			.025	.29
			(.009)	(.12)
Other Textiles			.055	.93 .73
			(.039)	(.27)(.37)

† Model IV results.   Model III results were not significant.

definition, they accentuate most of the conclusions of the preceding partial correlation analyses. For example, the regression coefficients of the lagged investment variable are generally higher in 1952 than for the other years, though significant coefficients appear for almost every industry in all of the years. Similarly, for the three primary variables besides lagged investment selected for special attention in Table VI–12, few significant values are recorded in 1952. Also, the observation that the capacity variable clearly performs best in 1951 while the residual funds variable does best in 1953 is again borne out. Finally, the sales variable unquestionably records its best performance in 1954, with the capacity variable doing surprisingly well and the residual funds variable doing surprisingly poorly.

The patterns of "significance," as exemplified by the *t* ratio, are also highly interesting. Specifically, there is a strong tendency for the regression parameter of a variable that passes this rather weak significance criterion to pass with notable honors. That is, most of the "significant" regression coefficients recorded in Table VI–12 actually have a *t* ratio of 2.0 or 3.0 rather than the minimum 1.0 requirement established for entry into the table.

It is also interesting to consider the range and central tendencies (to the extent they exist) for the different regression parameters. For example, while there is some tendency for the size of the regression parameters associated with the capacity variable to vary between industries and years, a significant coefficient for this variable usually is greater than .10 and less than .50 in value, with the mode tending to be somewhere between .30 and .40. Similarly, the residual funds variable, $T - L' - V$, tends toward values in the range between .20 and .40, although a notoriously large number of significant parameters are observable well beyond this range. The significant parameters for the sales variable are perhaps the most stable of those recorded. Specifically, they suggest that when sales are significant the tendency is for an increase of one dollar in sales to result in approximately a one- to four-cent increase in investment expenditures.

By contrast, the coefficients associated with lagged investment unquestionably display the least stability of all those reported, these coefficients tending to vary widely and erratically. Furthermore, several values greater than unity are recorded, a result which seems a bit difficult to believe on the basis of other knowledge and considerations. These greater than unity coefficients, in fact, strongly suggest that the lagged investment variable may be reflecting influences attributable to other, perhaps excluded, variables. In keeping with the preceding discussion, one variable for which lagged investment might be serving as a proxy is depreciation expense. However, this hypothesis is at least somewhat nullified by the fact that introduction of the change in net quick liquidity variable in the extended models tends to reduce many greater than unity regression parameters for lagged investment to levels well below unity. About the only exceptions are the heavy chemical and general industrial machinery industries in 1952. Partly because of the very wide range in the regression parameters observed for the lagged investment variables, results for both Model III and Model IV were reported for this variable in cases where the results deviated by more than 15%. With a few exceptions for the residual funds variable in 1954 (which are noted in the table) no significant parameters deviated between models by more than this percentage for any of the other three variables analyzed.

VI. *Conclusion and Summary*

The empirical findings that emerge from the cross-section analyses reported in this chapter are of somewhat mixed quality and character, being both affirmative and negative in nature. From the standpoint of the over-all objectives and strategy of this study, the most important conclusion is in many ways also the least conclusive. Specifically, the pattern of year-to-year results of the cross-section study lends confirmation, but only mild confirmation, to the accelerator-residual funds hypothesis. That is, accelerator-type variables — capacity, change in sales, and sales — all do better than the measure of residual funds in the buoyant year of 1951; however, these accelerator variables also perform comparatively well in 1954 which along with 1953 must be ranked as the most depressed year in the sample. Similarly, residual fund variables perform reasonably adequately on the whole in 1953 but only provide a semi-adequate explanation of investment in 1954.

Two negative conclusions of rather substantial interest are the rejection of any special role for depreciation expenses as a determinant of investment and the utter failure of any conventional model — accelerator, expectational, or fund flow — to explain investment in 1952. The rejection of a special role for depreciation expense is mainly interesting in terms of its policy implications. Apparently a corporate tax decrease granted in the form of depreciation expense should not be expected to be substantially more effective than other forms of corporate tax relief in stimulating investment outlays by manufacturing corporations.

The extremely negative findings with respect to all conventional models in 1952 are a much more difficult matter to interpret. Of the variables included in the basic, four-variable models analyzed in this chapter, only lagged investment displays any systematic relationship with current investment in 1952. Obviously, it is difficult under such circumstances to substantiate any interpretation of lagged investment as a proxy for lagged values of the basic accelerator, fund flow, expectational, or other underlying behavioral variables. At a minimum, the suggestion is clear that if the behavioral variables have any influence on current investment in 1952, it is not of recent vintage. Another interesting aspect of the 1952 results was the tendency toward highly negative partial correlations between change in net quick liquidity, included as one of the two additional variables in the extended versions of the basic models, and investment. This combination of high partial correlation between current investment and the change in net quick liquidity stock suggests the possibility that an entirely different, rather unconventional model of investment behavior is required to explain short-run investment patterns in 1952. In this model the emphasis would be upon continuity effects, that is, commitment to large-scale investment programs as started in immediately preceding years, and the availability of an excess stock of liquid funds. This new model was labeled the liquidity stock-lagged adjustment model and would seem to be worthy of further analysis if conditions similar to those existing at the end of 1951 ever occur again.

There was also some evidence that the sharply differentiated results in 1952 were partially attributable to a somewhat greater dominance of large firms in investment that year. Specifically, there was limited evidence that the large firms in the sample tended to be relatively heavy investors in 1952. By contrast, in 1951 when continuity effects may have been at their minimum (partial regressions between lagged investment and current investment being somewhat lower in that year) and where acceleration effects were most pronounced, small firms perhaps were the relatively heavy investors. In short, there is at least some slight suggestion that small firms tend to be more flexible in their investment planning and also more sensitive to the current business climate, timing their investment outlays to occur during periods of cyclical upswing.

Another basically negative conclusion was not so unexpected, strongly confirming the experiences of the 1946–1950 investment study. Specifically, none of the models employed displayed any overpowering ability to explain the underlying investment pattern since in almost all instances the multiple correlation coefficients were rather low. One explanation of these low correlation coefficients is that the cross-section samples embody a considerable range of corporations that differ sharply in their underlying motivational or utility preference structures. Furthermore, this underlying behavioral heterogeneity is apparently not at all adequately controlled or accounted for by the conventional industry stratification schemes employed in this study.

Another not unexpected negative finding concerns the performance of the change-in-sales variable. While there seemed to be some hope for this variable on the basis of the preliminary simple correlation analyses reported in the preceding chapter, the variable did not perform at all adequately in the partial analyses. Specifically, by almost any conventional standard, both the capacity and absolute sales variables represented better formulations of accelerator or expectational influences.

In sum, a rather substantial range or variety seems to be observable in manufacturing investment behavior in the period from 1951 to 1954. No simple theory seems to be an adequate representation of the observed patterns. Even so eclectic and broad a theory as the bifurcated accelerator-residual funds theory only performs moderately well and completely fails in 1952, a year of sharply divergent and unusual investment patterns. Manufacturing investment, in short, seems to be subject to a multiplicity of influences — accelerator, fund flow, expectational, and others — that are less than well-defined (such as the strong continuity and liquidity effects observable in 1952). The appropriate blending of these different influences seems to depend, moreover, on particular cyclical and business conditions.

Chapter VII | Investment Behavior, 1948–1958: A Time-Series Analysis

I. Introduction

In the preceding chapters the accelerator-residual funds theory has been tested against cross-section data on investment behavior of individual manufacturing firms in the years 1951 through 1954. In this chapter the theory will be analyzed against quarterly time-series data on manufacturing, both total and for component industries, for the period from 1948 to 1958.[1]

The objective of these time-series analyses is to shed more light on the relative usefulness of the accelerator-residual funds hypothesis. There is no presumption intended that these time-series analyses will provide evidence that makes possible a definitive discrimination

[1] The middle of 1948 represents the earliest date for which reasonably good quarterly data on manufacturing investment can be obtained, and the first quarter of 1958 was the latest date for which good data were available at the time when these time-series analyses were actually processed. However, in the next two chapters the predictive power of the time series developed here are tested against data for 1959, 1960, and 1961, all of which became available after the initial analyses were completed. Since the data for the latter three years were not employed as part of the original analysis, indeed were not available at the time of these analyses, the forecasting tests based on these latter three years are reasonably pure in the sense that they represent an evaluation of the extrapolability of the original models into a period of experience which was not available and therefore could not have affected the original design of the underlying models. A description of the data is presented in Chapter IV.

among alternative hypotheses. For reasons that will be elaborated in this and succeeding chapters, such discrimination seems virtually impossible with time-series data alone. Hypothesis testing with time-series data is at best hazardous; at times it can even be misleading or improper. Accordingly, the results reported in this chapter should be accepted as the basis for substantive statements about the validity or invalidity of different hypotheses only with the greatest care and circumspection.

As previously noted, the specification of an economic model for empirical testing is usually not a simple or an obvious matter. A number of choices or adaptations almost invariably must be made, and the character of these decisions may crucially affect the final results. Accordingly, in Section II of this chapter the concern is with the problem of selecting particular empirical formulations for final testing against the time-series data. Following this, in Section III, a presentation is made of the actual results obtained by fitting the specified models to both the aggregate of manufacturing data and that for the component industries. In Section IV, the underlying sample, composed of 38 quarterly sets of observations, is divided into two distinct subgroups, one ostensibly pertaining to periods of cyclical improvement in investment and the other to periods of decline or recession, the objective being to test better the bifurcated character of the accelerator-residual funds hypothesis. Finally, in Section V, a summary and evaluation of these analyses are presented.

II. *Empirical Specification of the Model*

The essential ingredients in any formulation of the accelerator-residual funds hypothesis are measures of capacity utilization and free residual funds (i.e., cash thrown off from operations after meeting dividends and, possibly, other high priority obligations). With a distributed lag or delayed reaction in the investment pattern hypothesized, a lagged value of the dependent investment variable also might be included. In addition, both for purposes of contrast and because previous time-series results (see Chapter II) have suggested their pertinency, various potential measures of expectational influences on investment seem worthy of empirical test-

ing. A particularly promising expectational variable would appear
to be some measure of equity or stock price, used as a barometer
of business optimism or confidence.[2]

In designating appropriate measures of capacity utilization and
free residual funds, a choice must be made from a number of alternative specifications of these variables. In addition, in a time-
series analysis a decision also must be made whether, and to what
extent, all of the different explanatory variables should be lagged.
A straightforward empirical method of specifying lags and choosing between alternative measures of the same variable is, of course,
simply to compare the relative degree of correlation between different variables and the dependent variable, in this case investment.

[2] That a stock price variable should be a reasonably good measure of business
expectations has been suggested in several previous studies. For example, as
mentioned earlier, stock price was easily the best time series variable investigated
in the earlier Meyer-Kuh study. Similarly, the role of stock price in the models
developed in this chapter might be construed as an aggregate version of the
individual firm equity values that proved generally successful in Yehuda Grunfeld's study of business investment contained in *The Demand for Durable Goods*,
Arnold C. Harberger, ed. (Chicago: University of Chicago Press, 1960). It
should be noted, however, that Grunfeld's argument that a firm's equity value
is a superior measure of expectations to profits is essentially irrelevant to the
tests of the accelerator-residual funds hypothesis presented here. Obviously,
profits is both a measure of expectations and of funds available for investment
financing. Because of this hybrid character, the residual funds theory has been
framed to the greatest extent possible in this study in terms of purer forms of
liquidity flow than straight profits. Furthermore, for reasons that will be
explained subsequently, it was concluded that the change in stock price is a better
measure of expectations than either the absolute level of stock prices or any
profit measure. When expectations are measured by the change in stock price,
rather than the absolute stock price, there is, moreover, no serious collinearity
between the expectations and liquidity flow measures used in this study. This
fact is of significance because Grunfeld considered it highly important that his
measures of equity value and profits (which, it should be recalled, are not the
same as the measures of fund flows used here) were so highly collinear that it
was possible for him to absorb completely all the influences of his profit variables
through the measure of equity value. This circumstance also may have been
attributable to the fact that he also included in his analysis the asset value of the
firm as a variable; by the nature of the construction of this variable as the sum
of previous investment up to time $t-1$ and the high auto-correlation of his dependent investment series, a spuriously high correlation was induced between
these two variables, raising questions about the over-all reliability of his results.
As will be shown by some detailed residual analyses performed in this chapter,
the residual fund and stock price variables clearly measure very different influences and have very different impacts upon the performance of the over-all
investment model under different cyclical conditions.

Specification of the residual fund variable is particularly difficult because the availability of data makes a wide range of alternatives possible. Specifically, the same range of residual funds variables is available for times-series analysis as with the cross-sections. The following possibilities actually were subjected to preliminary testing: net profit, P; net profit plus depreciation expense or gross cash throw-off, T; cash throw-off less cash dividend payments, $T - V$; cash throw-off less cash dividends and the estimated cash needed for working capital purposes *exclusive* of inventory requirements, $T - V - N'$; and cash throw-off less cash dividends and the net estimated cash needed for working capital purposes *inclusive* of inventory requirements, $T - V - N$. The choice of an appropriate lag for the residual funds variables was quite simple because in almost all instances a one-period lag of the cash flow and free fund variables proved to have at least as high or higher correlation with investment than all other lags tested. A tabulation of the simple correlations between investment and various cash flow measures lagged one period is shown in Table VII–1.

Cash throw-off less cash dividend payments clearly has the closest correlation with current investment of the five different residual

TABLE VII–1

Simple Correlations Between Investment and Various Measures of Cash Flow and Free Residual Funds in a Time-Series Analysis of Aggregate Manufacturing *
[Quarterly Data, 1949 (III) through 1958 (IV)]

Investment with:	Correlation
Net profits, P_{t-1}	.259
Cash throw-off (net profits plus depreciation expense), T_{t-1}	.428
Cash throw-off less cash dividend payments, $(T - V)_{t-1}$	.540
Cash throw-off less cash dividends and working capital needs exclusive of inventories, $(T - V - N')_{t-1}$	.205
Cash throw-off less cash dividends and working capital needs inclusive of inventories, $(T - V - N)_{t-1}$	−.163

* As indicated by the notational subscripts, all of the cash flow variables have been lagged one quarter.

fund formulations tested. This correlation of .540 is with 38 observations easily significant at the 1% level by conventional statistical tests. There is the danger, of course, that this high simple correlation could be spurious in the sense that it is attributable to other, third influences upon investment. However, an exhaustive check both of the simple intercorrelations and of the multiple correlations between the different cash flow and free residual funds variables and their performance in corresponding multiple variable models (which include variables measuring capacity utilization) tended to corroborate the conclusion suggested by the simple correlations, namely that $T - V$ is easily the best of the five different cash flow variables tested.

In this regard, a summary of the multiple regression models tested against the aggregate manufacturing data for the complete 38-quarter period from the middle of 1949 through the end of 1958 is shown in Table VII–2. The relative weakness of the "fully adjusted" cash throw-off variable, $T - V - N$, is shown in these results by the poor performance of this variable in models 21 through 24; specifically, the variable has a negative sign in every case, thus violating *a priori* expectation, and is always insignificantly different from zero at a 5% confidence level. While the simple cash throw-off variable, $T - V$, does not perform uniformly well, it usually does have a positive sign in the multiple regression equations and also is significant in a majority of cases, as shown by the results recorded for models 1 through 14.

The failure of the ostensibly "more sophisticated" cash flow variables that incorporate adjustments for working capital and other needs can be construed, of course, as something of a rejection of the more extreme formulations of the residual funds hypothesis. Such a conclusion, however, may be at least somewhat premature. In the first place, the adjustments for working capital and other needs are something less than sophisticated [3] and the performance

---

[3] The working capital requirements were estimated by performing simple linear regressions of working capital, both inclusive and exclusive of inventory requirements, on sales, federal income tax liabilities, short-term bank borrowing, and the change in sales, and using the discrepancy between the estimate of working capital needs obtained from the function and the actual holdings of working capital as an estimate of the excess or deficiency of working capital. That is, the excess or deficiency of working capital was considered to be the error term obtained from the regression for a particular time period.

TABLE VII-2

Comparison of Partial Regression Coefficients for Various Investment Models Tested Against Aggregate Manufacturing [Quarterly Data, 1949 (III) through 1958 (IV)] †

Model No.	$(T-V)_{t-1}$	$(T-V-N)_t$	C_{t-1}^M	C_{t-2}^M	C_{t-1}^P	C_{t-2}^P	S_t'	S_{t-1}'	S_{t-2}'	r_{t-3}	SP_{t-1}	I_{t-1} or I_{t-2}	R^2
(1)	.2405		3107.5							−191.9*		.818	.893
(2)	.2480		2379.0							−260.3*		.897	.896
(3)		−.0964*	4979.5								27.28	.655	.942
(4)	.3088			3142.3								.722	.892
(5)	.2984			2256.4						−243.6*		.851	.898
(6)	.5757						−.0303*	−.0816*	.0146*				.565
(7)	.4611						−.9194*	−.0186*		−46.6*	−12.8*	.843	.803
(8)	.3292											1.000	.877
(9)	.1386						.0210*			−645.5	6.17*	1.015	.941
(10)	−.0953*		5873.8								26.39	.557	.936
(11)	−.0684*		3090.1*	912.9*							18.5	.642	.955
(12)	.0811*				3734.1						2.28*	.761	.857
(13)	.0260*				1612.6*	698.8*					1.81*	.829	.931
(14)	.0886*				1232.4	5275.2		−.0160*			6.8*	.949	.943
(15)			7005.2								23.3		.697
(16)				2579.9							38.4		.857
(17)							.0213*	.0089*	.0368	−258.9*	−1.80*	1.027	.939
(18)							.0196*			−422.4	14.50	1.017	.929
(19)			4357.9								21.7	.702	.939
(20)				4102.6							26.4	.603	.936
(21)	−.0299*		4143.2							−236.2*	21.3	.714	.942
(22)	−.0439*									−362.6	25.7	.616	.942
(23)	−.0639*							.0013*			17.2	1.006	.878
(24)	−.1724*						−.0707*	−.0345*	.0395*	−838.6	24.5		.638

* *Not* significant at a 5% confidence level on a *one* tail test (as specified by the *a priori* expectation on sign).
† All models seasonally adjusted by introduction of three seasonal "dummy" variables, the coefficients for which are not shown for purposes of simplicity.

of $T - V - N$ and $T - V - N'$ might have been better if really reliable estimates of these needs had been available. At least some evidence that a fund flow formulation, with its emphasis on financial considerations, has at least as much explanatory power as a more purely expectationally oriented formulation is provided, furthermore, by the facts that (a) the basic cash throw-off variables perform better than simple net profits; and (b) cash throw-off less cash dividend payments performs better than cash throw-off itself. Further evidence to this effect is also provided by the extremely low, and more often than not negative, simple correlations between current investment and change in sales and change in profit variables, both of which might be expected to be reasonably good representations of expectational influences. The change in profit variable always records a negative simple correlation with investment, thus violating basic *a priori* expectations, while the best simple correlation between a change in sales variable and investment is with a two-period lag, even then achieving a value of only .339. In addition, inclusion of these change in sales and change in profit variables in more complete multiple variable formulations does not alter the basic conclusions. (Again see Table VII–2 for some relevant evidence.) On the basis of these various considerations, plus the fact that the fundamental *a priori* expectation of this study is in favor of the residual funds hypothesis, profits, change in sales, and change in profits were excluded as separate measures of expectational influences in the final models. Furthermore, only the cash throw-off less cash dividends payment variable, $T - V$, of the different cash flow and free fund variables is employed in the basic time-series regression models.

As for formulations of the capacity utilization concept, two different capacity utilization measures were tested: an index of capacity utilization as measured by the ratio of the Federal Reserve Board Production Index to the McGraw-Hill Capacity Series (interpolated from an annual basis to a quarterly basis using the *SEC–FTC* series on manufacturing investment); and the ratio between the value of the Federal Reserve Board Production Index for a given period and the previous peak value for that same series.[4]

[4] A more detailed description of the sources and derivation of these capacity series will be found in Chapters III and IV. In particular, it should be noted that

The two most promising "lags" for these capacity measures are one and two quarters. A tabulation of the simple correlations between current investment and these capacity utilization measures lagged both one and two quarters is shown in Table VII–3.

TABLE VII–3

Simple Correlations Between Investment and Measures of Capacity Utilization:
Time-Series Analysis of Aggregate Manufacturing
[Quarterly Data, 1949 (III) through 1958 (IV)]

Investment with:	Correlation
Capacity as measured by the ratio of the Federal Reserve Board's Manufacturing Production Index to the McGraw-Hill Capacity Series:	
lagged one quarter, C_{t-1}^M	.181
lagged two quarters, C_{t-2}^M	.236
Capacity as measured by the ratio of the Federal Reserve Board's Manufacturing Production Index to its own previous peak value:	
lagged one quarter, C_{t-1}^P	.336
lagged two quarters, C_{t-2}^P	.421

These simple correlations strongly suggest that the capacity measure obtained by taking the ratio of the Federal Reserve Board Manufacturing Production Index to its own previous peak value, the ratio lagged two quarters, provides the best explanation of current investment. However, when tests were performed with more complete multivariable models, these initial impressions were not fully sustained. When the McGraw-Hill and the previous Peak Period capacity indexes are included alternatively in otherwise identical regression models, the McGraw-Hill Index invariably performs better in the sense of having a higher partial correlation with

the deLeeuw index discussed in Chapter IV tended to record values about halfway between the two indexes employed here, a hardly surprising result since the deLeeuw index is in essence a complex average of the other types of capacity indexes. Accordingly, it seemed better to use the purer types of indexes in the actual empirical testing since the behavior of the deLeeuw index can always be inferred, in essence, from the observed empirical behavior of the other indexes.

investment and more significant regression coefficients than the Peak Period Index. The apparent explanation is that the McGraw-Hill Index has a much lower intercorrelation with the residual funds variable, $T - V$, than the Peak Period Index. Also, the McGraw-Hill Index is negatively correlated with investment lagged two periods while the Peak Period Index's correlations with lagged investment ranges from near zero to slightly positive values. In addition, both the Peak Period Index and the McGraw-Hill Index when lagged one period rather than two are much less positively correlated with lagged investment and have slightly less positive correlations with the cash throw-off variable, $T - V$, lagged one quarter.

The relative effectiveness of the different measures of capacity utilization in a partial regression format is indicated particularly well by the results reported in Table VII–2 for models 11 through 22. For example, models 15 through 16 differ only in that the McGraw-Hill Index is used in place of the equivalent Peak Period Index and yet the multiple correlations for the two equations are substantially different. Similarly, while models 17 and 18 suggest that a reasonably high correlation can be obtained for a simple change in sales formulation of the acceleration concept, this is achieved mainly by putting an extremely heavy weight on lagged investment; in fact, the coefficients of the change in sales variables themselves are almost invariably insignificant. On the other hand, the evidence that a one-period lag with accelerator variables performs better than a two-period lag is not so clearcut. As can be seen, however, particularly in the results for models 11 and 13, and by comparing models 19 and 20 with 21 and 22, there is usually very little to choose between a one- or two-period lag, although the one-period lag performs slightly better. On the basis of these various comparisons the McGraw-Hill Capacity Index lagged one period was employed as the principal, though not exclusive, measure of capacity utilization in most of the time-series analyses.

Two other variables, stock prices and the interest rate, are suggested both by theoretical considerations and by the results of previous empirical investigations.[5] In the preliminary analyses

[5] See Chapter II above and Meyer and Kuh, *The Investment Decision*, Chapter 11.

both the prime bank rate and the rate of interest on Moody's triple A industrial bonds were tried with lags up to four quarters as alternative measures of interest rate influences on manufacturing investment. Similarly, Standard and Poor's Index of 425 industrial stock prices lagged one, two, and three quarters was accepted as a measure of stock market influences. Another variable tested in some of the final models was capital stock as measured by gross fixed assets lagged two quarters; as explained in Chapter II this variable can play a role in lagged adjustment or reaction coefficient formulations of the acceleration principle. As before, a summary of the tests performed can be found in Table VII–2.

III. *Alternative Time-Series Models*

Both the preliminary analyses just reported and the results of the previous cross-section analyses strongly suggest that a regression model of the following form should be both interesting and provide a reasonably adequate explanation of postwar investment patterns in the manufacturing industry:

(I) $\qquad I_t = f_1[(T - V)_{t-1}, C^M_{t-1}, r_{t-3}, SP_{t-1}, I_{t-2}].$

The notation is as defined previously and the function is assumed to be linear, at least to a first approximation. Major alternatives would be models involving substitution of other measures of accelerator influences for C^M_{t-1} as follows:

(II) $\qquad I_t = f_2[(T - V)_{t-1}, C^P_{t-2}, r_{t-3}, SP_{t-1}, I_{t-2}]$

(III) $\qquad I_t = f_3[(T - V)_{t-1}, S'_{t-1}, S'_{t-2}, S'_{t-3}, r_{t-3}, SP_{t-1}, I_{t-2}].$

The tabulation of the multiple regression results presented in Table VII–2 have been grouped to correspond to these three basic models. Thus, equations 1 through 3 in the table relate to Model (I) and its variants; equations 4 and 5 to Model (II); and equations 6 through 9 to Model (III). The remaining three groupings in Table VII–2, 10 through 14, 15 through 20, and 21 through 24, are reasonably self evident and either represent tests of alternative concepts of specific models or were employed as part of the preliminary analyses just discussed.

Several interesting points are immediately observable from an inspection of Table VII–2. First, and most importantly, a wide range of sensible formulations of the models will provide reasonably good explanations of the variations in investment. Virtually all the coefficients of multiple determination are in the range of .90 to .95. The only notable exceptions occur when change in sales is used instead of one of the capacity variables as the basic acceleration concept, and even then the percentage of variation explained rarely drops below 80%. The change-in-sales variables also have the unattractive feature of often recording signs contrary to *a priori* expectation and of being statistically insignificant. On the other hand, these disadvantages are perhaps partially compensated by the somewhat better performance of the residual fund variable when it is incorporated into a model in which the acceleration effects are represented by changes in sales.

Both the capacity and the lagged investment parameters prove to be consistently significant, and the residual fund flow and the stock price variables record only slightly inferior performances. The capacity variable's consistent significance is all the more remarkable since its simple correlations with investment are relatively low, .181 for a one-period lag and .235 for a two-period lag, as contrasted with the residual funds variable's .540 simple correlation with investment.

The interest rate variable does not consistently record significant coefficients when measured against a 5% confidence level test. However, the interest rate variable just misses this level of significance in most cases, almost invariably being significant at a 10% or 15% level. Furthermore, the interest variable's coefficients consistently agree with the usual *a priori* hypothesis by being negative in sign, a result not commonly observed in many previous empirical studies.

The interaction effects that are observable between the interest rate, stock price, capacity utilization, and residual funds are also interesting. For example, as Model 3 reveals, inclusion of all four variables in one model usually results in at least two of the four variables not being significant at the 5% level and at least one of the four variables recording a sign opposite to that which might be expected *a priori*. The residual funds variable, moreover, tends to be the variable most adversely affected. However, if the change in sales version of the acceleration concept is used instead of a capacity utilization model, the residual funds variable is not greatly affected by introduction of the other variables. It is clearly the combination of including *both* stock price and capacity utilization variables simultaneously with residual funds that tends to reduce the explanatory power of the latter. Thus, residual funds is always significant at the 5% level when, as in Models (1), (2), (4), and (5), it is included with a capacity variable and without stock price. It is similarly significant in Models (7) and (9) when incorporated in models with stock price but without capacity variables (change in sales being used in these cases as the measure of accelerator effects). Conversely, residual funds is *never* significant when included in models with both capacity and stock price measures such as numbers (3) and (10) through (14).

The most pronounced and interesting interrelationships are, in fact, those occurring between the residual funds and stock price variables, for it is the high degree of collinearity between these two variables that poses the most difficult problems from the standpoint of model specification. Indeed, the degree of this collinearity is so great that specification of a time-series model that embodies really authentic structural characteristics for these two variables is essentially impossible. It would perhaps not be entirely improper to extend this cynicism to the point of saying that structural specification of time-series models is virtually impossible for all the variables included in the present investment analyses because of the limited amount of information available in the historical series and the complexity of the models required.

A little additional light can be cast, though, on the individual roles of the stock price and residual funds variables by comparing the residuals obtained from the time-series analysis before and after including the stock price variable in a particular model, using for this purpose Model 2 in Table VII–2. (This model with stock price included is, of course, Model 3 in the same table.) A comparison of the before and after residuals as shown in Table VII–4, indicates that there are two periods in which inclusion of the stock price variable effectuates a significant reduction in the size of the residuals: these are from the third quarter of 1950 through the second quarter of 1952 and from the third quarter of 1955 through the

TABLE VII-4

Residual Analyses Before and After Including Stock Price

Year and Quarter	Actual Value	without stock price in the model (Model 2 in Table VII-2)			with stock price in the model (Model 3 in Table VII-2)		
		Estimated Value	Residual	% Error	Estimated Value	Residual	% Error
4901	1947.06	2164.90	−217.85	−11.19	2116.64	−169.58	−8.71
4902	2083.83	2408.47	−324.65	−15.58	2212.42	−128.59	−6.17
5001	1692.85	1476.33	216.52	12.79	1535.26	157.59	9.31
5002	2000.00	1896.52	103.48	5.17	1885.93	114.07	5.70
5003	2100.57	2306.41	−205.84	−9.80	2126.20	−25.63	−1.22
5004	2727.67	2826.15	−98.47	−3.61	2646.97	80.71	2.96
5101	2287.38	2135.17	152.21	6.65	2280.39	6.99	0.31
5102	2863.26	2862.20	1.05	0.04	2864.11	−0.85	−0.03
5103	2855.06	2786.74	68.32	2.39	2848.24	6.81	0.24
5104	3340.96	3101.54	239.42	7.17	3227.00	113.96	3.41
5201	2705.88	2537.66	168.22	6.22	2583.35	122.53	4.53
5202	3145.64	3031.71	113.93	3.62	3107.81	37.83	1.20
5203	2786.82	2839.90	−53.09	−1.90	2883.35	−96.54	−3.46
5204	3334.71	3348.08	−13.37	−0.40	3323.14	11.56	0.35
5301	2730.81	2705.62	25.19	0.92	2736.59	−5.78	−0.21
5302	3113.57	3243.32	−129.76	−4.17	3300.21	−186.64	−5.99
5303	2863.73	3137.65	−273.92	−9.57	3139.25	−275.52	−9.62
5304	3317.17	3475.46	−158.29	−4.77	3362.67	−45.50	−1.37
5401	2581.91	2451.62	130.29	5.05	2351.95	229.96	8.91
5402	2853.29	2865.39	−12.09	−0.42	2685.19	168.10	5.89
5403	2642.36	2713.78	−71.42	−2.70	2544.54	97.81	3.70
5404	2959.08	2978.17	−19.09	−0.65	2918.71	40.37	1.36

TABLE VII-4 (continued)

Year and Quarter	Actual Value	without stock price in the model (Model 2 in Table VII-2)			with stock price in the model (Model 3 in Table VII-2)		
		Estimated Value	Residual	% Error	Estimated Value	Residual	% Error
5501	2224.53	2350.23	−125.70	−5.65	2357.92	−133.39	−6.00
5502	2734.83	2858.84	−124.01	−4.53	2880.91	−146.07	−5.34
5503	2814.56	2804.62	9.94	0.35	2813.20	1.36	0.05
5504	3345.12	3249.66	95.47	2.85	3401.99	−56.86	−1.70
5601	2777.46	2781.00	−3.53	−0.13	2919.51	−142.05	−5.11
5602	3431.99	3247.26	184.72	5.38	3355.41	76.58	2.23
5603	3479.13	3162.52	316.61	9.10	3284.58	194.55	5.59
5604	3932.50	3654.16	278.34	7.08	3788.17	144.34	3.67
5701	3077.26	3270.25	−192.99	−6.27	3202.00	−124.74	−4.05
5702	3624.78	3633.87	−9.09	−0.25	3532.23	92.55	2.55
5703	3447.98	3192.15	255.83	7.42	3225.24	222.74	6.46
5704	3638.77	3670.66	−31.89	−0.88	3644.92	−6.15	−0.17
5801	2470.59	2840.89	−370.30	−14.99	2581.77	−111.19	−4.50
5802	2484.36	2612.49	−128.13	−5.16	2639.83	−155.47	−6.26
5803	2253.81	2082.33	171.48	7.61	2209.89	43.92	1.95
5804	2463.87	2431.30	32.57	1.32	2617.66	−153.79	−6.24

NOTE: Estimated Value and Residual may not sum to Actual Value due to rounding.

third quarter of 1957 inclusive. On the other hand, using the stock price variable impairs the performance of the model for the period from the second quarter of 1953 through the second quarter of 1955 inclusive. For all other periods — the last two quarters of 1949 and the first two quarters of 1950, the last quarters of 1952 and the first quarter of 1953, and the last quarter of 1957 and all of 1958 — the performance of the model is little affected by inclusion or exclusion of the stock price variable. Specifically, in the very early 1949–1950 period and the very late 1957–1958 period the performance is about equally bad whether or not stock price is included, while in the second half of 1952 and the first quarter of 1953 the model performs extremely well both with and without stock price.

Some correlation would appear to exist between the state of the business cycle and the extent to which stock price is a helpful variable. When the economy is undergoing very rapid expansion or enjoying generally favorable business conditions, as from the third quarter of 1950 on through the middle of 1952 and from the middle of 1955 through the third quarter of 1957, stock price seems to be definitely beneficial. Specifically, its inclusion in these periods of relatively great buoyancy and economic optimism tends to reduce an otherwise strong tendency for the model to underestimate investment. By contrast, while there was a distinct tendency to overestimate investment during the relatively depressed years of 1953 and 1954 when stock price was not included in the model, the inclusion of stock price in the model tended to result in either systematically larger overestimates or, somewhat surprisingly, absolutely large underestimates of investment.

From the standpoint of the residual funds-accelerator hypothesis the really significant aspect of these residual analyses is the extent to which the positive contribution of the stock price variable to explaining investment is revealed as occurring during periods of expansion when the residual funds variable by hypothesis is supposed to be of limited influence. That is, a stock price variable in the model is desirable in place of a residual funds variable at just the times when the residual funds variable would not be expected to be of importance under any circumstances. Contrarily, when the residual funds variable is hypothesized to be of importance, inclusion of the stock price variable seemingly does at least as much harm as good. Accordingly, the high degree of collinearity between the stock price variable and the residual funds variable and the fact that the inclusion of both a stock price and a capacity variable will essentially eliminate any substantial influence for the residual funds variable does not appear to be a fundamental contradiction of the residual funds-accelerator hypothesis. It should be remembered, moreover, that reasonably adequate explanations of the 1948–1958 investment series can be obtained from a large variety of investment models, as Table VII–2 makes abundantly clear. The historical experience of that period is just not sufficient to the task of decisively choosing from the large number of available possibilities. Furthermore, there are reasons for suspecting that any serious delimitation of possibilities might be ill-advised since each variable seems to have its particular period of importance, a point that will be further elaborated when discussing interest rate influences.

The stock price variable is also a maverick in other ways. For example, unlike the other included variables, no satisfactory method was developed for deflating this variable to take account of changing price levels. Accordingly, as entered into the model without deflation it has much stronger trend characteristics than the other included variables. As such, it might be expected to reflect any excluded effects that followed a trend pattern. These considerations, as well as the obviously high degree of collinearity between the stock price variable and the other variables, suggest a reformulation in which the percentage change in stock price be used as an explanatory variable instead of the absolute stock price level. Specifically, an alternative version of Model 3 in Table VII–2 can be specified in which the percentage change in stock price lagged one period, ΔSP_{t-1}, is used instead of the absolute level of stock price. The following regression results:

$$I_t = -3051.6 + .243\,(T-V)_{t-1} + 3500.60\,C^M_{t-1} + 107.1\,r_{t-3}$$
$$+\ 14.9\,\Delta SP_{t-1} + .793\,I_{t-2} + \text{seasonal dummies} \qquad R^2 = .885.$$

It should be noted that the stock price variable in relative differenced form can be included in the same model with capacity without extinguishing the residual funds variable. In fact, all the coefficients are significant at the 5% level except the interest rate coefficient which, being positive, is unsatisfactory on other grounds as well. In all other respects, however, this model would appear to be as good as or better than any tested and therefore has been used with the time-series data on the individual manufacturing industries.

The actual results for the individual industries, shown in Table VII–5, are notable in several respects. First, and most disturbingly, a very pronounced tendency exists for the coefficients of multiple determination to be considerably lower for the individual industry regressions than in either the sample formed by pooling all the individual industry-years of observation into one sample (the results for which are shown in the final line of Table VII–5) or the aggregate for all manufacturing industry, as shown by the results discussed previously. Thus, the results obtained from individual industry analyses strongly corroborate recent findings by Grunfeld and Grilliches [6] to the effect that it is easier to build models with considerable explanatory power for aggregates than it is for constituent components of these aggregates.

Also notable is the fact that on a deaggregated basis the residual funds variable, $T - V$, records a considerably better over-all performance than the capacity utilization variable, C_{t-1}^M. With the exception of the coefficient for the motor vehicle and equipment industry, the residual fund variable's regression coefficients all would be significant at the 10% confidence level. By contrast, the capacity variable misses significance by a considerable margin in all but three cases: electrical machinery, food and related products, and petroleum and coal.

The interest rate variable also performs well in the deaggregated samples. The interest rate coefficients usually miss 5% significance only by a very small margin. Again, the coefficients for this variable are almost invariably negative and so in agreement with the usual *a priori* theory; the only exceptions are the food and related products and chemical industries.

In the deaggregated samples the percentage change in the stock price variable performs only in a mediocre manner in all but the stone, clay, and glass industry. The observed regression coefficients

[6] Zvi Grilliches and Yehuda Grunfeld, "Is Aggregation Necessarily Bad?" *Review of Economics and Statistics*, Vol. 42, No. 1 (February 1960), pp. 1–13.

TABLE VII-5

Regression Coefficients for Individual Manufacturing Industries:
Quarterly Time-Series, 1950 to 1958 (inclusive)

Industry	$(T-V)_{t-1}$	C^M_{t-1}	Variables † r_{t-3}	ΔSP_{t-1}	I_{t-2}	R^2
Paper	.757	−173.6*	−25.9*	−40.4*	.675	.933
Chemicals	.121*	1348.4	24.5*	137.5*	.780	.898
Petroleum and Coal	.250	1067.6	−74.0*	170.3*	.810	.910
Rubber	.158*	30.9*	−8.3*	−3.7*	.790	.802
Iron and Steel	.122*	140.7*	−30.8*	75.5*	.876	.750
Nonferrous Metals	.368	81.7*	−14.3*	−85.9*	.890	.656
Other Machinery	.410	61.3*	−33.4*	60.3*	.727	.941
Electrical Machinery	.127*	112.0	−7.8*	70.9*	.938	.873
Motor Vehicles & Equipment	−.087*	135.9*	−28.3*	61.0*	.894	.682
Other Transportation	.300	−11.2*	−46.9*	73.7*	1.110	.878
Textiles	.267	−43.7*	−18.2	49.8*	.623	.873
Stone, Clay, and Glass	.249	89.2*	−9.9*	150.2	.798	.872
Food and Related Products	.156*	531.1	25.6*	−38.6*	.165*	.468
All Above (pooled into one sample)	.165	12.1*	−36.1	3.4*	.823	.933

† Seasonal dummies were included in the models but their regression coefficients are not recorded.
* *Not* significant at the 5% level on a one-tail test.

for the variable range rather widely in size and, with the one exception of stone, clay, and glass, are statistically insignificant at a 5% level. As with the interest rate variable, however, the coefficients are usually in agreement with the accepted theory or expectations. Once again, moreover, in the individual industry as in the aggregate models, inclusion of both a percentage change in stock price and a capacity variable does not eliminate the influence of the residual funds variable.

The lagged investment variable performs consistently well, being insignificant only in the case of food and related products. Furthermore, the coefficients associated with this variable, with the exception of other transportation and of food and related products, tend to be within a range that might be expected in advance.

The individual industry parameters reported in Table VII–4 can be transformed into "dimensionless coefficients" by computing elasticities for the cash throw-off, interest, and capacity variables at the mean values for each industry. The results obtained from such calculations are shown in Table VII–6.[7] The reported elasticities are more or less consistent with most previous studies of manufacturing investment, the only major exception being the relatively large interest elasticities.

The results obtained from analysis of the two different types of sample used in this study, time-series and cross-section, can also be compared. Such comparisons are presented in Table VII–7 for both the capacity utilization and the cash throw-off variables in all industries for which a reasonably good matching could be made between the cross-section and time-series analyses. The cash throw-off variable comparisons are made directly in terms of the regression coefficient estimates obtained by the two different estimation schemes (since the scales employed in the two different

[7] This table, while developed from the data and analyses of this study, first was presented in Kuh and Meyer, "Investment, Liquidity, and Monetary Policy." The figures found under the heading "Long-Term Capacity Elasticity Inclusive of Distributed Lag" in the table are derived by attributing to capacity that portion of the explanation of the model accounted for by the lagged investment variable, I_{t-2}, and are calculated by the methods developed by Koyck, *Distributed Lags and Investment Analysis*, Chapter II. These all-inclusive capacity elasticities are recorded as much for the record as by virtue of any firm belief in their validity since both serious statistical and conceptual objections and questions could be raised about these numbers.

TABLE VII-6

Estimated Investment Elasticities in Manufacturing Industries †

Industry	Cash Throw-off Elasticity	Interest Elasticity	Simple or Short-Term Capacity Elasticity	Long-Term Capacity Elasticity Inclusive of Distributed Lag ‡
Iron and Steel	.126	−.322	.395	2.55
Nonferrous Metals	.424**	−.545	.587	5.32
Electrical Machinery	.183*	−.210	.592**	8.49
Other Machinery	.588**	−.489	.043*	.14
Motor Vehicles and Equipment	−.085	−.342	.365	3.32
Other Transportation Equipment	.345**	−.567**	−.064	.58
Stone, Clay, and Glass	.308**	−.276	.613	2.95
Food	.207*	+.391	2.240**	2.67
Textiles	.255**	−.538**	−.405	−1.07
Paper	.829**	−.597*	−.970	−2.95
Chemicals	.119*	+.230	2.416**	24.20
Rubber	.276*	−.645**	.557	2.56
Petroleum and Coal	.268**	−.342	1.253*	6.60
All Manufacturing	.257**	−.165	.685*	2.28

† Calculated at mean values for the variables.

‡ No significance tests are reported for this column since the reported elasticities are based on a composite calculation from two regression coefficients.

* The regression coefficients used in calculating these elasticities were significant at the 5% level in a conventional one-tail test of significance.

** The regression coefficients used in calculating these elasticities were significant at the 1% level in a conventional one-tail test of significance.

analyses are essentially the same for this variable) while the capacity comparisons are in terms of elasticities at mean values. It can hardly be overstressed that these comparisons between cross-section and time-series estimates are subject to a number of imperfections and must not be taken too literally. However, they are perhaps somewhat suggestive. There is, in fact, remarkable agreement in the central tendencies of the estimates obtained by the two different techniques.

The comparisons also illustrate, however, a number of less desirable aspects of the obtained estimates. Specifically, the range of the estimates is quite considerable for both techniques. This oc-

TABLE VII-7

A Comparison of Time-Series and Cross-Section Results
for Capacity and Residual Fund Variables

	(1) Simple or Short-Term Time-Series Capacity Elasticities	(2) Long-Term Time-Series Capacity Elasticities	(3) Simple Mean of "Significant" X-Section Capacity Elasticities	(4) Range of "Significant" X-Section Capacity Elasticities	(5) Cash Throw-off Coefficients: Time-Series	(6) Simple Mean Cash Throw-off Coefficients: Cross-Section	(7) Range of X-Section Cash Throw-off Coefficients
Iron and Steel	.395	2.55	.71	.38 – 1.03	.122	.35	.18 – .69
Electrical Machinery	.592	8.49	.98	.93 – 1.02	.127	.18	.10 – .32
Other Machinery	.043	.14	1.86	1.02 – 3.55	.410	.22	.04 – .43
Motor Vehicles and Equipment	.365	3.32	1.62	.79 – 2.44	–.087	.47	.19 – .96
Textiles	–.405	–1.07	2.60	2.30 – 2.90	.267	.72	.72
Paper	–.970	–2.95	.43	.33 – .54	.757	.35	.21 – .48
Chemicals	2.416	24.20	2.89	.85 – 4.12	.121	.23	.19 – .27
Rubber	.577	2.56	3.25	2.30 – 4.20	.158	.35	.10 – .60
All Manufacturing	.685	2.28	1.79*	.33 – 4.20	.165	.36*	.04 – .96

* A simple average of the industry data in the column above giving each industry a unitary weight.

curs, moreover, in spite of the fact that all cross-section estimates that are "statistically insignificant" have been eliminated. (Coefficients less in value than their standard error were considered insignificant.) The wide variation in the cross-section estimates probably can be attributed to sociological, psychological, and economic influences that are not incorporated in the simple investment models employed in these analyses. Given the high degree of over-all (i.e., multiple) correlation between the specified models and the time-series data, however, it is a bit difficult to explain the wide range in the time-series results on these grounds. Rather, a high degree of collinearity in the time-series data is a more likely explanation of the instability in the time-series estimates. Indeed, collinearity seems to be a singularly dominant characteristic of the time-series, a circumstance that is hardly novel for economic data. The problem of collinearity is accordingly singled out for more intense attention and analysis in the chapters that follow.

IV. *Upturn and Downturn Models: An Extension of the Time-Series Analysis*

A partial answer to the multicollinearity problem, as well as an important and highly useful extension of the empirical testing of the underlying accelerator-residual funds model, can be obtained by bifurcating the underlying time-series data into two separate categories corresponding, as closely as possible, to periods of business upswing and downswing, respectively. Under the accelerator-residual funds theory the expectation would be that a capacity utilization variable would dominate the upswings while the residual funds variable would provide the best explanation of investment in the downswing. At least some reduction in collinearity, therefore, would be immediately achieved by using the capacity variable only in the upswing model and residual funds only in downswings.

Expectations about the role of the interest rate and stock prices during the two different cyclical periods are more difficult to specify. Previous studies [8] would suggest that interest rate influences would be greatest near the peak of the upswing and perhaps also in the initial turn or decline from that peak. Thus the interest rate

[8] See Meyer and Kuh, Chapter 12.

should be most important in an upswing model but possibly not negligible in a downswing model. To the extent that the interest rate relates only to outside funds, however, which apparently are in less demand during periods of downswing for reasons developed in Chapter V, an interest rate variable might not be at all influential in the downswing model. Such a view would be further strengthened to the extent that residual funds place a floor on expenditures during periods of downswing or that investment-demand does not exceed internal funds at such times. Also, the residual analyses in Table VII–4, and other considerations suggest that the stock price variable is more justified in the upswing than downswing model.

The remaining variable included in previous analysis, lagged investment, can play several different roles, as explained in Chapter II and as suggested by the strong continuity results obtained from the cross-section analyses for the year 1952. Exact interpretation of this variable, other than to say that in some sense or another it specifies a continuity effect in investment planning, is in large measure a matter of choice.

On the basis of these considerations the models actually chosen for analysis with the bifurcated samples were as follows:

Downswing Model:

(IV) $I_t = f[(T - V)_{t-1}, I_{t-2} \text{ (and, optionally, } r_{t-3})]$,

Upswing Model:

(V) $I_t = f[C^M_{t-1}, r_{t-3}, SP_{t-1}, I_{t-2}]$.

The models were assumed linear to a first approximation and, for purposes of actual fitting, three additional dummy variables are added to take account of seasonal effects.

The sample, of course, must be bifurcated into its component upswing and downswing periods before the models themselves can be fitted. For this purpose the basic data employed were two capacity utilization series, the McGraw-Hill capacity index and the Previous Peak index. For reference these indexes can be found in Table IV–3. Of course, the information obtained from these capacity utilization indexes must be interpreted in the light of general information about the behavior of the business cycle during these years. A strong argument also can be made for defining the periods of upswing and downswing so they appear in relatively sustained runs; that is, it would be a bit difficult to believe that the economy could move back and forth from an upswing to a downswing and back to an upswing orientation in successive quarters. While any scheme of classification will involve some arbitrary elements, the classifications, for the most part, were reasonably simple and straightforward except for 1956. As noted in Chapter IV, ambivalent, somewhat contradictory, and erratic tendencies in the capacity utilization indexes were displayed in this year. Nineteen fifty-six was also a year that was difficult to characterize even in the general business cycle literature, the vogue of the day being to call the economic experiences of that and the first half of 1957 "rolling readjustment."

As a first approximation the sample was divided according to whether the value of the McGraw-Hill index, C_t^M, was greater than or equal to .73 or less than .73. Quarters in the first category were placed in the upturn category while those in the latter were characterized as downturns. This scheme, as can be seen by looking at Table IV–3, divides the sample exactly in half, placing 19 observations in each category. It results in the downswing category containing the last two quarters of 1949, the first quarter of 1950, all of 1954 and the first quarter of 1955, and every quarter from the second quarter of 1956 on to the fourth quarter of 1958, the end of the sample period. Upswings were represented by the last three quarters of 1950, all of 1951, 1952, and 1953, and the last three quarters of 1955 and the first quarter of 1956.

This categorization is also essentially the same as that obtained by making the division according to whether the four-quarter moving average of the alternative peak period capacity utilization index was greater than or equal to .99 or less than .99. The only exceptions occur during the difficult 1956 and 1957 periods when the two capacity indexes tended to behave differently.

The categorizations have the additional advantage of being more or less in agreement with general knowledge of the behavior of the business cycle during this period, again with the notable exception of the controversial 1956 and 1957 periods. In this connection, there is no inherent reason, of course, why general cyclical upturns and downturns must be synchronized with upturns and downturns in capacity utilization or upturns and downturns in investment. For example, while the general business cycle probably did not turn downward until the middle of 1957 or after, it is entirely possible that investment planning switched from a capacity orientation to a residual funds or a cash flow orientation well before the general downturn occurred.

Whatever the relative merits or demerits of the categorization scheme, it seems sensible enough to proceed with it as a good first approximation to the kind of bifurcation that is desired. Unfortunately, execution of the needed computations on an electronic calculator under the scheme was not quite perfect (for reasons that are yet to be determined!), with the first quarter of 1956 being improperly classified by the computer program as a year of downswing when, in fact, according to the criteria it should have been designated as a quarter of upswing. It seems doubtful that correction of this error would make a substantial difference in the results, but its existence should be borne in mind while interpreting the reported results.

The simple correlations between different variables in the two different periods are shown in Table VII-8. Inspection of these

TABLE VII-8

Bifurcated Sample Simple Correlations
(Downswings above diagonal: upswings below)

	I_t	I_{t-2}	C_{t-1}^M	$(T-V)_{t-1}$	r_{t-3}	SP_{t-1}
I_t	1.000	.736	.285	.848	.253	.698
I_{t-2}	.763	1.000	−.025	.554	.566	.635
C_{t-1}^M	.121	.002	1.000	.232	−.686	−.258
$(T-V)_{t-1}$	−.024	−.385	−.064	1.000	.219	.789
r_{t-3}	.628	.730	−.157	−.080	1.000	.623
SP_{t-1}	.440	.283	−.439	.504	.550	1.000

figures provides a means of checking the initial plausability of the underlying hypotheses that residual funds have a more prominent influence on investment during downturns than upturns and that capacity utilization's influence is just the contrary. In Table VII-8 the simple correlations obtained for the downswing periods are shown above the main diagonal while those for the upswings are shown below.

On the whole the simple correlations more or less agree with those hypothesized by the accelerator-residual funds theory. In particular, the behavior of the residual funds or cash throw-off variable, $T - V$, is almost exactly as hypothesized: during the periods of downswing the simple correlation between cash throw-off and current investment is higher than that between current investment and any other variable and, contrarily, the simple correlation between cash throw-off and investment during periods of upswing is lower than that to be found between any of the other hypothesized explanatory variables and investment. On the other hand, the behavior of the capacity variable, C^M, is not so clearly in agreement with the underlying hypotheses. The simple correlation between capacity and investment is slightly higher during the downswings than the upswings; however, the pattern of intercorrelations of the other explanatory variables is far more favorable for the capacity variable during periods of upswing than periods of downswing. The intercorrelations are lower and often negative during the upswing periods but, with one exception, are substantially positive during the downswings. It is also obvious from Table VII–8 that inclusion of stock price in the downswing model might have resulted in a collinearity problem since the intercorrelation between stock price and cash throw-off is a very substantial .789.

The results obtained from the multiple regression analyses themselves are as follows:

Downswings: [9]

$$I_t = 490.7 + .409\,(T - V)_{t-1} - 433.3\,r_{t-3} + .877\,I_{t-2}$$
$$(.126)\phantom{+ .409\,(T - V)_{t-1}}(199.3)(.217)$$
$$+ \text{(seasonal corrections)} \qquad R^2 = .900,$$

Upswings: [10]

$$I_t = 747.7 + 2563.3\,C^M_{t-1} + 19.2\,SP_{t-1} - 935.0\,r_{t-3} + .868\,I_{t-2}$$
$$(700.6)(3.4)(274.1)(.094)$$
$$+ \text{(seasonal corrections)} \qquad R^2 = .977,$$

---

[9] The seasonal corrections are obtained by using dummy variables and are as follows: $-420.2Q_1 - 66.1Q_2 - 448.1Q_4$ where Q_1, Q_2, and Q_4 are the dummy variables for the first, second, and fourth quarters respectively.

[10] The seasonal corrections are: $-318.0Q_1 + 153.5Q_2 - 395.8Q_4$.

where all variables are as defined before, the numbers in parentheses beneath the regression coefficients are standard errors, and R^2 is the coefficient of multiple determination. On the whole these models perform remarkably well in the sense that the coefficients of multiple determination are satisfactorily high and all of the regression coefficients are significant by the conventional tests and have the right signs.

Without the stock price or interest rate variables the following results are obtained:

Downswings: [11]

$$I_t = -442.4 + .507\,(T-V)_{t-1} + .570\,I_{t-2} + \text{(seasonal corrections)}$$
$$(.132)\phantom{(T-V)_{t-1} + }(.185)$$
$$R^2 = .862,$$

Upswings: [12]

$$I_t = -99.0 + 1562.0\,C^M_{t-1} + .677\,I_{t-2} + \text{(seasonal corrections)}$$
$$(1132.7)\phantom{C^M_{t-1} + }(.086)$$
$$R^2 = .904.$$

The main information added by these truncated models is the importance to the performance of the capacity variable in the upturns of being imbedded in a larger model. While the capacity utilization variable's regression coefficient is quite significant in the full upswing model, it is not significant in the truncated model. By contrast, the cash throw-off variable's performance is little affected by the inclusion or exclusion of the additional variable, the lagged interest rate, in the downswing model. In this context it is to be noted, moreover, that while the coefficient of multiple determination in the truncated upturn model is higher than that for the truncated downturn model, this higher correlation is achieved mainly by the attachment of greater significance to the seasonal adjustment factors and lagged investment which offset the relatively poor performance of the central capacity utilization variable. Apparently a more complicated explanation is needed of investment in the upswing of the cycle than the downswing. Under any circumstances, though, these results are further dramatic evidence of the

[11] The seasonal corrections are: $-240.6Q_1 + 85.0Q_2 - 219.3Q_4$.
[12] The seasonal corrections are: $-308.0Q_1 - 225.3Q_2 - 281.7Q_4$.

degree and importance of collinearity in the underlying time-series data.

The truncated model results also indicate that a rather special role may be played by the interest rate variable. This role is best revealed by inspecting the residuals that are obtained from the regression equations with and without interest rate included. Such "residual analyses" are shown for the downturn case in Table VII–9 and for the upswing in Table VII–10.

In both the down- and upswings it is clear that addition of the interest rate variable to the regressions greatly reduced the auto-correlation of the residuals. Without the interest rate the Durbin-Watson coefficients are highly significant, that is, the degree of auto-correlation in the residuals cannot be accepted as being generated by a random mechanism. By contrast, with the interest rate variable in the models, the Durbin-Watson coefficients move to values that are essentially insignificant or, at least, considerably less significant. In the downswings, moreover, the reduced auto-correlation of the residuals is mainly effectuated by a reduction in the continuously high negative errors observed during 1958. Without the lagged interest rate variable the regression model tends to overestimate investment substantially during this period, whereas with it the residuals, with the exception of the first quarter of 1958, become relatively small and with no pronounced tendency toward either overestimation or underestimation. The results also seem to document the widespread feeling that the Federal Reserve Board may have delayed a bit too long in 1957 in reversing a tight monetary policy.

In the upswing the main impact of the introduction of the interest rate is to reduce the systematic tendency toward overestimation of investment in 1953 that occurs when the interest rate is not included in the model. Again, 1953 was a year of interesting experiments in monetary policy.

To provide a further check on the legitimacy of the findings concerning the role of the interest rate, residual analyses with and without the interest rate also can be performed for Model 2 of Table VII–2 tested against the time-series data for the *entire* period. Such analyses are reported in Table VII–11. Again a reduction in auto-correlation occurs when the interest rate is introduced but the

TABLE VII-9

Bifurcated Investment Model: Downturn Residuals Analyses with and without the Interest Rate

Year and Quarter	Actual Value	Without Interest Rate in Model			With Interest Rate in Model		
		Estimated Value	Residual	% Error	Estimated Value	Residual	% Error
4903	1947.06	1963.78	−16.72	−0.86	2156.74	−209.68	−10.77
4904	2083.83	2333.84	−250.01	−12.00	2284.74	−200.92	−13.96
5001	1692.85	1344.25	348.60	20.59	1381.22	311.63	18.41
5401	2581.91	2219.07	362.84	14.05	2189.66	392.25	15.19
5402	2853.29	2750.65	102.65	3.60	2812.03	41.27	1.45
5403	2642.36	2736.59	−94.23	−3.57	2814.13	−171.77	−6.50
5404	2959.08	2838.18	120.90	4.09	2948.27	10.81	.37
5501	2224.53	2310.92	−86.39	−3.88	2372.24	−147.71	−6.64
5601	2777.46	2810.28	−32.81	−1.18	2773.57	3.90	.14
5602	3431.99	3326.28	105.71	3.08	3341.86	90.13	2.63
5603	3479.13	3294.55	184.58	5.31	3340.39	138.74	3.99
5604	3932.50	3505.33	427.18	10.86	3654.61	277.90	7.07
5701	3077.26	3214.19	−136.93	−4.45	3280.09	−202.83	−6.59
5702	3624.78	3603.69	21.09	.58	3672.18	−47.40	−1.31
5703	3447.98	3319.38	128.60	3.73	3251.51	196.47	5.70
5704	3638.77	3594.53	44.24	1.22	3574.51	64.26	1.77
5801	2470.59	2925.90	−455.31	−18.43	2827.82	−357.23	−14.46
5802	2484.36	2713.81	−229.45	−9.24	2568.36	−84.00	−3.38
5803	2253.81	2456.03	−202.23	−8.97	2207.57	46.24	2.05
5804	2463.87	2806.17	−342.31	−13.89	2525.91	−62.05	−2.52
		Durbin-Watson Coeff. 1.3234	No. Data Cases 20	Deg's of Frdm. 14	Durbin-Watson Coeff. 1.7616	No. Data Cases 20	Deg's of Frdm. 13

NOTE: Estimated Value and Residual may not sum to Actual Value due to rounding.

TABLE VII-10

Birfurcated Investment Model: Upswing Residuals Analyses with and without the Interest Rate

Year and Quarter	Actual Value	Without Interest Rate in Model			With Interest Rate in Model		
		Estimated Value	Residual	% Error	Estimated Value	Residual	% Error
5002	2000.00	2030.80	−30.80	−1.54	1945.66	54.34	2.72
5003	2100.57	2177.91	−77.35	−3.68	2169.53	−68.96	−3.28
5004	2727.67	2751.23	−23.56	−.86	2733.19	−5.52	−.20
5101	2287.38	2306.70	−19.32	−.84	2345.76	−58.38	−2.55
5102	2863.26	2778.55	84.71	2.96	2834.93	28.32	.99
5103	2855.06	2703.93	151.13	5.29	2789.50	65.55	2.30
5104	3340.96	3194.27	146.69	4.39	3334.88	6.07	.18
5201	2705.88	2653.12	52.76	1.95	2660.49	45.39	1.68
5202	3145.64	3026.77	118.87	3.78	3062.58	83.06	2.64
5203	2786.82	2808.27	−21.45	−.77	2812.20	−25.38	−.91
5204	3334.71	3350.90	−16.19	−.49	3390.21	−55.50	−1.66
5301	2730.81	2764.25	−33.45	−1.22	2717.82	12.99	.48
5302	3113.57	3177.88	−64.31	−2.07	3143.84	−30.27	−.97
5303	2863.73	3013.54	−149.81	−5.23	2929.87	−66.14	−2.31
5304	3317.17	3421.19	−104.02	−3.14	3281.57	35.60	1.07
5502	2734.83	2843.30	−108.46	−3.97	2870.29	−135.45	−4.95
5503	2814.56	2717.09	97.47	3.08	2719.63	94.93	3.37
5504	3345.12	3348.04	−2.92	−.09	3325.78	19.34	.58
		Durbin-Watson Coeff. 0.8567	No. Data Cases 18	Deg's of Frdm. 11	Durbin-Watson Coeff. 2.5853	No. Data Cases 18	Deg's of Frdm. 10

NOTE: Estimated Value and Residual may not sum to Actual Value due to rounding.

TABLE VII-11

Residual Analyses for All Time Periods with and without the Interest Rate

Year and Quarter	Actual Value	Without Interest Rate in Model			With Interest Rate in Model		
		Estimated Value	Residual	% Error	Estimated Value	Residual	% Error
4901	1947.06	2129.92	−182.86	−9.99	2164.88	−217.82	−11.19
4902	2083.83	2385.35	−301.53	−14.47	2408.46	−324.64	−15.58
5001	1692.85	1452.91	239.94	14.17	1476.29	216.56	12.79
5002	2000.00	1891.55	108.45	5.42	1896.61	103.39	5.17
5003	2100.57	2304.45	−203.89	−9.71	2306.43	−205.86	−9.80
5004	2727.67	2868.90	−141.23	−5.18	2826.17	−98.50	−3.61
5101	2287.38	2161.97	125.41	5.48	2135.15	152.23	6.66
5102	2863.26	2875.91	−12.65	−.44	2862.21	1.05	.04
5103	2855.06	2784.93	70.13	2.46	2786.74	68.32	2.39
5104	3340.96	3079.95	261.00	7.81	3101.52	239.44	7.17
5201	2705.88	2529.17	176.71	6.53	2537.63	168.25	6.22
5202	3145.64	3013.73	131.91	4.19	3031.69	113.95	3.62
5203	2786.82	2815.78	−28.96	1.04	2839.89	−53.07	−1.90
5204	3334.71	3332.70	2.01	.06	3348.06	−13.36	−.40
5301	2730.81	2734.12	−3.31	−.12	2705.60	25.21	.92
5302	3113.57	3264.60	−151.03	−4.85	3243.32	−129.75	−4.17
5303	2863.73	3165.44	−301.71	−10.54	3137.65	−273.92	−9.57
5304	3317.17	3515.48	−198.30	−5.98	3475.46	−158.29	−4.77
5401	2581.91	2506.86	75.05	2.91	2451.60	130.31	5.05
5402	2853.29	2866.40	−13.11	−.46	2865.38	−12.09	−.42
5403	2642.36	2692.35	−49.99	−1.89	2713.78	−71.42	−2.70

TABLE VII–11 (continued)

Year and Quarter	Actual Value	Without Interest Rate in Model			With Interest Rate in Model		
		Estimated Value	Residual	% Error	Estimated Value	Residual	% Error
5404	2959.08	2937.73	21.35	.72	2978.17	−19.08	−.64
5501	2224.53	2300.62	−76.09	−3.42	2350.22	−125.69	−5.65
5502	2734.83	2828.05	−93.22	−3.41	2858.86	−124.02	−4.53
5503	2814.56	2792.01	22.56	.80	2804.66	9.90	.35
5504	3345.12	3260.94	84.18	2.52	3249.68	95.44	2.85
5601	2777.46	2778.95	−1.49	−.05	2781.01	−3.55	−.13
5602	3431.99	3232.23	199.76	5.82	3247.29	184.70	5.38
5603	3479.13	3139.17	339.96	9.77	3162.55	316.58	9.10
5604	3932.50	3603.20	329.31	8.37	3654.18	278.33	7.08
5701	3077.26	3234.92	−157.65	−5.22	3270.27	−193.00	−6.27
5702	3624.78	3619.23	5.55	.15	3633.89	−9.11	−.25
5703	3447.98	3231.33	216.65	6.28	3192.18	255.80	7.42
5704	3638.77	3694.55	−55.78	−1.53	3670.68	−31.91	−.88
5801	2470.59	2849.15	−378.56	−15.32	2840.89	−370.30	−14.99
5802	2484.36	2660.02	−175.66	−7.07	2612.48	−128.11	−5.16
5803	2253.81	2135.70	118.11	5.24	2082.32	171.48	7.61
5804	2463.87	2464.87	−1.01	−.04	2431.21	32.67	1.32
		Durbin-Watson Coeff. 1.3655	No. Data Cases 38	Deg's of Frdm. 31	Durbin-Watson Coeff. 1.5055	No. Data Cases 38	Deg's of Frdm. 30

NOTE: Estimated Value and Residual may not sum to Actual Value due to rounding.

improvement is not as pronounced as in the bifurcated analyses. Similarly, the size of the estimation errors in 1953 and 1958 is reduced with the interest rate included but not as pronouncedly as before.

In general, it appears that if the interest rate rises to a relatively high level, as it did during early 1953 and late 1957, an adverse impact occurs on investment approximately three quarters later that cannot be accounted for by capacity utilization, fund flow, or other variables commonly included in investment models. Furthermore, there is some evidence that these interest rate influences are most likely to be felt near the very end of a general period of cyclical improvement, like 1953, or during the early phases of a general cyclical downturn, such as the first part of 1958. (It should be reemphasized here that periods of *general* upswing and downswing are not necessarily synchronized with periods of upswing and downswing in capacity utilization and investment patterns.) In short, there is evidence that monetary policy has exerted at least a negative influence on investment when applied very vigorously and under certain cyclical conditions.

V. *Summary*

Reported in this chapter were a series of different analyses of time-series data on manufacturing investment, finances, sales, and profitability. These data pertained both to specific industries within the manufacturing sector and to the aggregate for all of manufacturing and were composed of quarterly observations for the postwar period from 1949 through the end of 1958.

In order to define the exact form of the regression functions, a choice first was made of appropriate lags and alternative formulations of the principal explanatory variables, capacity utilization and cash throw-off. On the basis of an empirical evaluation, a capacity utilization measure based upon the McGraw-Hill capacity index and a simple cash throw-off variable, profits plus depreciation expense less dividends, were selected for primary analysis. Furthermore, for both these variables fairly short, one-period lags seemed to be most useful. In fact, the only explanatory variable that seemingly worked better with a longer lag was the interest rate which clearly was at its best with a rather substantial three-quarter lag.

Of the two central types of variables in the residual funds-accelerator model, cash throw-off and capacity utilization, the residual funds or cash throw-off variables usually recorded higher simple correlations with investment than capacity utilization variables, but the capacity utilization variables consistently provided a better explanation of investment when embedded in more complete or complex models. The residual funds variable, though, clearly was superior even in multiple variable models when individual or component manufacturing industries were analyzed. In fact, the performance of the capacity utilization variable was notoriously poor in the less aggregated samples. Comparison of the results obtained with the aggregate and individual industry data also strongly confirmed previous findings that it is easier to build a model "explaining" an aggregate than its individual components, at least to the extent that explanation is measured by the usual statistical standards of multiple correlation and significant regression coefficients.

Potentially pertinent results from the standpoint of evaluating the accelerator-residual funds hypothesis also were obtained when the time series for all manufacturing was divided into two groups, one pertaining to periods of cyclical expansion or upswings and one to periods of cyclical decline or downswings. The observed tendency for the capacity variable to perform better in a more complex model was again observable in the analyses of the bifurcated samples. Specifically, the capacity utilization variable only became significant in the upswing models when it was embedded in a fairly complete model including a stock price index and the interest rate as additional explanatory variables. By contrast, the cash throw-off variable provided a reasonably adequate explanation of investment in even the simplest downswing models.

The change-in-sales variable, the central variable in simple accelerator models, was, generally speaking, an empirical failure. Usefulness of the change-in-sales variable in explaining the variations in investment over time was singularly limited even when rather complex and extended lag structures were employed. Not only were the regression coefficients for the change-in-sales variables almost invariably insignificant, but the signs of these coefficients were more often than not negative, thus violating theoretical specification.

In a certain sense, the consistently best explanatory variable for investment was also a rather uninteresting one, lagged investment. As noted previously, lagged investment is best construed as a proxy for other variables or as representative of continuity effects in the investment process. The continuity and proxy roles are not, of course, necessarily exclusive. Whatever interpretation is accepted for the lagged investment variable, it was consistently significant and generally behaved more or less as expected. Indeed, only the residual funds variable in a few analyses associated with recession period data displayed a closer relationship with investment in all of the analyses and situations tested.

The stock price variable also recorded consistent and significant relationships with investment. However, this variable almost invariably was collinear with other variables included in the analysis, particularly residual funds. Where an attempt was made to circumvent this collinearity problem, and also to improve the conceptual qualities of the stock price variable by converting it into a percentage change, the results were somewhat less favorable but still significant to at least some degree. There is apparently an expectational influence at work in business investment decisions that is well measured by stock price levels or changes.

This expectational influence, furthermore, seems to be quite independent of and different from the financial constraint considerations represented by residual fund flows. While residual fund flows and stock price levels proved to be highly collinear, a detailed examination of the residuals obtained from an accelerator-residual funds investment model, with and without stock price included as an additional explanatory variable, indicated that the stock price variable tended to improve the explanatory ability of the equation mainly during periods of cyclical expansion. In fact, during recessionary periods, inclusion of the stock price variable either made little substantive difference or actually made the model less effective. Since the change in stock price seemed to be almost as effective as an explanatory variable as the absolute stock price and was not collinear with residual funds, a strong implication exists that the major role of the stock price variable is as a measure of expectations and not as a proxy or alternative measure of the same considerations as the residual funds variable. In short, both stock price and residual funds seem to have a role: one as a measure of expectations and the other as a measure of financial considerations. Still, it was unfortunate that the collinearity between the absolute values of these two variables was so great that a clearer determination could not be made of the relative roles and importance of these different influences.

The lagged interest rate variable, while not always associated with regression coefficients that were highly significant, usually did have coefficients with a negative sign, as hypothesized by conventional economic theory. To this extent, at least, the results of the present analysis could be considered superior to estimates of interest rate regression coefficients obtained in many previous empirical studies of investment behavior. Furthermore, the interest rate variable was most useful, not unexpectedly, when interest rates were high and just before or just after the upper turning point of the business cycle.

When the time-series results were compared with the cross-section results reported in previous chapters, there was some, but very limited, agreement between the regression estimates obtained from the two different sources. It was perhaps suggestive, though, that the central tendencies of the two different sets of estimates proved to be reasonably similar.

In general, the results of the time-series analyses reported in this chapter were far from conclusive. In a sense they prove above all else that one can obtain a fairly adequate explanation of manufacturing investment behavior over the period from 1949 to 1958 with almost any standard investment model. There was, in fact, only one apparent exception to this rule, a simple change-in-sales accelerator model.

If forced on the basis of this highly limited evidence to select one investment hypothesis as more promising in a majority of circumstances than any other, it would be difficult to escape the conclusion that some type of *capacity* formulation of the acceleration principle is superior to any other simple alternative. Even the effectiveness of the capacity variables, however, was crucially dependent upon being embedded in models which incorporated a number of other investment influences as well, particularly those relating to the interest rate and expectational influences as measured by stock prices. Furthermore, the next most useful variable to capacity utilization would appear to be some measure of residual funds. Again, though, a definite time constraint seems to pertain: the residual funds variable, as hypothesized, seems to be primarily useful in explaining investment levels during recession periods.

This tendency toward distinct time limitations on the effectiveness of different explanatory variables was even more noticeable with the stock price and interest rate variables. As already noted, these variables tended to make a positive contribution under very specific circumstances. The stock price variable was mainly useful during the highly buoyant and expansionary periods from mid-1950 through mid-1952 and mid-1955 through the third quarter of 1957. The interest rate variable, on the other hand, was primarily effective in 1953 and 1958 both when interest rates were high and when the cyclical position was one very near to or just beyond the upper turning point. As shown in preceding chapters, a rather similar time specialization of the models was also noted in the cross-section analyses. In particular, none of the standard investment models performed well in explaining the investment behavior observed in the cross-section samples for 1952. At that time, the principal determinants of investment behavior seemed to be the size of the prior liquidity stock and the existing commitment to investment programs already under way. All of these considerations strongly suggest that no simple investment model will ever be fully adequate to explain all the convolutions and turns observable in actual business investment behavior. Eclectic and rather complex models are apparently needed.

Such a conclusion is not at all comforting, moreover, since these time-series analyses also seem to confirm the view that time-series data are incapable of discriminating among a very wide range of explanatory hypotheses. That is, historical time series on investment behavior apparently do not incorporate sufficient evidence to permit the making of important structural distinctions. While cross-section data hold promise of filling some of these gaps in the historical experience, that promise would appear to be quite limited, at least in the case of investment analyses as shown by the results of the present study and by most previous cross-section studies of investment behavior.

In sum, while a number of potentially interesting and suggestive results have been observed in both the time-series and cross-section analyses, satisfaction is at least mitigated by a lurking suspicion that confirmation could be found for almost any and all hypotheses. This would seem to be particularly true of the time-series studies, based as they are on highly collinear data. To the extent, of course, that the cross-section analysis provided at least some partial or limited confirmation of the time-series results, or vice versa, these suspicions are somewhat lessened. Furthermore, to the extent that one has reasons — empirical, theoretical, emotional, or otherwise — for placing particular confidence in a particular theory, a further basis may be said to exist for choosing among a number of explanatory hypotheses displaying equal empirical prowess. The very serious problem remains, however, of how to integrate the different results and the different pieces of information obtained from these widely different sources into models that are *useful* for forecasting and policy purposes. These problems are at least considered, though less than fully answered, in the next two chapters.

Chapter VIII | Multicollinearity and Constrained Regression Estimation

I. *The Nature and Effects of Collinearity*

Of all the obstacles to the correct specification and estimation of structure in time-series models, multicollinearity is certainly one of the most important and universal. If this point needed further confirmation, the results of the preceding chapter surely provided abundant additional verification, at least in the particular context of manufacturing investment decisions. Indeed, collinearity of the underlying explanatory variables, which in turn created an inability to distinguish sharply between the empirical effectiveness of different investment hypotheses, was a dominant characteristic of the reported time-series results.

Multicollinearity arises in economic models when the independent or explanatory variables fail to be nonstochastic, as classical regression theory assumes, and are intercorrelated to some degree. Since economists must in general be satisfied with experiments conducted by nature, rather than under laboratory control, and since, in addition, substantial observation error is likely to exist, intercorrelations of notable magnitude are present in virtually all economic studies. In the most extreme case, when the rank of the correlation matrix is less than the number of variables, the correlation matrix is singular and the normal equations are therefore insoluble. This is ironically a fortunate (and in practice nonexistent) situation, for it clearly signals the presence of a harmfully collinear condition. The far more insidious and common case is that the intercorrelations are quite large, but the correlation matrix is not quite singular. Under such circumstances normal equations produce a determinant solution, but several difficulties generally will be encountered.

Since collinearity implies substantial covariation among independent variables, their total effect on the dependent variable may be divided rather arbitrarily, resulting in structurally improper coefficients. In essence, one variable implicitly acts to some degree as a proxy for others. The sum of the collinear variables' coefficients (normalized by their variances) will in general equal the "true" over-all effect of the variables, but the econometrician seeking structural specification usually demands that the individual coefficients, not the sum, closely approximate the "true" structural values. In addition, under collinear conditions, large standard errors for the coefficients normally will be estimated, usually quite properly, reflecting the paucity of information in the sample about individual coefficients. These large standard errors, of course, do increase the danger of incorrectly (from the standpoint of structural specification) rejecting a variable from the equation and allowing the remaining collinear variables to act as proxies for the rejected one.[1]

Collinearity is usually most severe with time-series data, because they are dominated by common trends or influences. The limited variation that may be observable often occurs, moreover, at times of heightened economic activity so that the period of erratic or nontrend related movement will be synchronized for many of the series employed in a model. Such synchronization creates, of course, the markedly high intercorrelations normally indigenous to

[1] When, in addition, autocorrelation is present, the standard errors will generally be underestimated. This can lead to the possibility of incorrectly including a variable in the model. However, the danger of including too many variables in a model is probably not nearly so great as those outlined above, and econometricians would seem rarely, if ever, to commit this type of specification error. See Henri Theil, *Economic Forecasts and Policy* (Amsterdam: North-Holland Publishing Co., 1958), p. 363.

time-series data.[2]   The combination of these high intercorrelations or the paucity of historical experimentation means that any slight alteration of the time series and their covariation patterns, especially during one of these crucial periods, can lead to substantial changes in the magnitude of the estimated regression coefficients, re-emphasizing the difficulty in structural determination.

Of course, structural validity need not be required of purely forecasting models (as contrasted with models aimed at evaluating competing public policy prescriptions and for which structural accuracy would seem obviously desirable).   The argument runs that in the realm of pure forecasting, any relationship, however coincidental, is satisfactory, so long as it remains stable during the prediction period.   What one is interested in is the prediction itself, not how it is obtained.   Thus, to cite a whimsical example, if there has been historically a stable relationship between the birth of rabbits in France and the purchases of automobiles in the United States, there is no reason not to take advantage of this fact.   There is certainly no obvious causal relationship between the two variables, but so long as this relationship, casual as it is, remains stable during the period to be predicted, one can very well forecast the purchase of cars in the United States by the birth of French rabbits.   The method, it is argued, is secondary to the results.

There are, nevertheless, several advantages of structural specification, *if it can be obtained*, in forecasting models.   First, the very nature of casual, "pseudo-structural" relationships as contrasted with realistic behavioral ones, suggests that they will be less stable and enduring, thereby increasing the possibility of a "parameter shift" between historical and future periods.   Predictions based on fortuitous, coincidental relationships can be used only with some uneasiness.   By contrast, models which base their explanatory power on established human behavioral patterns and technological or institutional constraints should be less apt to undergo marked changes.

The second advantage of structural specification, related somewhat to the first, concerns the identification of the occurrence of

[2] For some interesting evidence on the extent of such correlation see Edward Ames and Stanley Reiter, "Distributions of Correlation Coefficients in Economic Time Series," *Journal of the American Statistical Association*, Vol. 56, No. 295 (September 1961), pp. 637–656.

so-called "parameter shifts." Should the mechanism, causal or casual, by which predictions are generated change in some substantial amount from historical to prediction period, the model must be modified to reflect the change. Working with structural relationships usually simplifies the task of determining at what point circumstances have changed sufficiently to invalidate a particular forecasting model. In essence, the use of models embodying behavioral reality has the value of focusing the forecaster's attention on those elements of the economic environment which are crucial to the continued success of his predictions. Since the forecaster with knowledge of structure should be more aware of the relationships on which his forecasts are based, he is in a better position to appraise when the nature of behavioral reality has changed sufficiently to necessitate reestimation of the model. The difficulties encountered with postwar econometric consumption forecasts underline the potential value of this knowledge. Had more econometricians been aware that a positive correlation between income and household liquidity historically had aided their forecast results, they might usefully have altered their models to reflect the breakdown of this relationship, for the divergence of the liquid assets and income series in the postwar years itself was well predicted.

If exact structural specification were possible, given the tools and data available, models precisely embodying behavioral, technical, and institutional reality thus would be preferred. But there are several imposing obstacles to the specification of even an approximation to valid structural models, particularly when time-series data are employed. As pointed out before, the existence of multicollinearity makes the separation of effects common to several variables difficult, if not impossible. The division of these common effects, and therefore the respective coefficients, must be to some degree arbitrary.

Because of these and related considerations, Professor T. C. Liu has argued in a recent paper that true economic structure tends to contain far more explanatory variables than most models in the past have included.[3] He suggests that data limitations (in par-

[3] Ta Chung Liu, "Underidentification, Structural Estimation and Forecasting," *Econometrica*, Vol. 28, No. 4 (October 1960), pp. 855–865.

ticular, insufficient historical covariation between dependent and independent variables in time series) have made it impossible to include a large number of explanatory variables and still obtain "significant" structural estimates.

> Statistical difficulties (mainly intercorrelations between explanatory variables) which have plagued econometricians for decades, rather than economic theory or *a priori* information, are probably responsible for the tendency toward oversimplification of structural relationships . . . .[4]

The complexity of economic life, in short, implies that there are a great many variables and relationships which are relevant to a particular economic structure, but the paucity of good historical experiments precludes proper estimation.

The acceptance of Liu's argument leads to the conclusion that most attempts to specify structure correctly will have to proceed by including a greater number of explanatory variables than they have in the past. But it has been the experience of econometricians that multicollinearity is encountered with progressive severity as the number of independent variables is increased, since the additional variables often reflect different nuances of the same or closely related causal forces. As the preceding chapter made clear, collinearity difficulties are present to a marked degree even in the somewhat simplified and truncated investment models used here. The only apparent alternatives are either to abandon all efforts at structural estimation or develop alternative estimation procedures and data sources that better meet the collinearity problem. Clearly, the latter solutions are the preferable alternative. Their achievement, though, may be so difficult as to make abandonment of serious efforts to build "structurally accurate" forecasting models the more prudent course for those facing an immediate need to do actual forecasting. There is nothing inconsistent, moreover, in accepting such pessimistic advice as soundly practical for the present or short run, while proceeding with efforts to rectify the situation in the long run. At a minimum such efforts usually provide more exact information on the extent to which forecasting and structural accuracy are incompatible in the present state of economic knowl-

---

[4] *Ibid.*, p. 856.

edge as well as providing a further cumulation of experience and information for seeking the appropriate long-term objective of structural accuracy.

In the next section a very simple extension is made of some existing ideas for improving structural estimation in circumstances of collinear data. Specifically, the mathematical theory underlying a "least squares constrained coefficient" approach to the fitting of regression functions is expounded. Following this, in Section III, empirical results obtained from limited application of constrained regression to the investment models of this study are reported. Finally, Section IV considers the implications of the estimation methods developed in this chapter for structural specification in forecasting models and for certain possibilities of introducing Bayesian procedures into econometrics. This is done preparatory to testing more rigorously the comparative forecasting ability of different forms of constrained and unconstrained estimation in the next chapter.

II. *Regression, Constrained Coefficients, and Mathematical Programming*

There is substantial agreement that fruitful approaches to the solution of the time-series collinearity problem must employ "outside" information. In particular, many econometricians have turned to cross-section data in the hope that the greater covariation exhibited and larger number of observations available will tend to nullify the effect of any high intercorrelations among the explanatory variables. The results of these cross-section studies or other available sources of "extraneous" information (e.g., prior economic theory) often have been used in turn to fix the coefficients of one or more of a group of highly collinear variables in time-series studies. For example, important demand studies by Wold, Stone, Tobin and others have proceeded by using cross-sections to estimate the coefficient of one variable in a collinear model and then estimating the remaining coefficients from time-series data.[5] Some,

[5] Herman Wold and Lars Jureen, *Demand Analysis: A Study in Econometrics* (New York: John Wiley and Sons, 1953); Richard Stone, *The Measurement of Consumers' Expenditure and Behavior in the United Kingdom 1920–1938* (Cambridge: Cambridge University Press, 1954); and James Tobin, "A Statistical Demand Function for Food in the U.S.A.," *Journal of the Royal Statistical Society*, Series A, Vol. 113 (Part II, 1950), pp. 113–141.

however, have cast serious doubts upon the validity of using cross-section and time-series data to estimate coefficients in the same model. They suggest that the different data may in fact measure forces with completely different time horizons or reflect entirely different behavioral adjustments.[6] Still, there can be no doubt that the most promising solution to the lack of information which collinearity implies is finding new sources of information for the estimation of economic parameters.

"Extraneous estimation" is, moreover, merely a logical extension of the techniques which most econometricians have implicitly used in the past when confronted with multicollinearity. When collinearity has caused a coefficient to appear "nonsignificant" (as measured by its standard error) or just "unreasonable," the typical procedure has been to omit it from the equation. This is in effect employing a very particular but rather casually determined extraneous estimate, namely zero. Furthermore, any extraneous estimate, whether zero or nonzero, represents a form of constrained regression estimation; in essence, the extraneously estimated coefficient is restricted to one explicit point value.

In the constrained estimation method presented here a collinear variable's coefficient is also constrained, but in a more general way. Specifically, it would seem more intuitively satisfactory to force a variable to fall within certain limits, rather than assign it some fixed, arbitrary value — and especially zero — if the variable is hypothesized on other grounds to be an important determinant of the behavior under investigation.

Constrained regression is most readily analyzed by reconsidering the general problem of regression analysis in terms of its relationship to mathematical programming (a general term developed to encompass both linear and nonlinear programming methods). Such a reformulation is also helpful in the next chapter when relating forecasting objectives to different regression estimation procedures because, as will be shortly evident, it readily permits consideration of alternatives to least squares estimation methods.

In general, although by no means in all cases, standard mathe-

[6] Edwin Kuh and John R. Meyer, "How Extraneous Are Extraneous Estimates," *Review of Economics and Statistics*, Vol. 39, No. 4 (November 1957), pp. 380–393; and Grunfeld and Grilliches, "Is Aggregation Necessarily Bad?"

matical programming problems contain more variables in the objective function than there are constraints on the optimization procedure, so that the constraints are satisfied by a large number of solutions. The problem is to select that solution which has optimal properties. Regression analysis presents the converse problem. In this case the number of restrictions (i.e., the number of points through which the plane must pass) exceeds the number of variables. Since not all the constraints can be precisely satisfied at the same time, some compromise must be struck. The particular compromise selected will depend on the form of the error functions employed. The compromise can be expressed in mathematical terms, becoming an objective function which is to be optimized. The problem is simply to find a set of variables (i.e., coefficients) which provide the best compromise (as defined in the particular problem) to a set of restrictions, all of which cannot be satisfied at the same time.

Traditionally, least squares has been the method employed in regression analysis, mainly for reasons of computational tractability and simplicity. A standard computational procedure for obtaining least squares estimates of regression coefficients is inverting the correlation matrix of the independent variables and then post-multiplying by the vector of correlations between the dependent variable and the various independent variables. Mathematical programming, however, suggests another method. Consider a problem with dependent variable, y, n independent variables, $x_j, j = 1 \cdots n$, and m observations $(m > n)$. Associated with each observation will be an error, whose sign cannot be determined beforehand (i.e., it is impossible to determine prior to fitting the plane whether it will pass above or below the ith point). The quadratic programming formulation of the problem is therefore as follows:

Define $\quad b_j, j = 1 \cdots n; \ e_i, i = 1 \cdots m; \ $ and K by:

$$(8.1) \qquad \sum_{j=1}^{n} x_{ij}b_j + K + e_i = y_i \qquad \text{for all } i,$$

$$(8.2) \qquad \sum_{j=1}^{n} \bar{x}_j b_j + K = \bar{y},$$

$$(8.3) \qquad b_j \text{ unrestricted in sign} \qquad \text{for all } j,$$

$$(8.4) \qquad e_i, K \text{ unrestricted in sign} \qquad \text{for all } i.$$

Choose $b_j, j = 1 \cdots n$, and K to *minimize*

$$(8.5) \qquad \sum_{i=1}^{m} e_i^2.$$

In standard programming terminology (8.5) is the objective function and (8.1), (8.2), (8.3), and (8.4) are the constraints. The m constraints (8.1) require that the plane approximately pass through the points, and the constraint (8.2) requires that it pass through the means of the variables exactly, thereby establishing the constant, K.

A major computational advantage of using a mathematical programming algorithm in place of conventional least squares techniques is that the programming approach allows restrictions to be placed conveniently on the regression coefficients, b_j's. That is, defining L_j and U_j as lower and upper limits, respectively, on the coefficient b_j, (8.3) can be rewritten as:

$$(8.3') \qquad L_j \leqslant b_j \leqslant U_j \qquad \text{for all } j,$$

thereby incorporating the desired limits without causing any major increase in computational burden. This, in turn, permits an application, in a highly flexible manner, of *a priori* or extraneous information to the solution of the so-called "collinearity problem."

III. *Least Squares Regression with Constrained Coefficients: Some Empirical Results*

As just noted, least squares regression with constrained coefficients can be formulated as a mathematical programming problem of the type described by (8.1), (8.2), (8.3), (8.4), and (8.5). All that is necessary is that b_j constraints in (8.3') be described more precisely as follows: [7]

$$(8.6) \qquad b_{j\,\min} \leqslant b_j \leqslant b_{j\,\max}.$$

It is convenient, moreover, to let

$$c_j = b_j - b_{j\,\min}$$

[7] See also P. Wegner, "Memorandum No. LL27," *Littauer Statistical Laboratory,* Harvard University, mimeographed. There are, incidentally, some algebraic and typographical errors in this formulation so that caution should be employed when applying.

so that (8.6) can be rewritten as

$$0 \leqslant c_j \leqslant b_{j\,\text{max}} - b_{j\,\text{min}}.$$

This, in turn, permits a simplification of the objective function so that (in a vector and matrix notation as designated by capital letters corresponding to the original lower case notation) it becomes:

$$-2C'(X'Y - X'XB_{\text{min}}) + C'X'XC$$

or

$$C'(X'XB_{\text{min}} - X'Y) + \tfrac{1}{2}C'X'XC.$$

The corresponding constraints are:

$$C \leqslant B_{\text{max}} - B_{\text{min}}$$
$$C \geqslant 0.$$

It is worth noting that with the original variables defined in standardized terms $X'X$ is precisely the correlation matrix of the independent variables and therefore satisfies the positive semidefinite requirement of most quadratic programming algorithms; also, $X'XB_{\text{min}} - X'Y$ is merely an adjusted form of the righthand side of the traditional normal equations (expressed in terms of the correlation rather than moment matrix). The solution will be in terms of normalized regression coefficients which can easily be changed to the standard form by adjusting for their respective variances.[8]

The method of constrained regression is designed specifically to permit the inclusion in a single equation of all the variables which are believed *a priori* to be relevant without sacrificing too much structural specification to multicollinearity. Model 3 in Table VII–2 of the previous chapter is therefore used in the experiments that follow, since it is one of the most extended forms of the investment models used in this work and includes all major variables. Furthermore, the results originally obtained with this model were clearly influenced by the considerable collinearity of the included variables. There is, in short, no lack of challenge for constrained estimation with this model.

[8] The form of the general problem used here is the same as that employed by Philip Wolfe, "The Simplex Method for Quadratic Programming," *Econometrica*, Vol. 27, No. 3 (July 1959), pp. 382–398.

The job of specifying constraints for the included variables is a difficult one, but much aid can be gained from an examination of Tables VII–2, VII–7, and VI–12, which tabulate partial regression coefficients for various time-series and cross-section models. By use of these tables and accumulated theory, a first approximation to the structural constraints, shown in the top half of Table VIII–1, can be established.

TABLE VIII–1

Coefficient Constraints Used with Constrained Least Squares
Regression Technique

Constraint Set #1

$$.10 \leqslant I_{t-2} \leqslant .90$$
$$1500. \leqslant C^M_{t-1} \leqslant 4000.$$
$$.10 \leqslant (T - V)_{t-1} \leqslant .75$$
$$-200. \leqslant r_{t-3} \leqslant 0.0$$
$$0.0 \leqslant SP_{t-1} \leqslant 20.$$

$$\left. \begin{array}{l} Q_1 \\ Q_2 \\ Q_4 \end{array} \right\} \text{Unconstrained}$$

Constraint Set #2

$$.10 \leqslant I_{t-2} \leqslant .90$$
$$1500. \leqslant C^M_{t-1} \leqslant 3500.$$
$$.25 \leqslant (T - V)_{t-1} \leqslant .75$$
$$-100. \leqslant r_{t-3} \leqslant 0.0$$
$$0.0 \leqslant SP_{t-1} \leqslant 20.$$

$$\left. \begin{array}{l} Q_1 \\ Q_2 \\ Q_4 \end{array} \right\} \text{Unconstrained}$$

The limits on I_{t-2} are quite broad, reflecting the lack of any precise indication of the size of this coefficient. Distributed lag effects and replacement needs suggest that the minimum should be slightly positive and that the maximum should logically approach a value near one. Establishing bounds for the capacity variable is difficult since its dimension is not easily interpreted. Fortunately, analysis of the correlation matrix reveals that the capacity utilization variables' upper bound is the crucial one, since the inter-correlations between the capacity variable and interest rate variable often cause the former to assume values in this particular model well in excess of those suggested by prior knowledge and historical experience. The final value selected, 4000, is somewhat arbitrary, however. The coefficient of the residual funds variable must be prevented from becoming negative, since by hypothesis internal liquidity should have a positive effect on investment. The value established, .10, is a bare minimum and is raised in the second experiment. Existing theory strongly suggests that the upper limit on the interest rate variable should be zero, in spite of the positive zero-order correlation between it and investment. Again, the lower limit is both crucial and necessarily arbitrary, but even the most ardent supporters of monetary policy would probably not advocate values of less than -200. The limits placed on SP_{t-1} require, on the one hand, that its coefficient be positive and, on the other, that it not seem too excessive or destabilizing as a measure of expectations or available liquidity. Since Q_1, Q_2, and Q_4 are dummy variables, they are left unconstrained.

Because of the substantial intercorrelation of the variables, a second experiment, using different bounds, is also presented. These second constraints are found in the lower half of Table VIII–1. The major change is an increase in the lower limits of $(T - V)_{t-1}$ and r_{t-3}. Observation of the results reveals that these particular limits are of importance, since the final coefficients for these two variables fall at the limit. Such modifications can therefore be expected to provide interesting indications of the sensitivity of results to constraint specifications. The upper bound for C_{t-1}^M is also lowered in the second test, reflecting the somewhat arbitrary nature of the original selection, but this change proves to have no effect.

A comparison of the coefficients produced by the unconstrained and constrained least squares techniques, using the two sets of limits just discussed, can be found in Table VIII–2. The estimation of the coefficients is based on the same historical data used in the analyses of the preceding chapter. In the models for both constrained sets all the coefficients, with the exception of those for SP_{t-1}, r_{t-3}, and $(T - V)_{t-1}$, fall within two standard deviations of the original unconstrained values. Of the three which differ "significantly," the latter two are prevented from falling closer to their original values by the constraints. The former, SP_{t-1}, takes on a substantially smaller coefficient by virtue of the positive constraint

TABLE VIII-2

Comparison of Coefficients Produced by Constrained and
Unconstrained Least Squares Regression

Model	I_{t-2}	C^M_{t-1}	$(T-V)_{t-1}$	r_{t-3}	SP_{t-1}	Q_1	Q_2	Q_4	Constant
Constrained Set #1	.758	3820.6	.100	−200.0	14.42	−424.1	−364.8	68.8	−2112.58
Constrained Set #2	.794	3192.1	.250	−100.0	5.54	−346.3	−364.6	85.8	−2279.5
Unconstrained	.655	4979.5	−.096	−260.3	27.28	−492.7	−310.9	84.3	−2265.4
Standard Errors for Unconstrained Coefficients	.097	890.2	.084	153.5	5.68	80.3	89.82	73.7	

put upon the liquidity flow variable and the nature of the intercorrelation between the two variables.

Presented in Table VIII–3 are some "standard" measures of estimation accuracy for the three models. These numbers give some indication of the "price to be paid" for achieving improved structural qualities. Since, by definition, the unconstrained least squares model has the minimum variance property, its superior performance on the multiple correlation and standard error of estimate tests is hardly surprising. In fact, the two constrained models do remarkably well by comparison on these tests. The unconstrained ver-

TABLE VIII–3

Measures of Estimation Accuracy Constrained and
Unconstrained Least Squares Regressions Based
on "Historical" Data

Model	R^2	Standard Errors of Estimate	Average Absolute Error	Range
Constrained Set #1	.930	137.7	114.7	23.5%
Constrained Set #2	.905	160.5	132.5	31.2
Unconstrained	.942	125.4	103.4	18.9

sion also does at least as well or better on the other tests where no definitional reason exists for its superiority. In general, though, the "price" of structural improvement would not appear too great in this particular instance. A more pertinent or powerful test of the relative usefulness of the constrained models would be, of course, to compare their performance with the unconstrained as forecasters of activity beyond the historical period used for estimation periods. This is done in the next chapter.

IV. *Some Implications of Constrained Estimation*

While the results just reported from an application of constrained estimation are remarkably encouraging, in the sense that no extensive trade-off was observable between improving structural quality and certain standard measures of statistical accuracy, it would be presumptuous in the extreme to conclude that constrained estimation offers an obvious and simple solution to multicollinearity problems. Any attempt to estimate structurally meaningful coefficients makes the implicit (and generally unjustified) assumption that structure itself has already been properly, or at least approximately embodied in the model. Specifically, it is assumed that the proper nonlinearities and variables have been included, and the same assumption has been made in applying the constrained regression methods of this chapter to obtain more nearly structural parameter estimates. Yet it is precisely at this more basic stage, the formulation and testing of competing hypotheses as reflected in alternative model specifications, that multicollinearity poses the most insurmountable problem. If two variables show little covariation in the historical data, testing hypotheses based on their independent introduction is simply impossible. Where Nature has not performed the necessary experiments, hypothesis verification based on those data alone is infeasible. Most likely, as Liu points out, a hypothesis specifying too few variables, possibly some wholly incorrect ones, will be accepted and will be rejected only when the historical collinearity is broken.[9] At present the only tools available for avoiding such errors in hypothesis formulation and selection are the use of alternative bodies of data or other sources of theoretical and empirical knowledge.

Faced with substantial difficulty in properly hypothesizing behavioral reality, the forecaster is left in many cases with a choice between clearly nonstructural models, which nevertheless exhibit highly satisfactory historical fits, and crude approximations to structure, which describe history less well statistically. Such was the case to a limited extent with the unconstrained and constrained models in this chapter. And as has been suggested before and will become evident in the next chapter, models based on seemingly nonstructural, casual relationships often may be the better predictors. When the trade-off between rough structural representation and forecasting accuracy is large, the forecaster may find it very difficult indeed to select the crudely structural model over its unpretentiously nonstructural competitor.

[9] Liu, *op. cit.*

Moreover, the application of structural estimation methods like constrained regression to models which embody no more than empirically observed regularities can lead to a logical contradiction. The forecaster can find himself in the unfortunate position of placing structural constraints on essentially nonstructural parameters. That is, through a failure to specify nonlinearities properly or the improper deletion of relevant variables, a coefficient in a particular model may not validly fall within the limits placed upon it by the naive application of prior theory. Given the several forces for which a variable may act as proxy, it may be very difficult in many cases to establish reasonable bounds for coefficients. It is, in short, remarkable how little of substance is often known about even the probable dimensions of economic structure, let alone its detailed specification.

This paucity of definite structural information also at least raises questions about the possible usefulness of more subjective estimation methods in econometrics, if and as these emerge from recent developments in Bayesian statistics.[10] The Bayesian approach to regression analysis is to begin by setting "prior distributions" on the coefficients and then to proceed to take a sample which considers the conditional distribution of the observations given their individual means. Combining this conditional distribution with the prior marginal distribution on the coefficients, Bayesians obtain a conditional distribution of the coefficients given the sample, and the expected values of this distribution, weighted in light of error-cost considerations, provide point estimates of the regression parameters. The method of constrained estimation is not, of course, truly probabilistic in the sense that the Bayesian method is, or for that matter in the sense that classical regression is. Indeed, as explicitly or implicitly pointed out at several previous points, the nature of historical economic data normally available to economists raises serious questions about the validity of the usual probability applications in economics. The economist as a statistician perhaps is often best described as engaged in a form of curve fitting (with the emphasis on point estimation). The true test of his work is its

[10] Howard Raiffa and Robert Schlaifer, *Applied Statistical Decision Theory* (Boston: Division of Research, Harvard Business School, 1961), particularly Chapter 12.

reliability in predicting the effects of policy changes or future developments. Under such circumstances the importance of Bayesian procedures for econometrics lies in what impact they might have on these fitting procedures and, in particular, what the effect might be of greater incorporation of so-called *a priori* knowledge.

In this context, it is therefore potentially significant that constrained estimation would appear to produce results (i.e., curve fits) kindred to those that Bayesian regression might yield in certain circumstances. Essentially, the use of programming algorithms for estimation of regression parameters, some of which are constrained to values less than or greater than they would be without constraints, results in a sort of *minimum* modification of the unconstrained least squares estimate of the function while still adhering to the prescribed *a priori* limits on some (or all) of the coefficients. Several different Bayesian prior specifications of the error and parameter distributions might yield results in approximate agreement with these programming estimates. As long as the explanatory variables in the function to be estimated are not orthogonal, the most obvious specifications giving rise to these tendencies would seem to be approximate rectangularity over relevant ranges for the constrained parameters and prior error distributions and so-called diffuseness for the unconstrained parameters. In fact, as long as the prior distributions for the regression parameters are quite broad or ill-defined and the independent variables are fairly collinear, Bayesian estimates reasonably close to the constrained programming estimates would seem to be the normal expectation. Rectangularity and, to an even greater degree, diffuseness are, moreover, extremely weak or almost minimal priors in Bayesian terms. In this sense of imposing seemingly minimal priors and minimal modification of the unconstrained estimates, the constrained programming point estimates developed here are perhaps well described as "minimally subjective." As such, these estimates not only should be "least offensive" to objectivists but also probably incorporate about as much firm *a priori* information as is usually available today in econometric applications. Of course, if more precise information about the prior distribution of regression parameters becomes available, then exact Bayesian procedures for fitting regression coefficients might be employed usefully in econometrics,[11] leaving open the question of whether reliable probability statements can be made when using historical economic data.

The minimal subjectivity of the constrained programming estimates also should have an advantage when a need arises to communicate results for use by a large number of people with possibly different prior subjective estimates. That is, the minimal subjectivity property should insure that these estimates retain to a large degree the great advantage of the objective approach to statistical estimation: minimization of interpersonal communication problems when reporting research results. Since the typical situation in econometrics involves a large number of personal assessments and uses of research results, this property seems highly desirable. A final advantage of "minimal subjectivity" is that it is a logical first simple step in testing more subjective or, more accurately, less objective and traditional procedures in econometrics. Specifically, if the very slight modifications in traditional procedures represented by constrained regression do not bring forth much or any improvement, this at least suggests that the immediately important research problem for economics is not so much devising improved analytical procedures to make better use of existing knowledge of structure as improving the fund of such knowledge.

[11] A general Bayesian solution for regression estimation now is being coded for computer calculation by Charles Zartman of the Harvard Business School. This program will provide when completed a quite flexible format for introducing *a priori* information into regression estimation procedures. From a practical standpoint the essential question in deciding whether this additional flexibility is useful will be whether the available information permits complex prior specifications of the distribution of the regression parameters and the degree of collinearity in the underlying data. If complex prior specifications were unjustified while specification of regression parameter bounds were not and if the data were highly correlated, seemingly the usual cases in economics, the differences between the point estimates obtained by the methods developed here and those obtained by a more complete Bayesian procedure probably would be slight.

Chapter IX | Forecasting Investment: Concepts and Empirical Implications

I. Introduction: The Purposes and Evaluation of Economic Forecasts

Frequent reference has been made in preceding chapters to the forecasting problem. Indeed, it has been very strongly implied that in the absence of reliable probability methods, attributable to the nature of historical samples in economics, the ability to forecast accurately (in some sense yet to be defined) is one of the best tests available of empirically estimated economic parameters. In this chapter attempts are made to define more clearly the meaning of a good forecast and to compare the forecasting merits of alternative regression techniques.

An economic forecast is quite simply some statement concerning the condition of an unknown economic event or situation. The event (or events) will occur in the future and the statements usually are of a quantitative nature. Therefore, in the case of a true forecast, the model will have been specified beforehand, without the benefit of observing the data to be predicted. Econometricians are often quite tempted, in fact, to modify a model to fit the peculiarities of a particular set of historical data. The result often can be that the model fits the historical data but fails to perform well on data to which it is not fitted. To guard against this danger, it has been suggested that a model be fitted to one set of data and then used to predict a wholly different set, even if this means artificially subdividing the total data. Several economists have criticized this procedure as being unnecessary.[1] While noting the danger, particularly of misspecification, they feel that the cost of losing additional degrees of freedom (due to fewer observations on the historical data) is too great a price to pay. Furthermore, the price is considered to be unnecessary in the sense that the residuals from the fitted equation can always be computed and used as a measure of forecasting ability for any period included in the analysis. For reasons to be elaborated later, however, the size of the residuals at any particular point in time is dependent on the method of fitting employed in estimating the forecasting function. Several different tests exist, moreover, for evaluating forecasting performance. Indeed, given a particular test, a method of fitting can be devised that historically optimizes in terms of that test.[2] For any historical fit, therefore, a particular method of fitting has an inherent advantage when evaluated in terms of its own particular objective function or forecasting test. The only relatively neutral test is how the alternative functions, fitted by the different methods, perform on the various tests when extrapolated to new data, not included in the historical sample.[3] For these and other reasons, in the work that follows a subdivision of the data will be made. A good historical fit will suggest which models might be good predictors, but the actual ability to predict

[1] Guy H. Orcutt, Martin Greenberger, John Korbel, and Alice M. Rivlin, *Microanalysis of Socioeconomic Systems: A Simulation Study* (New York: Harper and Brothers, 1961); Charles Frederick Roos, *Dynamics of Economic Growth: the American Economy, 1957–1975* (New York: Econometric Institute, 1957); Carl F. Christ, "Aggregate Econometric Models," *American Economic Review*, Vol. 46, No. 2 (June 1956), pp. 385–408.

[2] That is, a given procedure must explicitly optimize some one or group of measures of accuracy when the accuracy calculations are based on the same sample as that used for the estimation of the coefficients. For example, assume that unconstrained least squares is used to estimate the coefficients from a sample of historical data and then measures of that function's ability to "predict" the same data are calculated. It naturally follows that the resultant R^2 must be greater and the standard error of estimate smaller than for any other method of estimation.

[3] Even when calculated on the basis of historical data, however, the various measures will indicate the comparative sub-optimality of the alternative estimation techniques.

successfully a set of new data will be the criterion by which the different methods are ultimately judged. These tests, however, still will be conditional in the sense that future values of the "explanatory" variables will be assumed to be known.

Although general requirements of forecasts often have been specified in the literature (usually under the inclusive term "verifiability"), the question still remains of what constitutes good prediction and whether it is possible to determine which of a set of predictions is optimal. To provide a framework in which to analyze these questions more easily, it seems advisable to give a brief outline of the relationship between forecasts and policy, using Theil's discussion of these problems as the point of departure.[4]

Consider a hypothetical "person" in whose hands are the policy decisions for a given economy. For the moment, say that the decision maker is limited to what may be broadly called "economic" questions, but the analysis can be generalized. He will be faced with a group of objectives, which for the purpose of explication will be assumed to be distinct and quantifiable. Assigned to these objectives is a vector of variables, y_i where $i = 1 \cdots n$.[5] In a complex world the policy maker will not be able to control these variables fully, but will have to be satisfied with influencing their values, in some hopefully predetermined manner, by means of another set of instrument variables over which he has full control. This set of instrument variables will be called x_j where $j = 1 \ldots m$. There will be, in addition, a group of influences on the Y vector over which our policy formulator has no control. These influences might include lagged values of the y_i's, lagged and current values of exogenous variables, and "random" disturbances. For purposes of simplicity all these influences will be lumped into a single vector, s_i, $i = 1 \cdots n$, one s_i being associated with each y_i. Furthermore, for any given equation the s_i has a specific value not dependent upon the system for its determination.

Assuming a completely "linear world," the relationships among

---

[4] Theil, *Economic Forecasts and Policy*, Chapters 7 and 8, gives a very detailed discussion of the theory on which this section is based.

[5] In all the work which follows, vectors will be denoted either by subscripted lower case letters or by unsubscripted capital letters. Matrices will be handled in the same manner, except that when subscripted, they will, of course, have two subscripts.

the above variables then can be expressed by the following system of equations:

$$y_1 = r_{11}x_1 + \cdots + r_{1m}x_m + s_1$$
$$y_2 = r_{21}x_1 + \cdots + r_{2m}x_m + s_2$$
$$\cdots\cdots\cdots\cdots\cdots\cdots\cdots\cdots\cdots$$
$$y_n = r_{n1}x_1 + \cdots + r_{nm}x_n + s_n$$

or in matrix notation:

(9.1) $$Y = RX + S.$$

The r_{ij}'s form a matrix of parameters, R, relating the policy maker's instrument variables to his objectives. Since not all of the m instrument variables have an effect on a particular y_i, some elements of R will probably be zero. These equations then specify that the various objectives are some linear function of the variables directly under the policy maker's control and of those over which he has no influence. These equations are of the reduced-form type, the righthand sides being wholly composed of exogenous or lagged endogenous variables and disturbances. (Though these equations are of the reduced form type, straightforward least squares estimation would be inappropriate if any parametric estimates were required for the S vector; these would seem to be more appropriately estimated by so-called extraneous or conditional estimation techniques.) [6] There is no loss of generality in omitting the remaining $(n - 1)$ of the y_i's from the righthand side of an equation for a given y_i. So long as the coefficient matrix of the y_i's in the original (nonreduced form) simultaneous system, from which (9.1) is derived, is nonsingular, the original system can be expressed in the reduced form (9.1).

For each specific set of x_j's there will correspond, of course, a set of outcomes (i.e., y_i's). Assuming that the policy maker is perceptive and rational, he should be able to evaluate the relative merits of the outcomes which result from his setting different values for the X vector. More formally, the policy maker has some welfare function, W_1, which initially might be expressed as

(9.2) $$w = W_1(y_1, \cdots, y_n).$$

[6] Stone, *Consumer Expenditures in the United Kingdom*, and Wold and Jureen, *Demand Analysis*.

This equation expresses welfare as a function only of the *outcome* of his various policy actions and places the decision making in a rather standard or classical statistical decision theory format. In general, however, in economics the levels of the instrument variables will have an effect on welfare in their own right, quite apart from their influence through the Y vector. Thus, in a more general case, (9.2) should be written

$$(9.3) \qquad w = W_2(y_1, \ldots, y_n; \; x_1, \cdots, x_m).$$

Viewed in the above framework, the question of what constitutes an optimal *decision* can be rather easily answered. If it is argued (idealistically) that the welfare function available to the policy maker reflects that of the total society, the best decision will be that vector of X's which maximizes (9.3) subject to the constraints (9.1).

An example may serve to clarify the above discussion.[7] The United States government since 1946 has been committed by law to seek to maintain full employment. It is possible that the government is able in some way to determine the level of *GNP* which corresponds to full employment. Say that *GNP* is the sum of consumption expenditures (C), private investment (I), and government expenditures (G). Assuming that *for any given period* the level of C and I will not depend on the current level of G, the government policy maker would estimate C and I and then set government spending at that level which would produce full employment *GNP*. Here, full employment *GNP*, an objective, is an element of the Y vector, G is an instrument variable and an element of the X vector, and C and I are variables exogenous to the system (at least in the short run) and part of the S vector. In this simple example, moreover, the parameters relating C, I, and G to Y are all exogenously specified as unity because the basic equation is a specified accounting identity. Total welfare will depend on how well the objective of full employment is satisfied (e.g., it depends on Y). But welfare quite clearly also might be rationally considered some function of the amount of government action that is found necessary to achieve this outcome (e.g., the level of X). Whether welfare is an increasing or decreasing function of X (i.e., G) will depend on the political

---

[7] This example is quite naive and grossly oversimplifies the presentation. Only one objective is included and no sense of simultaneity is achieved.

attitude of the policy maker. But there is little doubt that the functional relationship usually does exist.[8]

Independently of Theil, a rather natural alternative formulation of the above model was suggested by Holt, Modigliani, Muth, and Simon.[9] They stipulated that a single decision rule should be found that optimally relates forecasts of the S's to specifications of the X vector in a linear fashion. This could be expressed as follows:

$$X = \alpha S.$$

The decision rule, essentially, is substituted for explicit execution of the maximization procedure in each period. Decision rules are, in short, guides for the policy maker to follow in order to arrive quickly and expeditiously at a reasonably close approximization to optimal policies. Furthermore, in dynamic models (which are the central focus of the Holt, Modigliani, Muth, and Simon studies), it can be argued that the rules make the analysis more realistic.

Still another (perhaps slightly fanciful but not totally unrealistic) extension of these policy models would be to assume that the decision rules are not subject to change but are fixed by the nature of government or private institutions. Specifically, it might be argued that the decision rules used by policy makers and their subordinates in meeting their everyday tasks have been built up and codified over the years and are not subject to immediate or easy modification. Under such circumstances the only input into the welfare maximization problem that would be under the control of a policy-oriented official would be the forecasts embodied in the S vector. Under these circumstances it might be argued that the econometricians or other staff officials who supplied the s_i's should forecast, assuming that they knew the social welfare function and the nature of the bureaucratically fixed α's, in such a way as to move as high as

[8] The possibility that the policy maker's welfare function will differ from that of the general public cannot technically be overlooked, for it will certainly result in a loss of general welfare in the optimal situation. In a democracy, however, the man could in theory be removed. Theil, *op. cit.*, p. 351, discusses some of the implications of this problem.

[9] Charles C. Holt, Franco Modigliani, John F. Muth, and Herbert A. Simon, *Planning Production, Inventories and Work Force* (Englewood Cliffs: Prentice-Hall, 1960); and Charles C. Holt, "Linear Decision Rules for Economic Stabilization and Growth," *Quarterly Journal of Economics*, Vol. 76, No. 1 (February 1962), pp. 20–45.

possible on the social welfare function. This would be a case, moreover, in which deliberate bias in the forecast might be desirable. Obviously, there is much to be said about the dangers inherent in making the economist or the econometrician the "aristocrat of officialdom" in this fashion. Still, actual cases would seem to exist in which economic forecasts from government sources have come rather close to being biased or deliberately modified in order to condition behavior, both within government and without, in a way that was considered advantageous for the achievement of certain economic or social goals.

Specification of a decision process also specifies the relevant econometric estimation and forecasting problems. Adhering to the strict Theil model, the matrix of parameters which express the relation between the instrument and objective variables (R in the formulation above) first must be estimated. This amounts to predicting the effects of a given group of government policies (the X vector) on the set of objectives (the Y vector). This is generally named the "estimation problem" and will be so called here. Second, the various values of the S vector must be forecast. In the example outlined above, this would involve predicting both consumption and private investment for the given period.

The prediction of the effects of a given X vector (that is, the estimation of the R matrix) corresponds quite closely to the policy-choice use of econometric models. On the other hand, forecasting the value of the reduced-form constant terms (the S vector) is more akin to a "pure" forecasting use of models. Given that this study is focused on private investment decisions, which would seem best classified as a component of the S vector, the assumption is made in all that follows that the R matrix is either known exactly, exogenously specified, or at least specified conditional on the forecast of the S vector. In addition, it is assumed that the weighting scheme for consolidating a forecast of private manufacturing investment into an aggregate S is either known or is specified exactly. Attention thus is limited to the very specific problem of what is the best method of obtaining a forecast (generally by econometric means) of an influence not directly under the control of the public policy maker but which still must be entered into policy deliberations if optimal policies are to be established.

The most important implication of considering forecasting in a decision-oriented format is that the definition of a successful prediction becomes reasonably obvious, at least in theory. Good forecasts are not sought for their own sake, but rather as aids in improving policy decisions. When the forecasting problem is related to the whole decision process, an optimal forecast can be defined as one that recommends a set of policies that result in the maximization of the welfare function. Forecasts have a specific use, and the best forecast is the one which best satisfies this use.

The analysis, unfortunately, is far more theoretically elegant than practical. It implies that to be competent a forecaster must know the relevant welfare functions at least of the particular decision maker to whom he is supplying his predictions. And herein lies a formidable obstacle. Economists have always shied away from attempting to specify welfare functions. Even if one is willing to assume that some ordinal function of utility can be conceived, the problem of specifying it in econometrically tractable terms seems at present quite difficult.

Several alternatives suggest themselves. First, the problem could be handled in a general way by treating as separate cases the various broad forms that the underlying welfare functions might take. Attempts could then be made to prove (as is indeed possible in some cases) that under certain rather general assumptions concerning the welfare function and the constraints, specific procedures lead to welfare maximization. An excellent example is the proof by Theil that with a quadratic welfare function subject to linear constraints and under certain conventional assumptions about error distributions, least squares is an optimal procedure for estimating the R matrix.[10]

A second alternative is to follow methods analogous to those used in demand theory. The econometrician working in the area of demand theory is also faced with the problem of welfare functions, since demand functions are, of course, derived from underlying consumer utility functions. Fortunately, demand functions are easily (if not always accurately) measurable in terms of observable, real-world variables (prices, quantities traded, incomes). Rather than get tangled in a morass of speculation concerning the underlying welfare functions and income constraints, the econometrician

[10] Theil, *op. cit.*, p. 452 ff.

works directly with the "derived" demand functions themselves. While not the most basic approach to consumer behavior, it has turned out historically to be the most productive in an empirical sense.

An analogous, although not quite so obvious, parallel exists in the area of estimating forecasting models. As in the case of demand theory, the econometrician is faced with underlying welfare functions and in addition constraints of the form (9.1). From these basic functions it is possible to obtain a derived function, just as a demand function is obtained from utility curves. Related to each welfare function and its constraints is what will here be termed an "error-cost" function. This function expresses the relation between the size of a forecasting error and the "cost" to the policy maker of making this error. The error-cost function can be written:

$$(9.4) \qquad c_i = f(e_i) \qquad i = 1 \cdots n$$

which express this relationship for a particular observation, i. In (9.4) e_i is the observed estimation error (e.g., the difference between the actual and the predicted values of the variables under study) for the ith observation and c_i is the cost associated with this error. The total cost associated with a set of predictions and the errors which result will be some combination — linear or nonlinear — of the errors related to the individual observations.

Within the context of simple linear policy models like those considered here, the error-cost function (9.4) can be applied with equal facility to either estimation or forecasting problems, as defined above. Since the central focus of this study is upon understanding and forecasting *private* investment in the manufacturing sector, employing the error-cost function implies that costs are defined as being a function of the size of the forecast error in investment. Specifically, costs or welfare losses are measured in terms of deviations from the point forecasts for investment, implying quite plausibly that the policy or controlled variables (the X vector) are established by acting on the basis of these values.[11] These simplifi-

[11] In a probabilistic setting, basing decisions on point estimates in this fashion would only be fully justified if these point estimates could be established as certainty equivalents. To greatly understate the case, certainty equivalence simplifies the analysis of decision theory models, especially under dynamic conditions. Indeed, it could be argued that if econometricians couldn't have found certainty equivalence they would have had to invent it. As Theil states

cations are very much in keeping with existing practice in econometric applications where the custom has been to eliminate specific consideration of the welfare function by specifying exogenous public policy targets or goals in income and income growth, government expenditures, and unemployment and then measuring loss of welfare in terms of deviations from these goals.[12]

Once the error-cost function is considered, it is possible to treat the problem of maximizing welfare subject to a set of constraints simply as a problem of minimizing the cost of a set of estimates as defined by a particular error-cost function with a specified set of historical data. Of course, the problem of specifying the particular error-cost function associated with a given decision maker still exists and cannot be overlooked. But as with demand theory, it is usually far simpler to make intelligent statements about the form of this "derived" function than it is to specify the underlying welfare function. That is, demand functions in the case of demand theory and error-cost functions in the forecasting case have in some sense more real-life relevance and their alternative forms are intuitively grasped more easily. Of course, alternative cases still should be treated for there would seem to be no general error-cost function applicable to all decision makers. But it will be sufficient, at least for this

(*op. cit.*, p. 422): "Clearly few policy makers will appreciate their staffs providing them with information of a (more) elaborate and refined nature." A very real question can be raised, moreover, as to whether extensive worry about the existence or nonexistence of certainty equivalence is really a serious concern for economists. In essence, to worry about certainty equivalence one must have excess information to discard, information in this case about the characteristics of a probability distribution. The nature of economic data are such, however, that in many cases economists' knowledge of distributional characteristics, particularly beyond that of central tendency, is not very great. Harking back to earlier antecedents for an illustrative example, a Markoff theorem interpretation of least squares regression results is usually more easily justified with economic data than the more elaborate interpretations embodied in the classical normal regression model. In short, econometricians working with point estimates, and simply assuming certainty equivalence, are probably not in most applications really discarding any available information. Rather, they may be simply recognizing the limitations inherent in the data and information at hand.

[12] See the procedures followed by Theil and Holt in actual applications of their models; e.g. P. J. M. van den Bogaard and H. Theil, "Macrodynamic Policy-Making," *Metroeconomica*, Vol. II (December 1959), pp. 149–167, and C. Holt, *op. cit.* Theil and Holt define their errors as deviations from exogenously specified objectives which, in turn, could be rigorously derived only from the underlying welfare function.

preliminary effort, to consider merely the error-cost functions and not proceed to the more abstruse and nebulous area of welfare functions.

In a complete statistical decision context it would be necessary, of course, to specify the probability to be attached to any cost or welfare loss since the usual objective is to minimize aggregate *expected* cost. For reasons outlined at length in previous chapters, there is little reason to believe that very meaningful probability statements can be made on the basis of the usually available historical data in economics, particularly of the time-series variety. There is, moreover, a remarkable lack of knowledge of the relevant distributions needed to treat regression analyses in economics as one in which all variables, not just the dependent, are stochastic — which is almost surely the usual case with economic variables. Accordingly, the probability weighting problem will be ignored here and attention confined to minimizing simple unweighted cost functions of the type (9.4).

However viewed, the obvious forecasting or estimation objective in the present context is to generate values or employ procedures that result in a minimization of objective functions of the type (9.4). The specific objective will be to define forecasting procedures that, given an error-cost function and ignoring probability weights (or assuming them equal), generate forecast values which lead to a minimization of the stipulated cost relationships.[13] Again, the assumption of equal or nonexistent probability weights has several advantages. First, given the scarcity of information on such dis-

---

[13] If a probabilistic interpretation is given to the objective function this would mean that for a specified function, the logical way to proceed with estimation and forecasting is to find procedures for generating the historically best or optimizing estimation procedure for the given set of cost and probability specifications. As noted previously, it has been shown by Theil (p. 452 ff.) that under certain conditions setting policy using estimates yielded by simple least squares regression procedures will lead to the same degree of policy optimization as would be achieved by using knowledge of the entire distribution of the forecasts. Clearly, though, it could be achieved under other circumstances than those hypothesized by Theil, though perhaps very rarely with the same computational facility. Still, if one does accept probabilistic interpretations of econometric analyses, it would seem far better, especially now that modern electronic computers are available to reduce computational burdens, to proceed by trying to find the optimal estimation procedure under the most plausible specification of welfare functions and error distributions rather than to find the welfare functions and error distributions that correspond to the simplest computational procedure.

tributions in economic applications, it minimizes the input of unsubstantiable subjective judgments. Second, the objective function to be minimized in mathematical programming formulations can be considered to reflect error-cost relationships only, a substantial aid to conceptualization. Finally, certain computational and conceptual problems of a probabilistic character are avoided.

Clearly implicit in this discussion of forecasting is the notion that no single measure of forecasting success can be properly applied to all models and estimation techniques. In Section II this discussion is extended further and certain practical problems pertinent to the application of the general forecasting method to the specific models at hand are outlined. The remainder of the chapter is devoted to actual forecasting problems, undertaken from two different points of view. First, in Section III a comparison is made of the forecasting quality of the major time-series models presented in Chapter VII using the *same* estimation technique for all of the models. In the remaining sections the forecasting consequences of the various estimation methods developed in the previous chapter and the next section are examined. That is, a given model is estimated by *different* procedures and the forecasting results are compared on the basis of the various criteria of forecasting success. In Section IV, these tests of forecasting procedures are applied to the same range of investment models as in Section III but estimated with different specifications of the error-cost functions; however, no constraints are placed on the coefficients for the Section IV tests. Section V, by contrast, presents a comparison of the forecasting abilities of the constrained and unconstrained investment models developed in the last chapter; that is, Section V is essentially an extension of the previous discussion of multicollinearity problems. Finally, in Section VI, forecasting test results are reported for an aggregate investment function, appropriate for inclusion in a national income model, that grew out of the various investment findings reported in this study.

II. *Measures of Forecasting Accuracy*

As just noted, no forecasting problem can properly be considered *in vacuo*. In each forecasting situation a specification must be made in some manner of the error-cost function relevant to the problem and then of the best estimation procedure for that particular case. Within the specifically nonprobabilistic context of this study, the optimal strategy for the forecaster is defined as employing that set of coefficient estimates which produces the least costly combination of forecasting errors based on the sample of historical data available.

The selection of forecast criteria is necessarily rather arbitrary but has for the most part been limited to those which are quite familiar in statistics and econometrics: coefficient of multiple determination (R^2), standard error of estimate, average absolute error, range, and mean error. The last two are presented in percentage terms and are measured by the predicted minus the actual value divided by the actual value. Additionally, two other measures particularly suited to this type of analysis are presented. First, a variant of turning point measures is used in conjunction with an asymmetrical error-cost function. Specifically, a tabulation is made of under- and over-estimates at various points of the business cycle, thereby reflecting a nonsymmetrical error-cost relationship.

The second less well-known measure of accuracy used is the U coefficient developed by Theil.[14] It is a measure of the degree to which the forecasted series approximates the actual one, or more precisely, the amount by which α and β differ from 1 and 0, respectively, in the equation

$$P_i = \alpha A_i + \beta,$$

the P_i being observations on the predicted series and the A_i on the actual series. The Theil U coefficient is estimated by

$$(9.5) \qquad U = \frac{\sqrt{\sum_{i=1}^{n} (P_i - A_i)^2}}{\sqrt{\sum_{i=1}^{n} A_i^2} + \sqrt{\sum_{i=1}^{n} P_i^2}}$$

the notation being the same as above. By its definition, U is 0 for perfect predictions and, except for artificial cases, has an upper bound of 1. Furthermore, U can be decomposed into three com-

---

[14] Theil, *op. cit.*, p. 31 ff.

ponents, U^M, U^S, U^C which reflect the fractional loss of forecasting accuracy due to unequal means, variance, and covariation, respectively. The procedure is to define $\bar{P}$, $\bar{A}$, S_P, and S_A as the estimated means and standard deviations of the two series, r as the correlation coefficient between them, and D as the denominator of (9.5). Following Theil, these relationships can be defined:

$$U_M = \frac{\bar{P} - \bar{A}}{D}$$

$$U_S = \frac{S_P - S_A}{D}$$

$$U_C = \frac{\sqrt{2(1 - r)S_P S_A}}{D}$$

so that

$$U_M^2 + U_S^2 + U_C^2 = U^2.$$

U^M, U^S, and U^C are then defined by normalizing by U^2:

(9.6) $$U^M = \frac{U_M^2}{U^2} \qquad U^S = \frac{U_S^2}{U^2} \qquad U^C = \frac{U_C^2}{U^2}$$

and

$$U^M + U^S + U^C = 1.$$

The measures in (9.6) will prove particularly useful in analyzing the different sources of error among the various estimation techniques.

Several different estimation procedures corresponding to different error-cost functions might be used in the forecasting tests. The most obvious possibility, ordinary least squares, corresponds to specification of a quadratic error-cost function and represents the estimation procedure that will maximize, by definition, the historical multiple correlation and minimize the standard error of estimate. A second, constrained least squares, will maximize and minimize these same historical criteria except to the extent that such is prevented by the prior specification of limits on the range of certain coefficients. Computational procedures for obtaining estimates of the first type, that is ordinary least squares, are, of course, well known.   An algorithm for efficiently obtaining estimates of the second type, constrained least squares, was described in the last chapter.

Aside from a quadratic relationship between the size of error and the loss of welfare or increase in costs which is implicit in least squares, the most obvious alternative error-cost relationship is probably one described by a V; i.e., the costs of error are a simple linear function of the absolute size of the error.   Solution of this problem parallels very closely the quadratic problem presented in the last chapter.   Define b_j and b'_j, $j = 1 \cdots n$; e_{1i} and e_{2i}, $i = 1 \cdots m$; K_1; and K_2 by:

$$\sum_{j=1}^{n} x_{ij} b_j - \sum_{j=1}^{n} x_{ij} b'_j + K_1 - K_2 + e_{1i} - e_{2i} = y_i \qquad \text{for all } i$$

$$\sum_{j=1}^{n} x_j b_j - \sum_{j=1}^{n} x_j b'_j + K_1 - K_2 = \bar{y}$$

$$e_{1i}, e_{2i}, K_1, K_2, b_j, b'_j \geqslant 0 \qquad \text{for all } i, j.$$

Choose b_j and b'_j, $j = 1 \cdots n$; K_1; and K_2 to *minimize*

$$\sum_{i=1}^{m} e_{1i} + \sum_{i=1}^{m} e_{2i}.$$

In order to employ the simplex algorithm, the formulation of the last chapter is modified by the addition of the vector of b'_j's and e^2_i's and the constant K_2.   The inclusion of these variables permits the coefficients, constants, and individual deviations to be positive or negative while still adhering to the non-negativity constraint of the algorithm.   The nature of the algorithm assures that for any i either e_1 or e_2 will be 0; for any j either b_j or b'_j will be 0; and either K_1 or K_2 will be 0.   The regression analysis is thus formulated as a linear programming problem containing $2n + 2m + 2$ variables and $m + 1$ restrictions [15] in the simplest case where bounds are not placed

[15] A similar formulation of this problem is presented in Harvey M. Wagner, "Linear Programming Techniques for Regression Analysis," *Journal of the American Statistical Association*, Vol. 54, No. 285 (March 1959), pp. 206–212. He does not include explicitly the e_2, K_2, and b' variables which allow the use of the simplex method.   The problem, he points out, can be reformulated in terms of its dual as a bounded variable-linear programming problem with considerably fewer restrictions.

on the coefficients. Although the problem can become quite large, it can be handled by several computer codes.[16] Again, an important advantage of the programming solution is that it provides a simple means of incorporating extraneous information on the range of particular regression coefficients.

Another possible error-cost relationship is indicated by the common suggestion that the range of the errors (i.e., the difference between the greatest positive and greatest negative error) be minimized. This implies that up to a certain point the error-cost relationship is perfectly (or nearly) elastic and after that point becomes extremely inelastic. In short, small errors are costless relative to large ones. There is a good deal of similarity between this case and the quadratic or least squares case. Indeed, the minimum range problem can be considered to be the limiting case of the quadratic "error-cost" function.

This case is easily solved as a linear programming problem.[17] Define ep and en, the largest positive and negative deviations, respectively; b_j and b'_j, $j = 1 \cdots n$; K_1; and K_2 by:

$$-ep \leqslant y_i - \left(\sum_{j=1}^{n} x_{ij}b_j - \sum_{j=1}^{n} x_{ij}b'_j + K_1 - K_2 \right) \leqslant ep \qquad \text{for all } i$$

$$en \leqslant y_i - \left(\sum_{j=1}^{n} x_{ij}b_j - \sum_{j=1}^{n} x_{ij}b'_j + K_1 - K_2 \right) \leqslant -en \qquad \text{for all } i$$

$$\sum_{j=1}^{n} \bar{x}_j b_j - \sum_{j=1}^{n} \bar{x}_j b'_j + K_1 - K_2 = \bar{y}$$

$$ep, en, b_j, b'_j, K_1, K_2 \geqslant 0 \qquad \text{for all } j.$$

Choose b_j and b'_j, $j = 1 \cdots n$; K_1; and K_2 to *minimize*

$$ep + en.$$

Algebraic manipulations of the first two inequalities above will yield a problem containing $2n + 4$ variables and $4m + 1$ restrictions. For more than a small number of observations, the size of this problem becomes very large and might often exceed the capacity

[16] The problem was solved on the IBM 7090 computer using SCFM2, a linear programming code written by Standard Oil Company of California. It is available from the *IBM 7090 SHARE Library* in New York.

[17] Wagner, *op. cit.*, presents a problem similar to this.

of a computer program. However, Wagner has shown that the problem, formulated in terms of its dual, will produce the regression coefficients as a by-product.[18] The dual has $4m + 1$ variables, but only $n + 1$ restrictions. Computer linear programming codes generally can handle more variables than restrictions, so that the dual formulation is computationally more practicable.

There is reason to believe, however, that the method of minimizing the range is usually unsuitable. By its very nature the method tends to place undue emphasis on extreme observations. Of course, extreme observations could be eliminated which were "obviously" incorrect, but this leads to a rather arbitrary selection process and, consequently, to results that are difficult to evaluate objectively, if not of completely dubious value. Accordingly, this method has not been used in any of the forecasting tests that follow.

A property common to all of the error-cost functions underlying the analyses thus far has been symmetry. Whether the implied error-cost function has been quadratic, V-shaped, or U-shaped, a particular function assigns the same loss of welfare to a given error regardless of sign. Such reasoning has, in fact, underlain almost all regression analyses performed in the past. Yet there is no reason to assume universal symmetry of error-cost functions. In fact, historically, the very popularity of accuracy in predicting turning points as a measure of forecasting ability in economics strongly suggests an asymmetrical cost function. Furthermore, it is not difficult in the context of the present-day political-economic environment to construct circumstances in which such an asymmetrical function might appear highly plausible.

For example, with the current emphasis in many circles on resisting runaway inflation during a boom, a policy maker might be well-advised to consider it substantially more costly to underpredict investment during a boom than to overpredict. Boomtime underprediction might result in the forecast of a weakening economy. The inflation controls, presumably then being strongly applied, would be loosened and government spending might be stepped up. The result almost certainly would be an increase of inflationary pressure and a faster rise in price levels. On the other hand, overprediction of investment at such a time would result merely in a

[18] Wagner, *op. cit.*, pp. 210–211.

tightening of the inflation controls, and, given some substantial prejudice against inflation, might not be considered so serious an error. Precisely opposite arguments could be adumbrated for the recession case. Overprediction would be more costly since it would result in a reduction of government antirecession operations at a time when they were still needed. Underprediction, on the other hand, would lead to more government action, but at a time when inflation was not a great threat. Finally, the analysis suggests that the height of the boom or depth of the recession should have some effect on the cost of an error — a given-sized error being more costly at extreme points of the cycle.

More precisely, say the objective is to minimize the total weighted loss of welfare as defined by:

$$\sum_{i=1}^{m} w_i e_i^2$$

where

$$w_i = 1.0 + \left(\frac{y_i - \bar{y}}{\bar{y}}\right) \quad \text{for } e_i > 0 \qquad i = 1 \cdots m$$

and

$$w_i = 1.0 + \left(\frac{\bar{y} - y_i}{\bar{y}}\right) \quad \text{for } e_i < 0 \qquad i = 1 \cdots m.$$

Here y_i is an observation on the dependent variable. At the historical mean of the dependent variable (i.e., in neither a boom nor a recession), the cost function is precisely the same as the one implicit in least squares. Figure IX–1 shows the error-cost functions for simple least squares and hypothetical functions of the type described here which would be applicable in a boom and a recession. The "boom" function is for $\bar{y} = 2$, $y_i = 3$, and the "recession" function, for $\bar{y} = 2$, $y_i = 1$. In the empirical work the maximum value of

(9.7) $$\frac{y_i - \bar{y}}{\bar{y}}$$

is set equal to a parameter (less than 1) in order to prevent the possibility of the weight for the ith error becoming negative. Initially, the model is fitted by standard least squares techniques. All of the variables for each observation are then weighted according to the sign of the residual for that observation and the corresponding value of the dependent variable. (In determining the value of w_i, a series with the trend removed is used to prevent the introduction of spurious levels due to trend. In the actual fitting of the equations, however, the trend is kept in all of the variables.) For obvious mathematical reasons, it is best to weight all the variables for each obser-

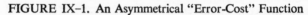

FIGURE IX-1. An Asymmetrical "Error-Cost" Function

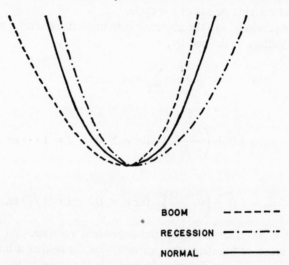

BOOM	– – – – –
RECESSION	— · — · — · · —
NORMAL	———————

vation by the square root of the proper w_i, normalized so that the sum of the square roots of the w_i's for any iteration equals the number of observations. One sensible criterion for termination of the process would be correspondence of the signs of the individual residuals for any two successive iterations. Unfortunately, when applied here the technique never produces a wholly convergent solution, even for quite small values of the weights. After a number of iterations, the results fall into a simple two-stage oscillation. However, the coefficients which result are never far apart and, of course, draw closer together when the size of the weights is reduced. Therefore, a small value, .15, for (9.7) is employed and the difference between the oscillating values of each coefficient is reconciled by means of a linear interpolation.[19]

In passing it should be noted that this type of asymmetrical function has some definite shortcomings. Specifically, it might be better to distinguish between the pre- and post-turning point situation when assigning a cost to an error. In the function derived here the size of the weight applied to an error is a function merely of the sign of the error and the level of the economy, as measured by the difference between the current value of the trend corrected dependent variable and its historical mean.

It is also worth noting explicitly at this juncture that data on which the empirical tests are based are divided into two distinct groups, the "historical" period comprised of third quarter 1949 to fourth quarter 1958 inclusive and the "future" or forecast periods containing observations either for first quarter 1959 through third quarter 1960 or first quarter 1959 through fourth quarter 1961.[20] The use of two prediction periods of differing lengths permits testing the effects of the length and cyclical characteristics of the forecast period on the forecasting results. The historical period data coincide precisely with those used to estimate the models presented in Chapter VII and it is upon a group of these models that the forecasting experiments are performed. However, the comparison of the forecasting ability of the various models and techniques is based on data for one of the future periods. That is, as a true conditional test of their usefulness as forecasting tools, the models are required to "predict" a set of data to which they were not fitted. While some justification for this process of artificial bifurcation has already been given, suffice it to say here that such a procedure properly

[19] Some nonlinear interpolation would probably be more correct, but in view of the small difference between the two estimates of each coefficient, it is likely that no serious error is committed by using a linear form.

[20] The models in Chapter VIII were estimated from time-series data published by the Department of Commerce in early 1961 and at that time could be extrapolated only to third quarter 1960 data. By the time work on the eleven-quarter extrapolation to third-quarter 1961 data was begun, the Department of Commerce had seen fit to revise its estimates of several of the crucial series for the period 1957 through 1960. Although the revisions do not in general alter the annual levels, they do change quarterly variation patterns somewhat. It has therefore been necessary to use the earlier published data with the seventh-quarter extrapolations and revised data with the eleven-quarter future period. Appendix B details the various series actually employed.

reflects more of the reality of the true forecasting situation. Clearly, no real-life forecaster is able to construct his model on the basis of the same data he is asked to predict. The procedure of bifurcating the data and "forecasting" the future opens up the possibility, moreover, that a particular regression technique may not prove optimal on the same criteria in both the historical and forecast periods.

III. *Forecasts Based on Alternative Model Specifications*

The analysis of the time-series data in Chapter VII indicated, among other things, that a strikingly large number of alternative specifications of investment models produce notably high coefficients of multiple determination. In fact, for the six models presented below, the lowest value for R^2 is .893, certainly not substantially less than the highest value .942. That the values of R^2 are uniformly so high and do not differ greatly tends to deprecate in some measure the usefulness of the coefficient of multiple determination as a method for discriminating among alternative formulations and points to the possible use of forecasting results as an alternative test. In the analysis that follows, six of the models tested in Chapter VII are retained for evaluation as forecasters. The six models divide into three groups, depending on treatment of expectational effects through stock price; specifically, absolute stock price, change in stock price, or no stock price variable can be employed. Raw absolute stock price was tested in two models, the difference being the inclusion or exclusion of the interest rate:

(I) $I_t = f_1(C^M_{t-1}, (T - V)_{t-1}, r_{t-3}, SP_{t-1}, I_{t-2})$
(II) $I_t = f_2(C^M_{t-1}, (T - V)_{t-1}, SP_{t-1}, I_{t-2})$.

The notation is the same as that used previously.[21] Substitution of the percentage change in stock price variable — $(SP_t - SP_{t-1})/SP_{t-1}$ — leads to:

(III) $I_t = f_3(C^M_{t-1}, (T - V)_{t-1}, r_{t-3}, \Delta SP_{t-1}, I_{t-2})$
(IV) $I_t = f_4(C^M_{t-1}, (T - V)_{t-1}, \Delta SP_{t-1}, I_{t-2})$.

Finally, with the stock price variable excluded, allowing the re-

[21] See Chapter II, Section 3.

maining variables to pick up expectational effects, the models become:

(V) $\quad I_t = f_5(C_{t-1}^M, (T - V)_{t-1}, r_{t-3}, I_{t-2})$

(VI) $\quad I_t = f_6(C_{t-1}^M, (T - V)_{t-1}, I_{t-2})$.

While the models essentially duplicate those analyzed in Chapter VII, they have been estimated by least squares from time series which differ slightly from those used earlier. The modification was necessary to make the historical period data compatible with the data for the full, eleven-quarter future or forecast period.[22]

The data modifications affect only the covariation patterns on one and a half year's experience and so do not have a marked effect upon the partial regression coefficients, as can be seen by comparing the results in Table IX–1 with those in Table VII–2. The interest rate

TABLE IX–1

Partial Regression Coefficients for Alternative Investment Models Tested against *Modified* Aggregate Manufacturing Data, "Historical" Period *

Model No.	C_{t-1}^M	$(T-V)_{t-1}$	r_{t-3}	SP_{t-1}	ΔSP_{t-1}	I_{t-2}
I	5026.9	−.0964 †	−242.7 †	27.36		.6510
II	5873.7	−.0962 †		26.60		.5602
III	3035.5	.2178	−88.71 †		20.40	.9844
IV	3380.2	.2137			20.87	.9514
V	2420.1	.2482	−177.6 †			.8927
VI	3097.6	.2412				.8208

* Seasonal "dummy" variables and constant terms deleted from table for clarity.

† *Not* significant at a 5% confidence level on a *one* tail test (as specified by the *a priori* expectation on sign).

variable consistently has a negative coefficient, supporting *a priori* expectations, but as before, it is not significant (at the 5% level). Moreover, the same patterns of intercorrelations are present and again produce undesirable results. Specifically, the inclusion of the absolute stock price variable causes negative coefficients to be estimated for $(T - V)_{t-1}$ and extremely large ones for C_{t-1}^M. To a lesser degree, the exclusion of the interest rate also results in an in-

[22] In all the models used the three seasonal dummy variables were employed, but generally not explicitly reported.

flation of the coefficients of capacity utilization. Models employing the change in stock price variable, with or without the interest rate (i.e., Models III and IV) contain coefficients which all have *a priori* correct signs and generally reasonable magnitudes. Quite disturbing, however, in both cases is the size of the lagged investment coefficient, which closely approximates one. For the investment process to be stable, one must clearly be the upper limit and values such as those estimated, .984 and .951, seem unrealistically large.

A tabulation of the various measures of estimation accuracy, as applied to the *historical* period, is presented in Table IX–2 for all models. Also shown is the fraction of coefficients whose sign is the opposite of that implied by *a priori* theory. Several interesting results are clear from the table.

As would be expected, the coefficient of multiple determination, standard error of estimate, and Theil U rank the alternative models in the same order. Of course, the correspondence of the ranking by R^2 and U need hold only for the historical period data, where the nature of the least squares algorithm allows no error due to a difference between the means of the actual and predicted series. Of greater interest, because the result is less obvious, is the fact that the average absolute error and, except in one case, range also rank the models in the same order as the other measures, corrected for degrees of freedom. The marked consistency of the rankings by these last two criteria with the ordering by corrected R^2, U, and standard error of estimate can probably be attributed to the efficiency characteristics of the least squares estimates, but the result is in no way necessary and, in fact, will be seen in later experiments to obtain to much less an extent.

The selection of the best candidates as forecasting models based on the evidence available at this stage is by no means simple nor unambiguous, in spite of the almost perfectly consistent ranking by the various criteria. One major difficulty is afforded by the marked similarity in the coefficients of multiple determination, although such a result is not unusual in the case of time series. More importantly, Model I, which has the superior measures of estimation accuracy, contains one coefficient whose sign contradicts prior theory, that for $(T - V)_{t-1}$, and two whose magnitudes are rather unrealistic, r_{t-3} and C_{t-1}^M. The interest rate shows a coefficient considerably smaller

TABLE IX-2

Comparison of Estimation Accuracy: Least Squares
Models Using "Historical" Period Data

Model No.	R^2	$R^2(C)$*	Standard Error of Estimate	Average Absolute Error	Mean Error†	Range	U	U^M	U^S	U^C	Fraction of a priori Incorrect Signs
I	.942	.924	125.8	103.0	.158%	19.3%	.0220	.000	.015	.985	$\frac{1}{5}$
II	.937	.920	130.9	110.5	.162	22.3	.0228	.000	.016	.984	$\frac{1}{4}$
III	.923	.899	144.7	123.6	.178	23.7	.0253	.000	.020	.980	$\frac{0}{5}$
IV	.922	.902	145.3	121.6	.168	23.7	.0254	.000	.020	.980	$\frac{0}{4}$
V	.895	.867	168.7	135.9	.313	28.8	.0295	.000	.028	.972	$\frac{0}{4}$
VI	.893	.869	170.8	134.2	.297	29.7	.0298	.000	.028	.972	$\frac{0}{3}$

* Coefficient of multiple determination (R^2) corrected for degrees of freedom.

† Measured as a percentage of the actual value and therefore need not be zero for the historical period.

than those generally estimated and the capacity utilization variable, one somewhat larger. Model II, which also describes the historical data well, contains one sign reversal and an even larger coefficient for C_{t-1}^M. On the other hand, the coefficients of Model VI, and to a lesser extent Model V, are all of reasonable magnitudes and sign, yet the measures of estimation accuracy are uniformly the least satisfactory of all the models. The forecaster is thus presented with a choice between models which possess substantial structural credibility and those which fit the historical data slightly more closely but which seem to sacrifice specification of structure.

The results obtained from using the six models to forecast the eleven-quarter future period (1959–I to 1961–III) are shown in Table IX–3. Immediately striking is the fact that, using any criterion, the ranking of the models as to forecasting accuracy differs substantially from the results based on the historical period (Table IX–2). Furthermore, there are marked differences in the models' forecasting accuracy with the future data whereas all were roughly equivalent with the historical data. With the future data, no model consistently ranks first by all of the criteria, but Models I, II, and VI rank ahead of the remaining formulations regardless of the forecasting measure used. More precisely, Model I registers the lowest average absolute error and mean error [23] (the latter being .37%, an almost perfect prediction of the mean level of investment), yet produces only the third best R^2 and standard error of estimate and the second lowest range. The lowest standard error of estimate and range is obtained by Model II, but the mean error is substantially increased to 7.4%. Model VI, while not optimal on any single criterion, produces the second highest R^2 and standard error of estimate and relatively satisfactory, specifically third best, values for all the other measures. Since it is also the model with the seemingly best structural characteristics, it is clearly the best forecasting model with some "structural accuracy." In fact, on the basis of the results reported in Table IX–3, the fundamental choice would appear to be between Model I, which has poor structural qualities but produces good forecasts, and Model VI, with good structural characteristics but only mediocre forecasting performance.

[23] A positive mean error reflects overprediction, since the measure is calculated by the difference between the predicted and actual value.

TABLE IX-3

Comparison of Forecasting Accuracy: Least Squares
Models Extrapolated to "Future" Period Data *

Model No.	R^2	Standard Error of Estimate	Average Absolute Error	Mean Error	Range	U	U^M	U^S	U^C
I	.770	161.5	144.6	0.37%	16.4%	.0296	.000	.046	.954
II	.840	134.9	196.3	7.4	15.3	.0421	.679	.000	.321
III	.579	218.7	368.0	−13.2	24.1	.0841	.739	.018	.243
IV	.633	204.0	294.2	−10.5	21.2	.0693	.675	.018	.307
V	.736	173.2	376.1	−13.6	18.9	.0815	.825	.027	.148
VI	.807	147.9	232.4	−8.1	18.1	.0515	.699	.022	.279

* "Future" Period is defined as 1959 (I) – 1961 (III).

The over-all heterogeneity of the results in Table IX–3 also hides a highly interesting pattern. In several cases, but by no means all, models which predict covariation best (e.g., have low standard errors of estimate) tend to have the largest mean biases and *vice versa*. That is, a model usually does not predict well both the level of investment activity and its cyclical fluctuation. Such a trade-off suggests that the best general measure of forecasting accuracy to use in these circumstances is the U coefficient, which weights both mean and covariation errors in addition to variation inequities. Ranked upon this criterion, Model I, dominated by the near perfect prediction of level, is clearly superior, Models II and VI noticeably less satisfactory, and Model III the least successful forecaster.

The notable success of Model I, particularly in predicting the mean level of investment, is rather difficult to interpret. This satisfactory performance might initially be thought to substantiate the hypothesis that, under conditions of structural continuity, the model which best describes historical experience should provide the best forecasts. There are, however, several reasons to suspect that Model I's performance is not a product of behavioral continuity but rather is due to a fortuitous balance of structural shifts and intercorrelation patterns.

There is also some rather clear evidence that the proper incorporation of capacity utilization and interest rate effects during the prediction period requires specification of coefficients different from those estimated from historical data. Specifically, moderate values of the C_{t-1}^M coefficient (i.e., about 3,000) lead consistently to marked underestimation, as can be seen in Models III through VI. It is only in Models I and II, where the coefficient appears excessive on prior grounds, that the underestimation tendency does not exist. Also, the inclusion of the interest rate with a negative coefficient of even small magnitude increases the underestimation of investment, although part of this is a result of the normally attendant decrease in the capacity utilization variable's coefficient. A comparison of the mean errors for Models V and VI reveals this fact very well.

Therefore, the successful performance of Model I should not be wholly credited to the continuity of historical behavior patterns. Rather, the inflated coefficient of C_{t-1}^M, restrained somewhat by the negative intercorrelation between it and r_{t-3}, together with the depressing effect of a large negative interest rate coefficient, contribute substantially to a nearly perfect forecast of level and lead to Model I's forecasting superiority. Model II, the same as I stripped of the interest rate variable, shows a moderate overprediction, as might be expected.

Rather disheartening is the failure of Models III and IV to produce better forecasting results. Both models contain coefficients of proper sign and, except for lagged investment, of acceptable magnitudes, and at the same time register good fits on the historical data. The marked tendency to underpredict investment level (mean errors are -13.2% and -10.5%, respectively) can be attributed to their smaller capacity utilization variable coefficients and in Model III to the additional depressing effect of the negative interest rate coefficient. Equally disturbing are the low corrected coefficients of multiple determination (.076 and .329 for Models III and IV, respectively), reflecting a failure to predict covariation pattern. Such errors of the second moments can be traced in large part to the abnormally high coefficients for lagged investment, which impart to the models substantial inflexibility and produce estimated series with variances notably smaller than that for the actual series.

Several conclusions might be drawn from the analysis. First, the results clearly indicate the difficulties caused by alteration of behavioral patterns from historical to forecast period (a proximate forecast period at that). In this connection it should be emphasized that the notable performance of Model I is probably in large part the outcome of a fortunate coincidence and should not be specifically attributed to the accuracy with which it fits the historical experience. If relationships change, it is very difficult, if indeed possible, to compare validly the forecasting ability of the models which contain a good deal of apparently *a priori* correct specification of historical structure with those which are more clearly pseudo-structural forecasting models. Nevertheless, the broad range of forecasting results and particularly the poor showing of Models III and IV focus attention on the sensitivity of forecasting results to model specification and, perhaps too, on the somewhat peculiar nature of the test period used. While the forecasts of Model I, and to a lesser degree of Models II and VI, are satisfactory, the performances of the other models are rather disappointing. At a minimum it can be said that the job of a forecaster in a dynamic economy like that of the United States is apparently a difficult one!

IV. *Forecasting with Alternative Cost Functions and Estimation Techniques*

The intrinsic forecasting quality of the models themselves, as just examined, can be compared with the forecasting performances of the alternative estimation techniques outlined in Section II and the preceding chapter. In view of the previously noted sensitivity of forecasting results to model specification, the six models employed in the previous section were utilized again in order to preserve consistency. In several cases, however, the least squares estimates of Chapter VII were used rather than the results just presented. In these cases, a seven rather than eleven quarter forecast period is used for all models in order to make the original historical and forecast period data fully compatible. For those models in which the historical data are compatible with both seven and eleven quarter future periods, both are presented.

The major coefficients of the six models, as estimated by least squares, minimum sum of absolute errors (*MSAE*), and nonsymmetrical error-cost function (*NSEC*) techniques, are shown in Table IX–4.[24] Possibly the most striking feature is the similarity of the coefficients estimated by the least squares and *MSAE* techniques. None of the coefficients of the six models (excluding seasonal dummies) differs "significantly" at the 5% level when estimated by these two methods, although caution should be exercised since the highly collinear data produce quite large standard errors. This qualification applies with particular force to Model III, where the sign for the interest rate coefficient changes and the coefficients for C_{t-1}^M and I_{t-2}, as estimated by the two techniques, differ by substantial amounts.

The coefficients produced by the *NSEC* technique tend to differ from the least squares coefficients less than they do from those of

[24] In all references which follow, including tables, "*MSAE*" will be used to denote the linear programming technique for minimizing the sum of absolute errors and "*NSEC*," the iterative least squares procedure used to handle the nonsymmetrical error cost function.

TABLE IX-4

Partial Regression Coefficients Produced by Alternative Estimation
Techniques: Aggregate Manufacturing Data, "Historical" Period *

Model and Estimation Technique	C_{t-1}^M	$(T-V)_{t-1}$	r_{t-3}	SP_{t-1}	ΔSP_{t-1}	I_{t-2}
Model I						
Least Squares	4979.5	−.0964	−260.3	27.281		.6554
MSAE	5692.6	−.1918	−276.6	33.089		.6285
NSEC	3517.79	−.0742	−528.5	25.540		.7531
Model II						
Least Squares	5873.8	−.0953		26.387		.5574
MSAE	6324.7	−.1259		26.494		.5661
NSEC	4869.6	.0044		16.844		.5837
Model III						
Least Squares	3035.5	.2178	−88.7		20.40	.9844
MSAE	4142.6	.2062	208.2		21.33	.8434
NSEC	1678.2	.2206	−361.2		18.55	1.0470
Model IV						
Least Squares	3380.2	.2137			20.87	.9514
MSAE	3108.1	.2199			16.78	.8659
NSEC	2784.5	.1975			20.00	.8565
Model V						
Least Squares	2379.0	.2480	−191.9			.8972
MSAE	2660.8	.2188	−64.2			.7970
NSEC	1301.3	.2533	−430.1			.9817
Model VI						
Least Squares	3107.5	.2405				.8184
MSAE	2991.3	.1974				.7731
NSEC	2854.1	.2210				.7609

* Constant terms and seasonal dummy variables are deleted from table for
clarity.

the *MSAE* method. Indeed, the least squares estimates usually lie
between those produced by the other two methods. Given the
asymmetrical bias which is being purposely built into the models by
the *NSEC* technique, deviations from the least squares coefficients
probably reflect the varying lead-lag relationships between the independent variables and I_t. Moreover, the high intercorrelations
among the explanatory variables suggest that individual lead-lag
relationships will be transmitted throughout the system. Thus, it is
not surprising that the interest rate and capacity utilization variables

show the most radical changes, for the high negative correlation between them requires that a decrease in one be accompanied by a compensating change in the other. A most noticeable effect is the substantial increase in the constant term in those models which contain r_{t-3}: in Models I and V the *NSEC* technique produces constants with values -653.2 and -233.0 respectively, compared with -2265.4 and -1500.5, the least squares results for the same models.

Table IX–5 tabulates the various measures of goodness-of-fit for the three estimation techniques, based on the historical period data. Least squares produces the highest coefficient of multiple determination and lowest U and standard error of estimate while the *MSAE* method results in the lowest average absolute error. In all cases these are, of course, reflections of the optimizing process built into each technique. A more interesting result revealed by the table is the fact that the measures of estimation accuracy do not vary substantially among the various techniques for a given model.

Empirical evidence on accuracy of forecasts, based on the seven quarter "future" period, 1959–I to 1960–III, is presented in Table IX–6 for the various models and estimation methods. The evidence concerning the relative merits of the least squares and *MSAE* techniques is somewhat ambiguous. On the one hand, *MSAE* produces average absolute errors that are noticeably smaller than least squares estimated counterparts in five of the six cases and about equal in the sixth. While not overly surprising, since it is this precise quality that the *MSAE* technique attempts to build into the model, the result is not a necessary consequence of the estimation procedure in nonhistorical periods. By contrast, in only one case does the least squares technique result in a lower standard error of estimate and higher R^2 then *MSAE*. This almost completely refutes what might be called neutral expectations, for it is a clear failure on the part of least squares to reflect in future period forecasts the optimal qualities purposely built into the models by the estimation technique.

It would appear, then, that *MSAE* performs far more satisfactorily than least squares, reflecting its own optimal qualities in the prediction period, whereas least squares, with the exception of one model, does not. An additional comparison of the results can be provided by recalling that the coefficient of multiple determination

TABLE IX-5

Comparison of Estimation Accuracy: Alternative Estimation Techniques Based on "Historical" Period Data

Model and Estimation Technique	R^2	Standard Error of Estimate	Average Absolute Error	Mean Error*	Range	U	U^M†	U^S	U^C
Model I									
Least Squares	.942	125.4	103.4	.15%	18.9%	.0219	.000	.015	.985
MSAE	.938	129.3	99.2	−.47	20.9	.0228	.014	.003	.983
NSEC	.934	134.1	110.0	.27	25.1	.0234	.000	.054	.946
Model II									
Least Squares	.936	131.5	110.1	.15	22.2	.0229	.000	.017	.983
MSAE	.931	136.8	106.6	−.53	26.7	.0241	.016	.004	.950
NSEC	.925	142.5	115.9	.46	19.2	.0249	.000	.161	.839
Model III									
Least Squares	.923	144.7	123.6	.18	23.7	.0253	.000	.020	.980
MSAE	.912	154.6	114.2	.40	26.5	.0270	.000	.044	.956
NSEC	.913	153.6	131.8	.29	25.0	.0268	.000	.032	.968
Model IV									
Least Squares	.922	145.3	121.6	.17	23.7	.0254	.000	.020	.980
MSAE	.916	151.1	117.1	.55	21.8	.0264	.000	.138	.862
NSEC	.913	154.1	122.8	.50	23.9	.0269	.000	.170	.830
Model V									
Least Squares	.896	168.0	134.9	.30	28.4	.0293	.000	.028	.972
MSAE	.890	172.5	131.9	.29	27.5	.0302	.001	.120	.879
NSEC	.891	172.3	140.8	.32	28.2	.0301	.000	.030	.970
Model VI									
Least Squares	.893	170.5	133.1	.30	29.5	.0298	.000	.028	.972
MSAE	.885	176.4	132.8	.30	28.4	.0309	.002	.135	.863
NSEC	.889	173.8	133.6	.55	26.7	.0304	.000	.124	.876

* Measured as a percentage of the actual value and therefore need not be zero for the historical period.
† All non-zero entries in these columns are caused by rounding error.

TABLE IX-6

Comparison of Forecasting Accuracy: Alternative Estimation Techniques
Tested against Seven-Quarter Future Period

Model and Estimation Technique	R^2	Standard Error of Estimate	Average Absolute Error	Mean Error	Range	U	U^M	U^S	U^C
Model I									
Least Squares	.771	169.1	151.6	−2.1%	17.5	.0342	.134	.087	.779
MSAE	.780	166.1	148.2	−1.2	18.0	.0320	.055	.027	.918
NSEC	.532	242.1	311.7	−10.6	23.0	.0764	.609	.095	.196
Model II									
Least Squares	.850	136.9	146.8	5.5	16.7	.0358	.522	.003	.475
MSAE	.817	151.4	127.2	2.6	18.9	.0307	.186	.064	.750
NSEC	.857	133.8	112.6	.6	16.6	.0249	.005	.055	.940
Model III									
Least Squares	.508	237.1	433.4	−15.7	24.1	.1009	.770	.045	.185
MSAE	.710	182.0	212.4	−5.7	22.0	.0468	.436	.028	.536
NSEC	.167	308.6	635.1	−23.1	33.5	.1505	.809	.033	.158
Model IV									
Least Squares	.587	217.2	359.8	−13.0	21.2	.0846	.733	.045	.222
MSAE	.606	212.2	307.4	−10.4	21.2	.0720	.657	.090	.253
NSEC	.710	182.0	217.4	−5.7	22.0	.0468	.436	.028	.536
Model V									
Least Squares	.667	204.2	429.0	−15.5	19.9	.0961	.815	.051	.133
MSAE	.753	175.8	309.9	−11.1	16.4	.0703	.757	.079	.164
NSEC	.411	271.4	620.1	−22.4	28.3	.1424	.839	.048	.113
Model VI									
Least Squares	.792	161.2	272.1	−9.6	18.5	.061	.729	.039	.232
MSAE	.805	156.2	272.7	−9.8	14.6	.062	.753	.081	.166
NSEC	.787	163.2	248.7	−8.4	17.9	.056	.674	.071	.255

and standard error of estimate are based on the second moments only, while the average absolute error refers only to the first moment. Fortunately, Theil's U coefficient is designed specifically to take account of prediction errors due to both first and second moment displacements. Using the U coefficient as the basis for comparison, the *MSAE* technique dominates least squares in five instances and in effect equals it in the sixth.

A second conclusion which can be drawn from Table IX–6 concerns the merits of the *NSEC* technique. The values of the dependent variable for the prediction period all fall below the historical mean for the series (with trend removed), so that on the basis of the definition used in developing the *NSEC* technique, as well as for other reasons, this period can be considered a "recession." Therefore, a nonsymmetrical cost function suggests that there should be as few positive $(P_i > A_i)$ residuals as possible. Table IX–7 tabulates

TABLE IX–7

Number of Predictions for which Estimated Value Exceeds Actual Value:
Least Squares vs. Nonsymmetrical Error Cost Technique

Model	Least Squares Technique	*NSEC* Technique
I	4	1
II	6	4
III	0	0
IV	0	0
V	0	0
VI	1	1

the number of positive residuals during the future period for each of the models as estimated by least squares and the *NSEC* method. It is clear that the desired bias is reflected in the *NSEC* forecasts, for in all cases the number of positive residuals for the *NSEC* technique never exceeds that for least squares and for two models is less.[25] Unfortunately, the desired bias is generally achieved at the expense of a significant tendency to underpredict I_t, particularly in Models I, III, and V. This result can be traced in large part to relatively negative coefficients for the interest rate variable. The systematic underestimation is reflected in the significantly higher mean errors

[25] The fact that least squares produces no positive residuals in three cases suggests that this test might not be sufficiently strong.

for the *NSEC* models and relatively higher values for U^M, particularly in Models III and V. On the other hand, the desired bias also is reflected with *NSEC* in Models II, IV, and VI, yet the prediction is as good as, and usually better than, with either of the other two estimation methods. In short, strictly on the basis of the results shown in Table IX–6, *NSEC* would appear to be the best way to fit forecasting models when the troublesome interest rate variable is excluded. Why this should be true is hardly obvious!

The rather poor performance of the least squares method is both somewhat surprising and possibly misleading. There is a strong suggestion that the results are quite sensitive to model specification and forecast period data characteristics, particularly for Models III and IV, where the coefficients estimated by the different methods differ most markedly. Alternatively, the superiority of the *MSAE* technique might be a function of the length of the forecast period. Evidence from two different tests of the length of forecast period hypothesis is presented in Tables IX–8 and IX–9. In the first table Models III and IV, for which compatible data are available, are extrapolated to an eleven quarter forecast period. The results extend those found in Table IX–6 for the same models and the seven quarter forecast period. In both cases *MSAE* dominates least squares with respect to all measures, reinforcing the earlier results.

As a second test of the effect of forecast period length on the prediction accuracy of the least squares and *MSAE* techniques, the coefficient of multiple determination, average absolute error, and U coefficient based on Model IV are shown in Table IX–9, for forecasts of two to eleven periods. Once again the evidence substantiates that presented earlier. *MSAE* completely dominates least squares in forecast periods of all length, producing higher R^2's and lower average absolute errors and U's.

The results of these tests point to the rejection of forecast period length as an explanation of the better performance of *MSAE* than least squares. It is therefore quite likely that sensitivity to model specification, combined with the peculiarities of the forecast period, explain the results. Those models with large capacity utilization and more positive interest rate coefficients prove the best predictors of the mean level of investment. For reasons which are not entirely clear, *MSAE* usually estimates larger coefficients for C_{t-1}^M and more

TABLE IX-8

Comparison of Forecasting Accuracy: Alternative Estimation Techniques
Tested against Eleven-Quarter Future Period

Model and Estimation Technique	R^2	Standard Error of Estimate	Average Absolute Error	Mean Error	Range	U	U^M	U^S	U^C
Model III									
Least Squares	.579	218.7	368.0	−13.2%	24.1%	.0841	.739	.018	.243
MSAE	.724	177.1	168.7	−3.5	22.0	.0381	.248	.016	.736
NSEC	.360	269.5	570.8	−20.5	33.5	.1292	.818	.011	.171
Model IV									
Least Squares	.633	204.0	294.2	−10.5	21.2	.0693	.675	.018	.307
MSAE	.662	196.0	252.5	−8.5	21.1	.0598	.605	.062	.333
NSEC	.635	203.6	245.0	−8.1	22.8	.0593	.568	.042	.390

TABLE IX–9

Forecasts Produced by Model IV for Periods of Varying Length:
Least Squares vs. Minimum Sum of Absolute Errors Technique

No. of periods	R^2	Average Absolute Error	U
		Least Squares	
2	.2218	235.8	.0714
3	.2094	172.6	.0560
4	.6243	231.6	.0627
5	.3996	302.5	.0793
6	.5196	355.7	.0875
7	.5872	359.8	.0846
8	.7170	359.0	.0802
9	.6737	326.9	.0762
10	.6478	307.0	.0721
11	.6334	294.2	.0693
	Minimum Sum of Absolute Errors		
2	.2968	188.3	.0551
3	.3145	129.5	.0430
4	.6269	193.6	.0533
5	.4267	252.9	.0665
6	.5454	300.8	.0739
7	.6060	307.4	.0720
8	.7263	314.4	.0697
9	.6833	281.5	.0662
10	.6713	265.8	.0628
11	.6618	254.5	.0603

positive coefficients for r_{t-3} than least squares. This fact is most probably in large part responsible for the dominance of *MSAE*. In view of these considerations, conclusions about the relative merits of least squares and the *MSAE* technique must be drawn with extreme caution. Based on the admittedly limited evidence, however, there is an indication that *MSAE* dominates the results, producing the more satisfactory forecasts for all the criteria employed.

In evaluating the results of the *NSEC* method, it should be remembered that the very nature of the cost function suggests that some systematic bias will be introduced by the estimation procedure. The magnitude of bias seems quite obviously to be a function of the particular model specification and in several cases proves to be quite substantial. Nevertheless, the desired bias is consistently produced. In this connection, it is indeed unfortunate that the forecast period does not contain some observations which can be classified as "business booms" in order that a more rigorous test could be effected.

V. *Forecasts with Constrained and Unconstrained Coefficients*

In the preceding chapter alternative estimates of Model I using constrained and unconstrained coefficients indicated that when fitted to the historical data there was little to choose between the two different sets of estimates. Multiple correlations and the standard errors of estimate were only slightly inferior when constraints were placed on the coefficients. The mean errors, moreover, were essentially the same for all models, and the average absolute error and range were only slightly inferior with than without constraints (see Table VIII–3). In short, on the basis of the historical evidence there was apparently little price to be paid in terms of forecasting performance for "improvements" in structure. The obvious question is whether the same can be said when tested by extrapolation to future data.

The results obtained from attempting to predict the seven quarter future period, first quarter 1959 through third quarter 1961, by means of the unconstrained and two constrained models are shown in Table IX–10. At first view they are something less than encouraging to the constrained estimation techniques. Neither of the two constrained models is able to predict either the covariation pattern or the mean level of investment better than the unconstrained version. For the two constrained sets the standard errors of estimate are 180.7 and 189.1, respectively, while that for the unconstrained equation is only 169.1. With respect to predicting the mean level of investment, all models tend to underestimate investment during the future period, but the constrained versions come out second best. The mean error for the unconstrained equation is 2.1% while that for the second constrained version is a high 7.1%. This dominance of the unconstrained technique is also reflected in its substantially lower value for the U coefficient, registering a value of .0342 as against the value of .0502 and .0537 for the two constrained versions.

On the basis of these results a forecaster clearly would have been well advised to use the unconstrained and less structurally satisfying

TABLE IX-10

Measures of Forecasting Accuracy: Constrained and Unconstrained
Least Square Regression Based on "Future" Period Data

Model	R^2	Standard Error of Estimate	Average Absolute Error	Mean Error	Range	U	U^M	U^S	U^C
Constrained Set #1	.739	180.7	220.5	−6.5%	19.8%	.0502	.519	.088	.393
Constrained Set #2	.714	189.1	245.8	−7.1	21.0	.0537	.536	.081	.383
Unconstrained	.771	169.1	151.6	−2.1	17.5	.0342	.134	.087	.779

model for his predictions. Historical continuity, in short, seemed sufficient in this period to insure that historical models with certain statistical properties carried these properties over at least into the short-run future.

There is also evidence that several relationships designated as structural actually changed during the prediction period, and in a way which fortuitously favored the unconstrained model. In particular, it is quite clear from previous results that a relatively large capacity coefficient was the best insurance of forecasting accuracy in this particular test period. Since one of the objectives of the constraints is specifically to reduce the size of the capacity utilization variable's coefficient, it almost automatically leads to an inferior forecasting performance. The relative inability of the constrained models to predict the mean level of investment can, in fact, be explained almost completely in terms of the reduction of the capacity utilization variable's coefficient and negative interest rate coefficients. While the interest rate coefficient is actually more negative in the unconstrained than constrained model, this is easily offset by the much larger capacity utilization coefficient when constraints are absent.

Modifications of the bifurcated time-series models presented in Chapter VII provide a further indication of the influence which the capacity variable has upon the predictions. The results obtained for the models without the interest rate, the inclusion of which as already pointed out tends to cause all models to underpredict, are:

Upswings:

$$I_t = 1400.8 + 3030.7 \ C_{t-1}^M + 13.87 \ SP_{t-1} + .594 \ I_{t-2}$$
$$\quad\quad\quad (961.) \quad\quad\quad (4.29) \quad\quad\quad (.069)$$
$$\quad + \text{(seasonal dummies)} \quad\quad\quad R^2 = .950.$$

Downswings:

$$I = 442.4 + .507 \ (T - V)_{t-1} + .570 \ I_{t-2} + \text{(seasonal dummies)}$$
$$\quad\quad\quad (.132) \quad\quad\quad (.185)$$
$$\quad\quad\quad\quad\quad\quad\quad\quad\quad\quad\quad R^2 = .862.$$

The residuals for predictions of 1959 (I) through 1960 (III) by these models are shown in Table IX–11, where R^2's, standard errors

TABLE IX–11

Residuals and Measures of Forecasting Accuracy for Bifurcated
Investment Models, Excluding Interest Rate

Upswing Model

Year and Quarter	Actual Value	Estimated Value	Residual	Percentage Error
1959–1	2046.7	439.8	−1606.9	−78.5
1959–2	2494.6	663.1	−1831.5	−73.4
1959–3	2486.6	669.6	−1817.2	−73.1
1959–4	2958.6	1193.5	−1765.1	−59.7
1960–1	2555.8	662.8	−1893.0	−74.1
1960–2	3120.3	972.9	−2147.4	−68.8
1960–3	3021.7	947.2	−2074.5	−68.7
R^2	Standard Error of Estimate		Mean Error	U
.768	170.5		−70.9%	.5353

Downswing Model

Year and Quarter	Actual Value	Estimated Value	Residual	Percentage Error
1959–1	2046.7	2532.4	485.7	23.7
1959–2	2494.6	2637.0	142.4	5.7
1959–3	2486.8	3066.8	580.0	23.3
1959–4	2958.6	2938.6	−20.0	−0.7
1960–1	2555.8	2468.3	−87.5	−3.4
1960–2	3120.3	2979.9	−140.4	−4.5
1960–3	3021.7	3015.7	−6.0	−0.2
R^2	Standard Error of Estimate		Mean Error	U
.440	264.7		6.3%	.0541

of estimate, mean errors, and U coefficients are also reported. The upswing model, which includes the capacity utilization variable with only a moderate coefficient, grossly underpredicts investment expenditures, registering a mean error of -70.9% and residuals as high as \$2,074 million. By contrast, the downswing model, excluding the capacity variable, on balance overpredicts investment, as reflected by the positive mean error, 6.3%. It is, incidentally, satisfying that the model developed to characterize periods of relatively low economic activity performs with overwhelmingly more success than the one descriptive of economic expansion, inasmuch as the prediction period is one characterized by somewhat depressed industrial activity.

Further evidence of the deleterious forecasting effects of a negative interest rate coefficient also is provided by testing the downswing model with the interest rate included. The estimated model is:

$$I = 490.7 + .409 \, (T-V)_{t-1} - 433.3 \, r_{t-3} + .409 \, I_{t-2}$$
$$ (.125) \phantom{(T-V)_{t-1}} (199.3) (.217)$$
$$ + \text{(seasonal dummies)} R^2 = .899.$$

When used to forecast the 1959 (I) through 1960 (III) period of mildly rising but nevertheless depressed investment activity, the results are extremely unsatisfactory. The tendency reported in Table IX–11 to overpredict is reversed when the interest rate is included and the mean error increases in absolute value from 6.3% to 14.9%. Furthermore, the model's ability to predict the covariation pattern is all but destroyed, R^2 dropping from .440 to .150 and the U coefficient rising from .054 to .109.

These difficulties with the interest rate variable are symptomatic of the general problem of obtaining sufficiently accurate structural specifications in economics to make such specification a positive aid to forecasting. As was pointed out previously, there is evidence to suggest that the effect of the interest rate on investment is highly nonlinear. While it may act as a crucial constraint at or near cyclical peaks, the interest rate appears to have little effect at troughs or throughout a major part of the cycle, at least at levels exhibited historically. It therefore should enter the investment model in a complex nonlinear fashion, thereby invalidating the simple linearity assumption made here and in almost all other empirical investment studies. Moreover, since economic activity at or near cyclical peaks describes a relatively small number of observation periods, the "spurious" or nonstructural positive correlation empirically observed during most other periods easily could dominate under the simplifying assumption of linearity. In turn this fact probably explains the frequency with which the interest rate is estimated with a positive partial regression coefficient and why models with a positive interest rate coefficient in this study consistently have produced superior forecasts. The period from 1959 (I) to 1961 (III) was one of mixed economic activity during which a slowly rising interest rate was accompanied by a very slowly increasing level of investment activity. With liquidity at high levels, the rising interest rate had little responsibility for any sluggishness of investment expenditures, and forecasting with a positive interest rate coefficient, no matter how structurally spurious, helped rather than hindered.

VI. *A Forecasting Model for Aggregate Investment*

A logical conclusion to the forecasting analyses of this study is the presentation of a forecasting model for aggregate business expenditures on plant and equipment in the United States. At the outset it was noted that one objective was to determine if a knowledge of business administrative rules and practices for the allocation of funds to fixed assets, often revealed only through the study of disaggregated, industry, and individual firm data, can provide aid in the formulation of an aggregate forecasting model. Specifically, it was hoped that the more deaggregative data would permit effective testing of alternative hypotheses — a testing which seemed precluded with time-series data because of their collinear character.

Along the way, and as discussed in some detail in the preceding section, it has become increasingly obvious that data limitations, foremost among several problems, often preclude the incorporation of both good structural specification and accurate description of historical experience in the same model. The forecaster is thus confronted with a paradox. While it generally becomes easier to describe historical behavior, and often predict successfully at the level of broad aggregates, it is difficult, if not impossible, to do so by means of models which are reasonable reflections of behavioral structure. In terms of the previous discussion, the trade-off between forecasting ability and structural specification is often most dramatic in aggregate time-series models.

Knowledge gained from the study of less aggregative behavior, nevertheless, might be of use. Specifically, the dominant importance found for capacity utilization, retained earnings, and lagged investment variables suggests that some formulation of each might profitably be included in an aggregate forecasting model. Based

on these and other considerations, the following quarterly model
was estimated by simple least squares: [26]

$$I = 2.16 + .192(RE + DE) + 6.99 \left(\sum^{4} \frac{GNP_t}{GNP_o} \right)_{t-1} + .748 I_{t-1}$$
$$\quad (.088) \quad\quad\quad (14.7) \quad\quad\quad\quad\quad\quad\quad\quad (.088)$$
$$R^2 = .857 \quad SEE = 1.24$$

where I is aggregate business investment in plant and equipment;
RE, corporate retained earnings; DE, corporate depreciation allowances; GNP, gross national product; R^2, the coefficient of multiple
determination; SEE, the standard error of estimate; the subscript o
denotes previous peak value; $\sum^{4}$, a four-period moving average
(centered on the last quarter); and the numbers shown in parentheses below the coefficients, their respective standard errors. As
before, the data are quarterly for the period 1949 (III)–1958 (IV) and
all relevant series are price deflated by the Department of Commerce index of producers' durable equipment prices.

The specified model probably should be considered as more forecasting than structural in nature. Although previous findings indicate
that stock price level or its change and interest rates have important
roles in the structure of the investment function, data limitations
make it impossible to include them satisfactorily in these aggregate
models. In fact, so strong is the correlation between stock price level
and the other independent variables that its inclusion causes all but
the lagged investment term to become highly nonsignificant. This
places the major forecasting burden on lagged investment, thereby
relying heavily on the autocorrelative qualities of the series under
study. Also, a more direct and better measure of private sector
capacity utilization might have been employed, but none are immediately obvious or available.

The forecasts for the period 1959 (I) through 1961 (III) produced
by the model are tabulated in Table IX–12. The results are quite
satisfactory. Although the R^2 is not outstandingly high, there is
essentially no mean error and the U coefficient, in this case domi-

[26] A model similar to this was suggested by the present authors to Gary
Fromm, who used it in his "Inventories, Business Cycles, and Economic Stabilization," in *Inventory Fluctuations and Economic Stabilization*, Part IV, material
prepared for U.S. Congress Joint Economic Committee (1962). Quarterly
depreciation was interpolated from available annual figures.

TABLE IX-12

Residuals and Measures of Forecasting Accuracy
for Aggregate Investment Model

Year and Quarter	Actual Value (in $ billion)	Estimated Value (in $ billion)	Residual (in $ billion)	Percentage Error
1959−1	34.5000	34.9258	0.4258	1.23
1959−2	36.3000	35.6504	−0.6496	−1.79
1959−3	36.8000	37.5111	0.7111	1.93
1959−4	37.0000	37.4126	0.4126	1.12
1960−1	38.3000	37.5523	−0.7477	−1.95
1960−2	39.3000	38.6662	−0.6338	−1.61
1960−3	38.4000	39.3481	0.9481	2.47
1960−4	38.5000	38.5230	0.0230	0.06
1961−1	36.3000	38.4356	2.1356	5.88
1961−2	36.9000	36.7436	−0.1564	−0.42
1961−3	37.8000	37.4136	−0.3864	−1.02

R^2	Standard Error of Estimate	Average Absolute Error	Mean Error	Range
.590	.825	.657	0.54%	7.8%

	U	U^M	U^S	U^C
	.0113	.050	.002	.948

nated by the lack of mean bias, is an exceptionally low .0113. The model produces forecasts which are on the average only about .5% too high, or roughly \$180 million over the actual value. Moreover, in all but two cases the error is less than \$750 million or roughly 2%. Furthermore, some might argue, rightly or wrongly, that the relatively large overestimate for 1961 (I) can be attributed to business apprehension at the imminent change in governmental leadership, an expectational factor difficult to incorporate into any model. In any case, few forecasters would be dissatisfied with the over-all results.

For the sake of completeness, the same aggregate model was refitted to data for 1949 (III) through 1961 (III) (which was the last quarter for which data were readily available at the time of writing). The results are:

$$I_t = -1.41 + .191(RE+DE)_{t-1} + 6.65 \sum^4 \left(\frac{GNP_t}{GNP_o}\right)_{(t-1)} + .736\,I_{t-1}$$
$$\quad (.069) \qquad\qquad (13.0) \qquad\qquad\qquad (.075)$$

$$R^2 = .849 \quad SEE = 1.20.$$

As would be expected from the accuracy of the predictions, this estimation of the model does not differ noticeably from the one based on the shorter time period. Since it incorporates more up-to-date information, this model probably would be the more advisable formulation for producing predictions of future investment levels.

Chapter X | Method, Theory, and Policy: Some Implications

I. *Introduction*

In the process of attempting the empirical specification of the investment characteristics of large United States manufacturing corporations three basic and distinct topics have been discussed. The first is, of course, simply the theory or concepts of investment processes themselves, the objective being to test many different theories of investment so as at least to reduce the empirically admissible range of hypotheses. The second is the improvement of the technical aspects of empirical estimation and forecasting in economics. The third, treated only in an implicit fashion thus far, is that of the implications of these various findings for the formation and design of public policies aimed at cyclical stabilization or promotion of economic growth.

In this final chapter an attempt will be made to summarize and develop some further implications of what has preceded. The endeavor will be organized under the three headings of method, theory, and policy, followed in Section V by a few final comments or afterthoughts.

II. *Method*

The first purely statistical finding was the inadequacy of conventionally simple statistical regression models as explanations of the complex and heterogeneous behavior embodied in cross-section samples. Finding this heterogeneity was hardly surprising. Indeed, one of the established "traditions" in the relatively new art of analyzing economic cross-section data is the finding of exceedingly low correlations and high standard errors of estimate. In the present study this inadequacy was illustrated both in the preliminary analyses, using simple two variable correlations, and in the multiple regression and partial correlation analyses employed in the subsequent multivariable analyses of the same data.

The tradition of low correlations in cross-section studies has been particularly pronounced in studies aimed at measuring or evaluating consumer behavior or business investment. These are both areas in which uncertainty, the availability of information, differences in risk preferences, and other utility determinants can and almost certainly do play a crucial role in influencing final decisions. The failure of simple hypotheses about consumption or investment to explain adequately the experience observed in cross-section samples strongly suggests that the valuations placed upon these many dimensions of risk, gain, and psychic comfort are very complex and differ rather markedly from one individual household or corporation to another. The implications of this heterogeneity for the design of econometric investigations of cross-section data are, of course, highly important.[1] Basically they strongly imply that the different economic units being observed differ substantially in their behavioral parameters.

Another technical finding that can hardly be classified as surprising was the limited compatibility of the parameter estimates obtained from the cross-section data with those from time-series. For reasons that have now been explored with reasonable thoroughness,[2] this incompatibility of cross-section and time-series data has many sources. Not the least of these is the fact that cross-section data seem to represent a much wider range of human experience than

---

[1] One of the present authors is now completing another study (Meyer, *The Measurement of Business Motivation*) using much of the same data as employed in this study to experiment with some alternative techniques for meeting this heterogeneity problem.

[2] Meyer and Kuh, "How Extraneous Are Extraneous Estimates?" *Review of Economics and Statistics*, Vol. 39 (November 1957), pp. 380–393. Grilliches and Grunfeld, etc.

time-series. Cross-section data apparently reflect both the longer-run adjustments of a more complete equilibrium as well as the shorter-run adaptations that are inherently more characteristic of time-series data. In addition, sociological, psychological, and technological factors, conventionally considered beyond the scope of economic theory, may be observable in cross-section data but essentially "averaged out" of aggregate time-series.

The incompatibility of the cross-section and time-series parameter estimates obtained in this study, however, can be overemphasized. Specifically, the compatibility, while limited, was greater than the *a priori* expectations of the investigators. The observed compatibility readily falls short, though, of the early and rather naive expectations of econometricians when first undertaking investigation of cross-section data in the anticipation that it would provide parameter estimates and information that could be easily and quickly incorporated into time-series studies.

Confirmation was also found in the time-series data for the general hypothesis that it is much easier to construct an explanatory model for an economic aggregate than for its parts. Specifically, the goodness of statistical fit as measured by the coefficient of determination tended to be better with the historical data from 1948 through 1958 for *both* the time-series analysis of *aggregate* manufacturing investment and for a *pooled* sample composed of the component industries of manufacturing than for analyses of the component industries conducted separately. In the case of the pooled data this is all the more remarkable because the number of degrees of freedom is technically, and probably actually, much larger for this sample than for the component industry samples. Apparently, the variation in investment between industry groups was more closely associated with the explanatory variables than that within individual industries.

The major methodological objective of the study, however, was not to find further substantiation for these reasonably well-established negative conclusions but to improve economic forecasting and the accuracy of its measurement. A particular objective was to progress beyond the conventional coefficient of determination as a measure of forecasting accuracy. Specifically, such alternatives as average absolute error, mean error, the range, and Theil's U coefficient were considered. In terms of historical data it became quite clear that a technique of estimation usually can be found that will provide the best performance in terms of a specified goal or measure of forecasting accuracy. The mathematical specification of the exact estimation technique or its algorithm, however, may not always be easy. Furthermore, recognition that better measures of forecasting performance than the coefficient of determination may exist and of the fact that these alternative forecasting measures can be related to different specifications of estimation techniques almost immediately leads into a decision theory orientation of the estimation problem.

In a decision theory format the optimal estimation method is the one which produces optimal policy rather than merely best forecasts. This further implies that the estimation method should vary according to the policy maker's welfare or cost function and the constraints relating his available economic policy instruments to his objectives. Further empirical study may uncover some universal form for the welfare function-constraint system, but for the present it seemed necessary to proceed by analyzing alternative "error-cost" functions, which summarize in more tractable form a particular system. The alternatives explored in this study are by no means exhaustive, and an obvious area for further work is the formulation and testing of estimation methods which are optimal with respect to other specifications.

Detailed discussion was devoted to estimation methods suggested by U-shaped, V-shaped, symmetrical, and asymmetrical quadratic error-cost functions. Using the investment models developed as part of this study, empirical results were presented for the latter three cases, corresponding to minimizing the sum of absolute errors, simple least squares, and an iterative least squares procedure. The relationship between regression analyses and mathematical programming proved extremely useful for the formulation and solution of several of these estimation problems. The minimization of the range, implied by the U-shaped cost function, was not analyzed further since the method gives undue weight to extreme observations and makes structural estimation difficult.

The basic conclusion was that while least squares may be as effective as any of the other methods studied, neither its superiority nor its inferiority is clear from the results presented. For example, minimizing the sum of absolute errors generally produces forecasts with smaller average absolute errors and as high coefficients of multiple determination and in some cases higher than, least squares. Since estimation with a minimum sum of absolute errors can be formulated as a linear programming problem, this procedure has the added advantage of yielding as a by-product (from the dual) the marginal increase of error which will result from altering a particular coefficient.

The results obtained from minimizing a nonsymmetrical error-cost function were less conclusive. In producing the desired bias, the technique yields several models whose forecasting ability compares quite favorably with least squares. The method, however, does have a tendency to alter several of the models radically so that an unsought persistent underestimation of investment results. The bias, being a systematic one, can be corrected, potentially in a rather straightforward manner, but its substantial size and seriousness should nevertheless not be overlooked. Also, the iterative procedure employed can undoubtedly be improved. The ideal situation would be the development of a purely analytical technique to minimize nonsymmetrical cost functions of this general type, although such a technique is not obvious. In general, both the form of the functions and the techniques for handling nonsymmetrical error-cost functions need a great deal of refinement, for the work presented here is of a quite elementary level.

The position was taken in this study that prediction models should seek to reflect structure properly insofar as is possible. Multicollinearity is possibly the most important obstacle to the correct specification of prediction models. A tabular method was presented for identifying severe multicollinearity in the models and some rather interesting results were observed. However, the method is far more qualitative than it is quantitative and therefore lacks rigor. Given the practical importance of the collinearity problem, more research in the future might be devoted to developing methods for quantitatively identifying the degree and precise nature of multicollinearity.

A constrained coefficient least squares estimation technique was developed as a method for estimating structural coefficients under conditions of marked collinearity. The method is a generalization of the more arbitrary technique, used in the past, by which one or more of the coefficients of a highly collinear set of variables is constrained to zero or to a value exogenously (e.g., cross-sectionally) estimated. The empirical results for investment functions derived from the constrained coefficient method were rather encouraging. For both the historical and forecast periods, the trade-off between the increased structural validity of the constrained models and the minimum variance property of the unconstrained models was found to be quite small. While continuity of historical covariance patterns might explain the dominance of the unconstrained models, arguments were advanced which attributed the result to a shift in structure between the two periods which was peculiarly favorable to the unconstrained models. The results are by no means conclusive and the method certainly seems worthy of further study through application to a broader range of models and bodies of data.

It cannot be claimed, however, that constrained least squares provides or can provide any fully adequate solution to the time-series collinearity problem. The only true solution is to find new and better sources of information. That, however, is easier said than done, as experiences with using cross-section estimates as a solution to the collinearity problem suggest.

An important consequence of so much collinearity in time-series data is that time series usually are just not of sufficient quality to permit the making of important structural distinctions. The common practice of conducting large-scale examinations of time-series data seemingly aimed at making such distinctions is therefore almost surely effort misdirected. Collinear time-series data also do not provide a good basis for accepting or rejecting different hypotheses. For example, as pointed out in Chapter VII, the sign on the residual funds variable, $T - V$, becomes negative when included in a time-series model with *both* capacity and an absolute stock price variable. To infer from this evidence, however, that the residual funds hypothesis should be rejected is simply wrong or at least premature. All that can be said is that in the historical sample under analysis the variables were so synchronized that it is impossible to include more than two of them in the same model. Models using any two of them do about equally well (though inclusion of the capacity variable usually accords a slight advantage) in explaining the historical patterns; so all hypotheses can be said to be consistent with the available evidence.

The experiments with constrained estimation and forecasting reported in Chapters VIII and IX strongly reinforce this conclusion that structural estimation of economic relationships is difficult or virtually impossible with time-series analyses. They also point to a corollary that follows quite naturally from the limitations of time-series analyses. This is to admit the inadequacy of existing knowledge of structure and not to be too compulsively concerned about integrating structural reality into models whose main objective is only to produce good forecasts. In short, it may be best simply to concentrate on producing good forecasting models for their own sake, not worrying too much whether the model captures some unknown structural reality with any great accuracy.

This is not by way of recommending, however, that all search for structure should cease or that if a "structurally more accurate" model produces as good forecasts as any other model available it should not be used. However, it must be recognized, as illustrated by the results reported in Chapter IX, a very real trade-off often may exist between structural quality and forecasting success.

Furthermore, given the primitive state of economic knowledge of structure, particularly of investment behavior at the aggregate level, it is not at all clear that economists even know when they are sacrificing structural accuracy. Virtually all theory of investment behavior pertains to micro-units. Unfortunately, a large number of unknown interactions and nonlinearities usually make it impossible to know just what the aggregated coefficients should be. Aggregate structure is, in short, not behavioral in the same way that micro-structure is and therefore full insight into its form is for the moment at least beyond available knowledge. These difficulties are also compounded by the fact that present time-series data are insufficient to estimate simple linear multivariable micro-models, let alone the complex interactions and nonlinearities needed to move from micro to aggregate parameters.

In sum, knowledge of micro-structure and theory may be a useful guide in searching for the empirical regularities from which to construct aggregate forecasting models. However, this usefulness should not be overestimated, for knowledge of aggregate structural coefficients (whatever they are) is quite limited and the quality of data from which the estimates are to be derived is quite low. Should the best model which retains "structural flavor" prove an unsatisfactory forecaster, there is, moreover, no major reason for hesitating about turning to other sources. Specifically, the best forecasting model often may be based on autoregression (lagged dependent variables), exogenous measures of intentions and expectations (such as the McGraw-Hill and OBE–SEC surveys), and one or two structural-type variables to aid in picking up turning points. In fact, one of the more important pieces of unfinished research suggested by this study is seeing what kind of improvement might be made in forecasting investment if questionnaire information on expectations and intentions were included in the aggregate forecasting equation reported at the end of Chapter IX.

The position advanced here, of skepticism about the present efficacy of structural estimates in forecasting, may seem quite heretical to some.[3] Those who find these views surprising should reflect, however, that when confronted with actual forecasting problems, economists have long displayed a propensity to adopt a pragmatic approach very much like that just advocated. Indeed, some observers might even contend that such pragmatism is the hallmark of the more successful practitioners of economic forecasting!

III. *Theory and Concepts*

Probably the most important finding about the underlying structure of manufacturing investment behavior and the problems associated with constructing a conceptual framework for its explanation is the insufficiency of simple models. This is particularly true of attempts to explain the complexity and heterogeneity usually found in cross-section data. A need seemingly exists for an entirely new approach to the problem of constructing a theory of investment that is adequate to explain differences among business firms with different strategies and objectives. Furthermore, a much wider range of technological, sociological, and psychological phenomena than are conventionally found in economic theory may be needed. The challenge of providing an adequate explanation of cross-section

---

[3] Similar views have been expressed, though, by others. In particular see Liu, "Underidentification, Structural Estimation, and Forecasting."

data is, in short, also a challenge to the legitimacy of the conventional limits placed upon economic theory.

As for the accelerator-residual funds hypothesis that has been the central focus of this study, only limited empirical confirmation was observable. In the cross-section data the theory performed reasonably well in explaining the relationships between investment and capacity and investment and residual fund flows under different cyclical conditions, but it failed utterly, as did all the conventional theories, to explain the 1952 experience. The performance of the hypothesis in explaining time-series data, as might have been expected on technical grounds alone, was considerably more impressive, including a rather good performance on the crucial bifurcated sample test.

The accelerator-residual funds theory is, if anything, though, clearly too simple rather than too complex. For example, failure to explain the 1952 cross-section data seemed to be linked to an inability of the theory to handle situations in which business firms were exceptionally liquid and already committed to rather large, long-run investment programs. Similarly, there were strong suggestions in both the cross-section and time-series results that expectational effects need to be more specifically recognized. This apparent need for more complex theories implies, of course, that even simpler investment hypotheses, such as naive accelerator models, are of limited value in explaining observed empirical behavior or, for that matter, formulating and developing public policy.

An adequate theory of investment behavior also seems to require the incorporation of monetary or interest rate effects, at least under certain circumstances. Specifically, the interest rate was an integral part of any model that provided a good empirical explanation of investment when high interest rates prevailed late in the upswing of the business cycle. Since good forecasts and structural understanding tend to be even more essential for public policy purposes late in the business cycle than at other times, this interest rate behavior pattern must be considered relevant, if not highly significant.

At least some information was obtained, moreover, on all of the four basic conceptual questions raised by the investment supply and demand analysis presented in Chapter I. The first of these four issues was the extent of any interest elasticity of demand for investment. As just noted, investment demand is apparently influenced in an important way by the interest rate when interest levels are high and the economy is near the upper turning point of the business cycle. On the other hand, there was little evidence of much interest elasticity for investment demand under other circumstances. In short, the relationship between investment demand and interest rates seems to be nonlinear and multiplicative with levels of business activity and liquid assets.

The second basic issue was defining which variables constitute the best measures of the general level of investment demand. While the interest rate is essentially a price variable, the level-of-demand variables are analogous to the income variables in a consumer demand equation or, following conventional characterizations, to "shift variables" in demand functions. In general, the empirical evidence strongly implied that capacity utilization and acceleration effects were the best measures of the level of investment demand. The accelerator effects, however, seemed to require substantial supplementation with measures of business expectations, the most promising of which seemed to be changes in equity or stock-price values. Furthermore, capacity or absolute sales formulations of acceleration concepts consistently performed better than simple change-in-sales accelerator models. In short, the general level of demand apparently is best represented by the rate of capacity utilization in combination with a measure of business expectations like movements in stock prices.

The third issue concerned the existence or nonexistence of a discontinuity in an individual firm's supply of funds function at the point where internal funds are exhausted. (It should be noted that the issue, insofar as this study was concerned, was strictly empirical; accordingly, some arguments that have been posed as to why this discontinuity will not exist under certain extremely unreal assumptions are not relevant.) [4] The probable existence of such a discontinuity was at least suggested by the sharp rise in external business borrowing and the increased importance of the interest rate observed at the end of cyclical upswings. The increased importance

[4] For a comprehensive discussion and evaluation of these arguments and their relevancy see John Lintner, "Dividends, Earnings, Leverage, Stock Prices and the Supply of Capital to Corporations," *Review of Economics and Statistics*, Vol. 44, No. 3 (August 1962), pp. 243–269.

of residual funds as a determinant of investment during periods of downturn is also considerably easier to rationalize if internal funds are valued differently from external funds. Accordingly, the observed evidence was at least consistent with the hypothesis that such a discontinuity or reduced supply elasticity exists.

On the fourth issue, relating to whether or not shifts in investment supply and demand functions are synchronized, the evidence suggests that a fair degree of synchronization does exist *except* at the very extremes of the business cycle. When the general business cycle is nearing its upper turning point, investment demand often seems to move ahead of the supply of internal funds, while on the downswing a contrary tendency exists for investment demand to fall below the rate at which internal funds are generated. Any excess of internal funds over investment demands during periods of recession seems to be used for the retirement of debt, particularly short-term, and improvement of liquidity stocks. There is, therefore, some justification for the notion that business firms attempt to set their dividend payoff and depreciation policies in a fashion which results in the supply of internal funds being adequate for investment needs on the average over the cycle. Debt is used mainly (though not exclusively and especially not in growth situations) to make short-run financial adjustments needed when investment outlays are unavoidably less than perfectly synchronized with fund flows. Furthermore, the degree to which businessmen will or can use debt as a short-run financial stabilizer may be related to the size of the firm since there was some limited evidence that smaller firms attempt to synchronize their fund flows and capital outlays more closely than large firms. One device for achieving this synchronization is for smaller firms to concentrate investment more in years of exceptional prosperity. In keeping with this pattern, large firms seemed to have been relatively heavy investors in 1952 when investment was not related to either fund flows or activity levels, but rather to the availability of liquidity stocks.

The supply and demand picture for business investment that thus emerges is one in which: (1) the supply of funds schedule is less elastic at the point where internal funds are exhausted; (2) the demand function is at least somewhat sensitive to interest or price effects at high rates and levels of activity; (3) the demand function shifts in response to changes in both capacity utilization and business expectations; and (4) demand shifts are synchronized to a large extent with changes in the position of the less elastic portion of the supply function. Such a simple summary, however, can be easily misleading. The essential problems in diagnosing investment patterns are knowing the relative juxtaposition of the different functions and accurately assessing the different elasticities at particular points in time. The number of possible configurations is almost infinite; indeed, it is perhaps accurate to say that no two periods of time have been or are likely to be exactly the same in terms of the weights placed on different determinants of business investment decisions. At one point of time (e.g., as in early 1952) it may have been the size of business liquidity stocks and of incomplete investment programs; at other times (late 1957 and possibly mid-1953) the state of external fund or debt markets may have been overriding; at still other times (1950–1951 and 1955–1956) the state of general business psychology or expectations might have been the single most important consideration. No simple theory, or even one as complex as the accelerator-residual funds theory, is likely to be accurate in all these different circumstances.

Still, the accelerator-residual funds theory, with its embodied simplifications, may have a role to play. Specifically, if there is one factor that seems to have more relevance in determining investment decisions in more circumstances than any other, it is almost surely the relationship of output to existing productive capacity. Furthermore, if there is a second factor of some universality, it would appear to be the state of internal business finances. But even these more general influences (particularly internal finances) have their distinct limitations with respect to time and stage of the cycle. Accordingly, circumspect forecasters and policy makers probably are well advised to think first of what is unique or special in a given circumstance and only secondly of what answers are yielded by formal application of existing theories and their empirical manifestations.

IV. *Policy*

In discussing policy, the customary distinctions between monetary and fiscal policy and between cyclical stabilization and economic growth are highly useful. Of the variables tested and found to be significant in this study, monetary policy can be expected to have a direct influence on the interest rate and, potentially at least, a substantial indirect influence on stock price. Direct monetary policy influences on investment achieved through the interest rate would seem to be mainly negative and limited to periods near the peak of the business cycle. The only possibility for exercising a positive impact through monetary policy might be if interest rates were quickly reduced near the peak of the cycle or shortly after the upper turning point so as to increase investment in the early stages of a cyclical downturn.

Proper application of monetary policy as a tool for cyclically restraining investment obviously will require an astute sense of timing. Among other difficulties, a considerable lag exists between a change in the interest rate and apparent realization of its effects. The question might be asked, moreover, whether a decrease in investment is ever really desired late in a cyclical upswing or early in a cyclical downswing, the times at which an increase in interest rates should be effective. The main justification for investment restraint in such circumstances would be as a weapon to combat price inflation occurring just before the cyclical peak. However, any carryover of investment depressants after the peak has been passed probably would not be considered desirable. Indeed, the only possible recent historical exception might have been 1958 when a "residual" price inflation seemed to occur early in the cyclical downturn. Even then, to have thus achieved price stability at a time when the economy was beginning to lose its momentum might have been considered rather costly in terms of both social and economic values.

The great advantage of fiscal policy over monetary policy as a means of regulating investment is that it has substantial positive as well as negative possibilities. Two types of fiscal action to stimulate investment seem possible: (1) direct stimulation by corporate or business tax relief; and (2) indirect stimulation by encouraging general consumer demand which, in turn, could be expected to increase capacity utilization and improve business expectations so as to shift the general level of investment demand upward.

The choice between using direct or indirect fiscal tools would seem to depend crucially, especially if the accelerator-residual funds hypothesis is tentatively accepted, on exactly what stage of the cycle existed. For example, in periods of mild recession, when residual funds or supply aspects dominate, direct techniques should be effective. Furthermore, and in keeping with what was observed about the timing of interest rate effects and the very special characteristics of 1952 investment patterns, any action that increases business liquidity may have a particularly pronounced effect upon investment in periods just after the upper turning point of the cycle or in periods when the economy is moving along a high plateau or upper cyclical ceiling. By contrast, in the early stages of a business upswing, when investment is often (though far from always) capacity-oriented and business funds are usually plentiful, an indirect approach to obtaining higher investment outlays via general stimulation of consumer demands would appear more promising. In such periods of expansion any increase in business liquidity effected by direct fiscal measures might be simply redundant.

In short, when increased investment is the objective, corporate tax relief or other forms of direct stimulus should be applied early in a downturn while general or consumer-oriented stimulants, including income tax reductions, would be most likely to have the desired effect late in a downturn or early in a recovery. To suppress or reduce investment demand the prescriptions would be almost exactly reversed. Specifically, an increase in business taxes, like an increase in interest rates, should be an effective restraint toward the end of the cyclical upswing, becoming increasingly effective after the early stages of business recovery have passed.

To take an illustrative example, the use of direct stimulants, like some sort of accelerated amortization or other business tax relief, probably would have worked reasonably well as a stimulant to business investment late in 1957 and early in 1958. If nothing else, such fiscal action would have helped counteract the depressing effects of the tight monetary policy of late 1957. Similarly, direct action to reduce the flow of liquidity to businesses in 1956 probably would have taken the edge off of the investment boom of 1955–1957 somewhat earlier. Indeed, the more generous depreciation clauses contained in the 1954 revision of the Internal Revenue Code may have been a fairly important offset during the 1955–1957 investment boom to the tight monetary policies of the period.

Contrasting examples of where indirect or general stimulation might have been potentially advantageous perhaps occurred in late 1953 and 1961; in these years business liquidity was quite high and capacity utilization remained relatively low. Therefore, a personal income tax reduction probably would have provided the surest, though admittedly indirect, inducement for business investment. Direct tax relief to business under the circumstances of 1953 and 1961 would have increased already plentiful supplies of funds and left essentially untouched the basic problems of increasing capacity utilization and improving business expectations.

Obviously, the proper use of fiscal policy as a tool for stabilizing business investment outlays requires as much sophistication and delicacy of timing as with monetary policy. The strong continuity in investment patterns suggested by the rather high coefficients recorded for lagged investment as an explanatory variable also implies that there is a limited scope for policy actions aimed at immediate or short-run investment stabilization. Under the best of circumstances only 20% to 40% of total manufacturing investment outlay would appear to be susceptible to short-run influences, say within one to three quarters. Of course, 20% to 40% of manufacturing investment, amounting as it does to approximately $3 to $5 billion a year at current levels, is a significant quantity, well worthy of public policy attention. Still, a considerable amount of sluggishness is always likely to exist in the movement of producers' durable expenditures over time.

Given this sluggishness and the timing difficulties alluded to, any really serious effort to achieve cyclical stabilization through policies aimed at modifying investment behavior would seem to be virtually impossible without employing highly flexible fiscal policies. The needed flexibility would be most easily achieved under a system in which the executive branch of the federal government operated with considerable administrative latitude in the setting of tax rates, and possibly transfer payments and other government expenditures as well. However, while administrative latitude is the most obvious method of achieving the desired flexibility, it is not necessarily the only one; nor is it necessarily the best because administrated flexibility is likely to be less predictable, thereby giving rise to potential uncertainty. Uncertainty, in turn, very well may have a deleterious effect on investment in and of itself because "waiting and seeing" is a not uncommon business reaction to relative indeterminacy, particularly when chances appear good that the indeterminacy may be shortly eliminated.

Automatic fiscal flexibility, as contrasted with discretionary, would not be easy to create legislatively but it surely should not be beyond the realm of possibility. The American fiscal system is already a rather complicated device with a considerable body of experience with automatic stabilizers. This very breadth and complexity presents a number of opportunities for creating different blends and balances between different fiscal and monetary policies.

In sum, *timing is of the essence* in stabilization policies. At the moment, monetary policy is clearly the most flexible of the available tools. Unfortunately, monetary policy mainly exercises a negative influence on investment decisions. To expect a policy device with this sort of serious limitation to bear the whole burden of stabilizing business investment outlays is clearly expecting a good deal. Even if monetary managers had the very best of wisdom and foresight, it would be virtually impossible for them to achieve investment stability with monetary policy alone. To pursue stability seriously as an objective, a policy tool which could more positively influence investment would be needed and a flexible fiscal policy, either automatic or under the executive branch's discretion, would seem to be indispensable.

Stability is not, of course, the only reasonable objective of public policy. Indeed, it could be argued that too much stability is undesirable. Recently, in fact, the focus of public policy as it affects business investment plans has been mainly on increasing the long-term growth of plant and equipment investment rather than short-run stabilization. Devices such as special tax credits for business investment outlays and revisions in the estimates of useful lives for tax reporting of depreciation charges have been much discussed and seriously considered.[5] By augmenting the probable flow of internally available funds, these devices would shift the discontinuity in the supply of funds schedule to the right on the average

---

[5] The revision of estimated useful lives for tax purposes actually was adopted as official policy after this was written. Also, special tax credits for investment have now been enacted.

over the cycle, at least initially. However, to derive a continued positive impact from such financial effects would require that the increased depreciation and lowered taxes were not fully reflected after an elapse of time in augmented dividends. Since there is quite a bit of evidence that dividend policy is slow to adapt to fund flow changes [6] and at least some evidence that depreciation charges are regarded as more than merely an accounting fiction by businessmen, a fair probability would seem to exist that the favorable financial implications of these investment incentives would persist for some time. Furthermore, to the extent that stockholders regard depreciation and special tax credits as legitimate charges against income, these policies might reduce the implicit cost assigned to funds retained by business managers, shifting the supply of funds schedule downward. Any special tax credit for investment outlays also decreases the cost of an investment outlay and thereby must increase its rate of return. This, in turn, should have at least some modestly favorable effects on investment demand.

The effectiveness of these inducements to invest depends, though, on the legitimacy of a number of less than fully substantiated assumptions about business and stockholder attitudes. To the extent, moreover, that shifts in investment supply and demand schedules are further synchronized by these policies, at least some of the positive impact may be dissipated. The extra retained funds simply might take the form of increased liquidity or other short-term holdings in a recession and reduced short-term borrowing during upswings. In short, if no substantial positive effects upon investment demand are exerted by these policies, the only result might be to increase the existing high degree of insulation of many corporations from external financial sources. This, in turn, should reduce the already limited effectiveness of monetary policy as a stabilizer. Indeed, by increasing the average level of business liquidity, most policies aimed at increasing investment growth by tax concession probably would decrease the general effectiveness of both fiscal and monetary stabilization efforts.

Determining the net effect of these conflicting tendencies is obviously difficult. A final evaluation is complicated, moreover, by the necessity to weigh stabilization against growth objectives. Taken

[6] See Lintner, "The Determinants of Corporate Savings."

together with the paucity of information on the validity of certain key assumptions, any final policy judgment almost necessarily must be subjective and at least a bit heuristic.

V. *A Postscript*

It is, of course, somewhat less than fully satisfying to conclude on such a note of uncertainty. A major message, in fact, of this final chapter, and one that was not fully intended or anticipated originally, is that we live in an economic world of great complexity and about which firm, well-substantiated knowledge is not very plentiful or easily obtained. This is hardly a communication that will prove inspiring, of course, to those who must in private or public life daily face and make decisions in spite of these complications. Nor can these decision makers be expected to be terribly sympathetic when the investigator pleads that his ignorance is the unavoidable result of an unkind Nature that refuses to perform historical experiments with the precision and controls of the laboratory.

The intention here, moreover, is not to argue that the economic world is totally devoid of all behavioral regularities. Identification of these regularities may not be an easy task and may require new tools and concepts, but it would still appear possible. Furthermore, in the present state of economic science in which there are often so many conflicting or alternative hypotheses, it is often a step forward if at least a few possibilities can be eliminated. It is, in short, perhaps better to know limitations than to exceed them. This study, hopefully, has contributed at least to a better knowledge of these limitations and even some small increment of information about the nature of regularities in business investment decisions and how these might be used to improve economic forecasting and policy.

The Sample: Industry Groupings and Included Firms

I. *Pulp, Paper and Related Products*

1. APW Products Co., Inc.
2. American Box Board Co.
3. American Seal-Kap Corp.
4. American Writing Paper Co.
5. Camp Manufacturing Co., Inc.
6. Champion Paper and Fibre Co.
7. Chesapeake Corp. of Virginia
8. Consolidated Paper Co.
9. Consolidated Water Power & Paper Co.
10. Container Corp. of America
11. Dennison Mfg. Co.
12. Dixie Cup Co.
13. Dobeckmun Co.
14. Eastern Corp.
15. Eddy Paper Corp.
16. Gaylord Container Co.
17. Glatfelter Co., P.H.
18. Hammermill Paper Co.
19. International Paper Co.
20. Keyes Fibre Co.
21. Lily-Tulip Cup Corp.
22. Marathon Corp.
23. Mead Corp.
24. Nashua Gummed & Coated Paper Co.
25. National Container Corp.
26. Oswego Falls Corp.
27. Rayonier, Inc.
28. River Raisin Paper Co.
29. Robert Gair Co.
30. Scott Paper Co.
31. S. D. Warren Co.
32. Sonoco Products Co.
33. Southland Paper Mills, Inc.
34. Standard Cap and Seal Corp.
35. St. Regis Paper Co.
36. United Board and Carton Corp.
37. Union Bag & Paper Corp.
38. West Virginia Pulp & Paper Co.

II. *Light Chemicals*

1. Abbot Laboratories
2. Allied Laboratories Inc.
3. American Home Products Corp.
4. Bon Ami Company
5. Bristol-Myers Company
6. B. T. Babbitt, Inc.
7. Colgate-Palmolive-Peet Co.
8. Cook Paint and Varnish Co.
9. Devoe Raynolds Co. Inc.
10. Ferro Corporation
11. General Paint Corp.
12. Glidden Company
13. Grand Rapids Varnish Corp.
14. Norwich Pharmacal Co.
15. Parke, Davis and Company
16. Patterson-Sargent Co.
17. Plough Inc.
18. Rexall Drug Company
19. Sterling Drug Inc.
20. Valspar Corporation

III. *Heavy Chemicals*

1. Air Reduction Co. Inc.
2. American Cyanamid Co.
3. American Potash and Chemical Corp.
4. Atlas Powder Company
5. California Ink Company
6. Celanese Corp. of America
7. Columbian Carbon Co.
8. Commercial Solvents Corp.
9. Consolidated Chemical Industries Inc.
10. Continental-Diamond Fibre Co.
11. duPont de Nemours & Co.
12. Harshaw Chemical Co.
13. Hercules Powder Co.
14. Heyden Chemical Corp.
15. Hooker Electrochemical Co.
16. Industrial Rayon Corp.
17. Interchemical Corp.
18. Koppers Co., Inc.
19. Lithium Corp. of America, Inc.
20. Mathieson Chemical Corp.
21. Monroe Chemical Co.
22. Monsanto Chemical Co.
23. National Vulcanized Fibre Co.
24. National Cylinder Gas Co.
25. Newport Industries, Inc.
26. Nopco Chemical Co.
27. Park Chemical Co.
28. Pennsylvania Salt Mfg. Co.
29. Pfizer & Co., Inc., Chas.
30. Publicker Industries Inc.
31. Sun Chemical Corp.
32. Union Carbide & Carbon Corp.
33. United Carbon Co.
34. United States Potash Co.
35. Victor Chemical Works

IV. *Petroleum*

1. Anderson-Prichard Oil Corp.
2. Atlantic Refining Co.
3. Cities Service Co.
4. Continental Oil Co.
5. Crown Central Petroleum Corp.
6. Deep Rock Oil Corp.
7. Gulf Oil Corp.
8. Lion Oil Co.
9. Mid-Continent-Petroleum Corp.
10. Mohawk Petroleum Corp.
11. Ohio Oil Co.
12. Panhandle Producing & Refining Co.
13. Phillips Petroleum Co.
14. Plymouth Oil Co.

15. Pure Oil Co.
16. Quaker State Oil Refining Corp.
17. Richfield Oil Corp.
18. Roosevelt Oil Refining Corp.
19. Shamrock Oil & Gas Corp.
20. Shell Oil Co.
21. Sinclair Oil Corp.
22. Skelly Oil Co.
23. Socony Mobil Oil Co.
24. Standard Oil of New Jersey
25. Standard Oil of Ohio
26. Standard Oil of California
27. Standard Oil of Indiana
28. Sun Oil Co.
29. Texas Co., The
30. Tide Water Associated Oil Co.
31. Union Oil Co. of California

V. *Rubber*

1. B. F. Goodrich Co.
2. Brown Rubber Co. Inc.
3. Dayton Rubber Co.
4. Firestone Tire & Rubber Co.
5. General Tire & Rubber Co.
6. Goodyear Tire & Rubber Co.
7. Hewitt Robins Inc.
8. Kleinert Rubber Co.
9. Lee Rubber & Tire Corp.
10. Mansfield Tire & Rubber Co.
11. Midwest Rubber Reclaiming Co.
12. Seiberling Rubber Co.
13. Thermoid Co.
14. United States Rubber Co.

VI. *Heavy Steel*

1. Acme Steel Co.
2. Alan Wood Steel Co.

3. Alleghany Ludlum Steel Corp.
4. American Brake Shoe Co.
5. Armco Steel Corp.
6. Barium Steel Corp.
7. Bethlehem Steel Corp.
8. Bliss & Laughlin, Inc.
9. Central Foundry Co., The
10. Continental Steel Corp.
11. Crucible Steel Co. of America
12. Detroit Steel Corp.
13. Detroit Gray Iron Foundry Co.
14. Duraloy Co.
15. Eastern Stainless Steel Corp.
16. General Steel Casting Corp.
17. Granite City Steel
18. Inland Steel Co.
19. Interlake Iron Corp.
20. Jessop Steel Co.
21. Jones & Laughlin Steel Corp.
22. Lukens Steel Co.
23. Midwest Piping & Supply Co., Inc.
24. Midland Steel Products Co.
25. Molybdenum Corp. of America
26. Moore Drop Forging Co.
27. National Steel Corp.
28. National Malleable & Steel Castings Co.
29. Pittsburgh Forgings Co.
30. Pittsburgh Coke & Chemical Co.
31. Poor and Co.
32. Republic Steel Corp.
33. Rotary Electric Steel Co.
34. Scullin Steel Co.
35. Sharon Steel Corp.
36. Superior Steel Corp.
37. Transue & Williams Steel Forging Corp.
38. Universal-Cyclops Steel Corp.
39. United States Steel Corp.

40. United States Pipe & Foundry Co.
41. Vanadium Corp. of America
42. Vanadium-Alloys Steel Co.
43. Wheeling Steel Corp.
44. Woodward Iron Co.
45. Youngstown Sheet & Tube Co.

VII. *Miscellaneous Fabricated Metal Products (Rivets, Screws, Wire, Roller Bearings, etc.)*

1. Aero Supply Mfg. Co.
2. American Screw Co.
3. Anaconda Wire & Cable Co.
4. Atlas Tack Corp.
5. Belmont Iron Works
6. Belden Mfg. Co.
7. Fanner Manufacturing Co.
8. General Cable Corp.
9. Hoover Ball & Bearing Co.
10. Lamson and Sessions Co.
11. Macwhyte Co.
12. Metal Textile Corp.
13. Metals Disintegrating Co., Inc.
14. Mullins Mfg. Corp.
15. National Tank Co.
16. Pheoll Manufacturing Co.
17. Pittsburgh Screw & Bolt Corp.
18. Rheem Mfg. Co.
19. Rome Cable Corp.
20. Timken Roller Bearing Co.
21. Union Wire Rope Corp.
22. United Carr Fastener Corp.
23. Van Dorn Iron Works Co.

VIII. *Special Industrial Machinery*

1. American Laundry Mach. Co.

2. Automatic Voting Machine Corp.
3. Babcock Wilcox
4. Balcrank Inc.
5. Brown McLaren Mfg. Co.
6. Cherry-Burrel Corp.
7. Continental Gin Co.
8. Daystrom Inc.
9. Food Mach. and Chem. Corp.
10. Foster Wheeler Corp.
11. Gellman Mfg. Co.
12. Hobart Mfg. Co.
13. Intertype Corp.
14. Kent Inc. Moore Organization, Inc.
15. Key Co.
16. Lanston Monotype Machine Co.
17. Manning, Maxwell & Moore, Inc.
18. Meyer-Blanke Co.
19. National Cellulose Corp.
20. National Rubber Mach. Co.
21. Tokheim Corp.
22. Victor Equipment Co.
23. Wayne Pump Co.

IX. *Light Electrical Goods and Machinery*

1. American Bosch Corp.
2. American Phenolic Corp.
3. Casco Products Corp.
4. Edison Inc., Thomas A.
5. Electric Storage Battery Co.
6. Electric Autolite Co.
7. Felt & Tarrant Mfg. Co.
8. General Instrument Corp.
9. General Railway Signal Co.
10. Globe-Union Inc.
11. International Resistance Co.
12. Kingston Products Corp.

13. Muter Co.
14. National Cash Register Co.
15. National Union Radio Corp.
16. Oak Mfg. Co.
17. Pitney-Bowes, Inc.
18. Rudy Mfg. Co.
19. Sprague Electric Co.
20. Tung-Sol Electric Inc.
21. Underwood Corp.

X. *Automotive Fabricators*

1. Budd Co.
2. Checker Cab Mfg. Corp.
3. Chrysler Corp.
4. Diamond T. Motor Car Co.
5. Divco Corp.
6. Fruehauf Trailer Co.
7. General Motors Corp.
8. Hastings Mfg. Co.
9. Liberty Products Corp.
10. Mack Truck Co.
11. Marmon-Herrington Co., Inc.
12. Motor Wheel Corp.
13. Pressed Metals of America, Inc.
14. Seagrave Corp.
15. Twin Coach Co.

XI. *Household Durables*

1. A. C. Gilbert Co.
2. American Safety Razor Corp.
3. Automatic Washer Co.
4. Cribben and Sexton Co.
5. Detroit and Michigan Stove Co.
6. Easy Washing Machine Corp.
7. Eureka Williams Corp.
8. George D. Roper Corp.
9. Gillette Co.
10. Ironrite Inc.
11. Knapp-Monarch Co.
12. Maytag Co.

13. McGraw Electric Co.
14. Silex Co.
15. Thor Corp.
16. Whirlpool Corp.
17. White Sewing Machine Corp.

XII. *Machine Tools*

1. Allied Products Corp.
2. Brown Sharpe Mfg. Co.
3. Bullard Co.
4. Cincinnati Milling Mach. Co.
5. E. W. Bliss Co.
6. Giddings and Lewis Mach. Tool Co.
7. Gisholt Machine Co.
8. Greenfield Tap and Die Corp.
9. Hanson-Van Winkle-Munning Co.
10. Hydraulic Press Mfg. Co.
11. McKay Machine Co.
12. Mesta Machine Co.
13. Monarch Machine Tool Co.
14. National Acme Co.
15. Seneca Falls Machine Co.
16. Simonds Saw and Steel Co.
17. South Bend Lathe Works
18. Sundstrand Machine Tool Co.
19. Superior Tool and Die Co.
20. Udylite Corp.
21. United Eng. and Foundry Co.
22. Van Norman Co.
23. Warner and Swasey Co.

XIII. *Heavy Electrical Machinery*

1. Century Electric Co.
2. Clark Controller Co.
3. Cutler-Hammer, Inc.
4. Elliott Company
5. General Electric Co.

6. Harvey Hubbell Inc.
7. Howell Elec. Motors Co.
8. I-T-E Circuit Breaker Co.
9. Jack and Heintz, Inc.
10. Joslyn Mfg. and Supply Co.
11. Master Electric Co.
12. Philadelphia Insulated Wire Co.
13. Reliance Electric and Engr. Co.
14. Sangamo Electric Co.
15. Speer Carbon Co.
16. Square D Co.
17. The Louis Allis Co.
18. Wagner Electric Corp.
19. Westinghouse Electric Corp.

XIV. *Basic Textiles*

1. Bates Mfg. Co.
2. Beaunit Mills Inc.
3. Blumenthal Co. Inc.
4. Belding Heminway Co. Inc.
5. Cannon Mills Co.
6. Century Ribbon Mills, Inc.
7. Collins and Aikman Corp.
8. J. P. Stevens Co.
9. Kendall Co.
10. Liberty Fabrics, Inc.
11. Mount Vernon-Woodberry Mills, Inc.
12. M. Lowenstein Sons Inc.
13. Robbins Mills Inc.
14. Verney Corp.
15. Wyandotte Worsted Co.

XV. *Other Textiles*

1. Adams-Millis Corp.
2. Armstrong Cork Co.
3. Bigelow-Sanford Carpet Co., Inc.
4. Claussner Hosiery Co.

5. Congoleum-Nairn Inc.
6. Davenport Hosiery Mills
7. Firth Carpet Co.
8. Gotham Hosiery Co.
9. Lees & Sons Co.
10. Mohawk Carpet Mills, Inc.
11. Mojud Hosiery Co., Inc.
12. Phoenix Hosiery Co.
13. Real Silk Hosiery Mills, Inc.
14. Van Raalte Co., Inc.
15. Wayne Knitting Mills, Inc.

XVI. *Automobile Parts and Accessories*

1. Ainsworth Mfg. Corp.
2. American Metal Prod. Co.
3. Arvin Industries, Inc.
4. Borg-Warner Corp.
5. Clark Equipment Co.
6. Cleveland Graphite Bronze Co.
7. Eaton Mfg. Co.
8. Federal Mogul Corp.
9. Gabriel Co.
10. Hurd Lock and Mfg. Co.
11. Lakey Foundry Co.
12. McQuay Norris Mfg. Co.
13. Michigan Bumper Co.
14. Muskegon Piston Ring Co.
15. Pierce Governor, Inc.
16. Soss Mfg. Co.
17. Sheller Mfg. Corp.
18. Standard Tube Co.
19. Stewart Warner Corp.
20. Thompson Products, Inc.
21. Universal Products Co., Inc.

XVII. *General Industrial Machinery*

1. American Chain and Cable Co.

2. American Machine and Metals, Inc.
3. Buffalo Forge Co.
4. Byron Jackson Co.
5. Chain Belt Co.
6. Chicago Pneumatic Tool Co.
7. Comb.-Eng. Superheater, Inc.
8. Dresser Industries, Inc.
9. Economy Baler Co.
10. Fairbanks, Morse and Co.
11. Gardner Denver Co.
12. Hein Werner Corp.
13. Ingersoll-Rand Co.
14. Link-Belt Co.
15. National Motor Bearing Co., Inc.
16. Reda Pump Co.
17. Thor Power Tool Co.
18. Walworth Co.
19. Worthington Pump & Mach. Corp.

XVIII. *Heavy Equipment, Engines, and Turbines*

1. Allis-Chalmers Mfg. Co.
2. Athey Products Corp.
3. Briggs and Stratton Corp.
4. Bucyrus Erie Co.
5. Caterpillar Tractor Co.
6. Cleveland Trencher Co.
7. Continental Motors Corp.
8. Cooper-Bessemer Corp.
9. Cummins Engine Co. Inc.
10. Deere and Co.
11. Emsco Derrick & Equip. Co.
12. Gar Wood Industries, Inc.
13. Hercules Motors Corp.
14. International Harvester Co.
15. J. I. Case Co.
16. Minneapolis Moline Co.

17. National Supply Co.
18. Oliver Corp.
19. Reed Roller Bit Co.

XIX. *Air Conditioners, Heating, Containers, and Related Products*

1. American Air Filter Co.
2. American Can Co.
3. American Radiator and Stand. Sanitary Corp.
4. Bell and Gosset Co.
5. Carrier Corp.
6. Continental Can Co.
7. Crane Co.
8. Crown Cork and Seal Co., Inc.
9. Detroit Steel Products Co.
10. General Bronze Corp.
11. Holland Furnace Co.
12. Hussmann Refrigerator Co.
13. Iron Fireman Mfg. Co.
14. Kawneer Co.
15. Otis Elevator Co.
16. Richmond Radiator Co.
17. Trane Co.
18. United States Air Conditioning Corp.
19. Yale and Towne Mfg. Co.

XX. *Electronics*

1. Admiral Corp.
2. Aircraft Radio Corp.
3. Dumont Labs, Inc.
4. Emerson Radio & Phono. Corp.
5. Lear, Inc.
6. Radio Corp. of America
7. Stromberg-Carlson Co.
8. Sylvania Elec. Prod.
9. Zenith Radio Corp.

Appendix **B** | *Time-Series Data*

THIS APPENDIX tabulates the data used with the time-series models in Chapters VII, VIII, and IX. The variable codes are discussed in Chapters III and VII. In keeping with the practice used throughout this study of bifurcating the series, Section I below tabulates the "historical" period and Section II, the seven-quarter "forecast" period. In Section III the series, modified in accordance with footnote 5, Chapter IX, are listed. Only those series and observations affected are shown. The last eleven quarters of the series in Section III comprise the extended forecast period used in Chapter IX. Section IV extends the series for r_{t-3}, SP_{t-1}, and ΔSP_{t-1} to the end of the eleven-quarter forecast period. Where applicable, figures are in millions of 1954 dollars.

I. *Original Data: "Historical" Period Observations*

Year	Quarter	I_t	I_{t-2}	C_{t-1}^P	C_{t-2}^P
1949	3	1947.	2152.	.92	.96
	4	2084.	2174.	.94	.92
1950	1	1693.	1947.	.93	.94
	2	2000.	2084.	.98	.93
	3	2101.	1693.	1.06	.98
	4	2728.	2000.	1.08	1.06
1951	1	2287.	2101.	1.02	1.08
	2	2863.	2728.	1.02	1.02
	3	2855.	2287.	1.00	1.02
	4	3341.	2863.	.97	1.00
1952	1	2706.	2855.	.98	.97
	2	3146.	3341.	1.00	.98
	3	2787.	2706.	.99	1.00
	4	3335.	3146.	1.02	.99
1953	1	2731.	2787.	1.08	1.02
	2	3114.	3335.	1.02	1.08
	3	2864.	2731.	1.01	1.02
	4	3317.	3114.	.99	1.01
1954	1	2582.	2864.	.94	.99
	2	2853.	3317.	.90	.94
	3	2642.	2582.	.91	.90
	4	2959.	2853.	.91	.91
1955	1	2225.	2642.	.93	.91
	2	2735.	2959.	.98	.93
	3	2815.	2225.	1.02	.98
	4	3345.	2735.	1.02	1.02
1956	1	2777.	2815.	1.02	1.02
	2	3432.	3345.	.99	1.02
	3	3479.	2777.	.99	.99
	4	3933.	3432.	.98	.99
1957	1	3077.	3479.	1.01	.98
	2	3625.	3933.	1.00	1.01
	3	3448.	3077.	.99	1.00
	4	3639.	3625.	.99	.99
1958	1	2471.	3448.	.94	.99
	2	2484.	3639.	.87	.94
	3	2254.	2471.	.87	.87
	4	2464.	2484.	.92	.87

Year	Quarter	C^M_{t-1}	C^M_{t-2}	FA_{t-1}	$(T-V)_{t-1}$
1949	3	.71	.74	49096.	2327.
	4	.71	.71	50520.	2865.
1950	1	.69	.71	51844.	1810.
	2	.72	.60	51936.	2903.
	3	.77	.72	52737.	3834.
	4	.82	.77	51914.	4054.
1951	1	.81	.82	52412.	2695.
	2	.82	.81	51736.	3543.
	3	.80	.82	52931.	3307.
	4	.77	.80	54406.	2580.
1952	1	.76	.77	56547.	2299.
	2	.77	.76	57085.	2668.
	3	.75	.77	50579.	2748.
	4	.76	.75	59951.	2844.
1953	1	.80	.76	61740.	2841.
	2	.81	.80	62037.	3190.
	3	.81	.81	62064.	3333.
	4	.79	.81	62890.	3255.
1954	1	.73	.79	65137.	2505.
	2	.70	.73	65122.	3002.
	3	.69	.70	65916.	3368.
	4	.69	.69	67095.	3096.
1955	1	.69	.69	68827.	2935.
	2	.72	.69	68239.	3794.
	3	.74	.77	68301.	4379.
	4	.74	.74	68940.	4104.
1956	1	.74	.74	69498.	3727.
	2	.73	.74	69278.	4106.
	3	.72	.73	69811.	4249.
	4	.70	.72	71005.	3761.
1957	1	.71	.70	72361.	3776.
	2	.70	.71	72818.	3993.
	3	.69	.70	73763.	3961.
	4	.68	.69	74807.	3721.
1958	1	.63	.68	76272.	3243.
	2	.58	.63	76725.	2568.
	3	.58	.58	77069.	2940.
	4	.60	.58	77721.	3448.

Year	Quarter	r_{t-3}	SP_{t-1}	S'_t	ΔSP_{t-1}
1949	3	2.71	14.29	1506.	−4.
	4	2.61	14.93	−273.	4.
1950	1	2.63	15.92	545.	7.
	2	2.55	16.83	6702.	6.
	3	2.52	18.18	5146.	8.
	4	2.51	18.35	2135.	1.
1951	1	2.53	20.01	408.	9.
	2	2.56	21.81	168.	9.
	3	2.60	22.14	−3226.	1.
	4	2.64	23.21	3839.	5.
1952	1	2.83	23.57	−2764.	2.
	2	2.80	24.23	611.	3.
	3	2.85	24.19	−321.	0.
	4	2.85	25.36	7145.	5.
1953	1	2.86	25.34	−1800.	0.
	2	2.87	26.23	1699.	4.
	3	2.92	24.66	−2372.	−6.
	4	3.01	24.04	−1141.	−3.
1954	1	3.27	24.44	−4099.	2.
	2	3.16	26.13	1482.	7.
	3	3.05	28.87	−1870.	10.
	4	2.88	31.27	4012.	9.
1955	1	2.81	34.62	771.	10.
	2	2.80	37.50	3773.	8.
	3	2.80	39.79	−1149.	6.
	4	2.92	45.46	3399.	14.
1956	1	2.98	46.85	−2685.	3.
	2	3.04	48.20	764.	3.
	3	3.06	50.13	−2950.	4.
	4	3.06	51.44	4228.	3.
1957	1	3.20	49.41	−2082.	−4.
	2	3.35	47.13	212.	−5.
	3	3.60	49.82	−1680.	6.
	4	3.58	49.86	−293.	0.
1958	1	3.68	43.71	−6374.	−12.
	2	3.96	44.32	−1259.	1.
	3	3.82	46.41	1405.	5.
	4	3.44	50.79	4327.	9.

Year	Quarter	S'_{t-1}	Q_1	Q_2	Q_4
1949	3	−642.	0.	0.	0.
	4	1506.	0.	0.	1.
1950	1	−273.	1.	0.	0.
	2	545.	0.	1.	0.
	3	6702.	0.	0.	0.
	4	5146.	0.	0.	1.
1951	1	2135.	1.	0.	0.
	2	408.	0.	1.	0.
	3	168.	0.	0.	0.
	4	−3226.	0.	0.	1.
1952	1	3839.	1.	0.	0.
	2	−2764.	0.	1.	0.
	3	611.	0.	0.	0.
	4	−321.	0.	0.	1.
1953	1	7145.	1.	0.	0.
	2	−1800.	0.	1.	0.
	3	1699.	0.	0.	0.
	4	−2372.	0.	0.	1.
1954	1	−1141.	1.	0.	0.
	2	−4099.	0.	1.	0.
	3	1482.	0.	0.	0.
	4	−1870.	0.	0.	1.
1955	1	4012.	1.	0.	0.
	2	−771.	0.	1.	0.
	3	3773.	0.	0.	0.
	4	−1149.	0.	0.	1.
1956	1	3399.	1.	0.	0.
	2	−2685.	0.	1.	0.
	3	764.	0.	0.	0.
	4	−2950.	0.	0.	1.
1957	1	4228.	1.	0.	0.
	2	−2082.	0.	1.	0.
	3	212.	0.	0.	0.
	4	−1680.	0.	0.	1.
1958	1	−293.	1.	0.	0.
	2	−6374.	0.	1.	0.
	3	1259.	0.	0.	0.
	4	1405.	0.	0.	1.

II. *Original Data:* *"Future"* or *"Forecast"* *Period* *Observations*

Year	Quarter	I_t	I_{t-2}	C_{t-1}^M
1959	1	2047.	2254.	.62
	2	2495.	2464.	.64
	3	2487.	2047.	.68
	4	2959.	2495.	.65
1960	1	2556.	2487.	.64
	2	3120.	2959.	.68
	3	3022.	2556.	.66

Year	Quarter	$(T-V)_{t-1}$	r_{t-3}	SP_{t-1}	ΔSP_{t-1}
1959	1	3809.	3.35	55.92	10.
	2	3738.	3.72	59.05	6.
	3	4622.	3.95	61.59	4.
	4	3698.	4.01	63.06	2.
1960	1	3421.	4.27	62.02	−2.
	2	3858.	4.36	60.19	−3.
	3	3949.	4.44	59.79	−1.

Year	Quarter	Q_1	Q_2	Q_4
1959	1	1.	0.	0.
	2	0.	1.	0.
	3	0.	0.	0.
	4	0.	0.	1.
1960	1	1.	0.	0.
	2	0.	1.	0.
	3	0.	0.	0.

III. *Modified Data: Observations for Series and Period Affected*

Year	Quarter	I_t	I_{t-2}	C^M_{t-1}	$(T-V)_{t-1}$
1957	1	3075.	3479.	.71	3776.
	2	3622.	3933.	.70	3989.
	3	3445.	3075.	.69	3958.
	4	3648.	3622.	.68	3717.
1958	1	2462.	3445.	.63	3251.
	2	2482.	3648.	.58	2559.
	3	2246.	2462.	.58	2938.
	4	2460.	2482.	.60	3436.
1959	1	2043.	2246.	.62	3803.
	2	2492.	2460.	.64	3725.
	3	2475.	2043.	.68	4618.
	4	2943.	2492.	.65	3680.
1960	1	2541.	2475.	.64	3404.
	2	3077.	2943.	.67	3837.
	3	2960.	2541.	.66	3894.
	4	3295.	3077.	.63	3591.
1961	1	2451.	2960.	.63	3297.
	2	2820.	3295.	.60	3019.
	3	2715.	2451.	.63	3958.

IV. *Extension of Series to End of Eleven-Quarter "Forecast" Period*

Year	Quarter	r_{t-3}	SP_{t-1}	ΔSP_{t-1}
1960	4	4.43	59.06	−1.
1961	1	4.34	58.67	−1.
	2	4.18	65.58	12.
.	3	4.17	59.82	6.

Selected Bibliography on Investment Decisions (mid-1956 through 1962)[*]

Bowman, Mary J. (ed.), *Expectations, Uncertainty and Business Behavior.* New York: Social Science Research Council, Committee on Business Enterprise Research, 1958.

Brockie, Melvin D. and Grey, Arthur L., Jr., "The Marginal Efficiency of Capital and Investment Programming," *Economic Journal*, Vol. 66, No. 269 (December 1956), pp. 662–676.

Brown, E. Cary, Solow, R. M., Ando, A., and Kareken, J., "Lags in Fiscal and Monetary Policy," Commission on Money and Credit.

Brown, Murray and Roseman, Herman, "Cross-Section Analysis of Manufacturing Investment During 1951–1955," *Proceedings of the Business and Economic Statistics Section of the American Statistical Association*, 1957, pp. 344–351.

Butler, William F., "Capacity Utilization and the Rate of Profitability in Manufacturing," *American Economic Review*, Vol. 48, No. 2 (May 1958), pp. 239–248.

Cohen, M., "Anticipations Data in the Capital Goods Field," *Proceedings of the Business and Economic Statistics Section of the American Statistical Association*, Washington, 1957, pp. 193–198.

Darling, Paul G., "Surrogative Measurements of Expectations: An Example in Estimating the Liquidity Influence on Investment," *Review of Economics and Statistics*, Vol. 38, No. 4 (November 1956), pp. 413–426.

---

[*] A selected bibliography on investment decisions pertaining to literature published prior to 1956 can be found in Meyer, John R. and Kuh, Edwin, *The Investment Decision* (Cambridge: Harvard University Press, 1957), pp. 269–277.

274   *Investment Decisions, Economic Forecasting, and Public Policy*

deLeeuw, Frank, "The Demand for Capital by Manufacturers," paper presented at Meeting of the Econometric Society, St. Louis, December 1960. Abstract in *Econometrica*, Vol. 29, No. 3 (July 1961), p. 474.

Duesenberry, James S., *Business Cycles and Economic Growth*. New York: McGraw-Hill Book Company, 1958.

Durand, David, "The Cost of Capital, Corporation Finance and the Theory of Investment: A Comment," *American Economic Review*, Vol. 49, No. 4 (September 1959), pp. 639–654.

Eckaus, R. S. and Lefeber, Louis, "Capital Formation: A Theoretical and Empirical Analysis," *Review of Economics and Statistics*, Vol. 44, No. 2 (May 1962), pp. 113—122.

Eisner, Robert, "A Distributed Lag Investment Function," *Econometrica*, Vol. 21, No. 1 (January 1960), pp. 1–29.

——, and Strotz, R., "The Determinants of Business Investment," *Impacts of Monetary Policy*, Commission on Money and Credit Research Monographs (Englewood Cliffs, New Jersey: Prentice-Hall, 1963).

Foss, Murray F. and Natrella, Vito, "Ten Years' Experience with Business Investment Anticipations," *Survey of Current Business*, Vol. 37, No. 1 (January 1957), pp. 16–24.

Friend, Irwin and Kravis, Irving B., "Entrepreneurial Income, Saving, and Investment," *American Economic Review*, Vol. 47, No 3 (June 1957), pp. 269–301.

Fromm, Gary, "Inventory Fluctations and Cyclical Instability," paper presented at Meeting of the Econometric Society, December 1961. Abstract in *Econometrica*, Vol. 30, No. 3 (June 1962), p. 587.

Gehrels, Franz and Wiggins, Suzanne, "Interest Rates and Manufacturers' Fixed Investments," *American Economic Review*, Vol. 47, No. 1 (March 1957), pp. 79–92.

Gordon, Myron J., "The Savings Investment and Valuation of a Corporation," *Review of Economics and Statistics*, Vol. 44, No. 1 (February 1962), pp. 37–51.

Grunfeld, Yehuda, "The Determinants of Corporate Investment," in Arnold C. Harberger (ed.), *The Demand for Durable Goods*. Chicago: University of Chicago Press, 1960.

Jorgenson, D., "Anticipations, Appropriations and Investment Behavior in U.S. Business: Quarterly 1947–1960," University of California at Berkeley, 1962, mimeographed.

Kisselgoff, Avram and Modigliani, Franco, "Private Investment in the Electric Power Industry and the Acceleration Principle," *Review of Economics and Statistics*, Vol. 39, No. 4 (November 1957), pp. 363–379.

Kuh, Edwin, "The Validity of Cross-Sectionally Estimated Behavior

Equations in Times Series Applications," *Econometrica*, Vol. 27, No. 2 (April 1959), pp. 197–214.

——, *Capital Stock Growth*, forthcoming.

——, "Theory and Institutions in the Study of Investment Behavior," *American Economic Review*, Vol. 53, No. 2 (May 1963), pp. 260–268.

——, and Meyer, John R., "Investment, Liquidity, and Monetary Policy," *Impacts of Monetary Policy*, Commission on Money and Credit Monographs (Englewood Cliffs, New Jersey: Prentice-Hall, 1963).

Lanzillotti, Robert F., "Pricing Objectives in Large Companies," *American Economic Review*, Vol. 48, No. 5 (December 1958), pp. 921–940.

Liebling, Herman I., "Financing Business in Recession and Expansion," *Survey of Current Business*, Vol. 38, No. 10 (October 1958), pp. 15–20.

Lindsay, Robert, "The Stability of Business Capital Outlays," *Review of Economics and Statistics*, Vol. 40, No. 2 (May 1958), pp. 159–163.

Lintner, John, "Dividends, Earnings, Leverage, Stock Prices, and the Supply of Capital to Corporations," *Review of Economics and Statistics*, Vol. 44, No. 3 (August 1962), pp. 243–269.

Liu, Ta Chung, "An Exploratory Quarterly Econometric Model of Effective Demand in the Postwar U.S. Economy," Cornell University, Ithaca, mimeographed.

——, "A Simple Forecasting Model for the U.S. Economy," *International Monetary Fund Staff Papers*, Vol. 4, No. 3 (August 1955), pp. 434–466.

Maisel, Sherman J., *Fluctuations, Growth, and Forecasting: The Principles of Dynamic Business Economics*. New York: John Wiley & Sons, 1957.

Modigliani, Franco and Miller, Merton H., "The Cost of Capital, Corporation Finance and the Theory of Investment," *American Economic Review*, Vol. 48, No. 3 (June 1958), pp. 261–297.

——, and Weingartner, H. M., "Forecasting Uses of Anticipatory Data on Investment and Sales," *Quarterly Journal of Economics*, Vol. 72, No. 1 (February 1958), pp. 23–54.

National Bureau of Economic Research, Conference on Research in Income and Wealth, *Problems of Capital Formation: Concepts, Measurement and Controlling Factors*, Studies in Income and Wealth, Vol. 19. Princeton: Princeton University Press, 1957.

Nerlove, Marc, *The Dynamics of Supply: Estimation of Farmers' Response to Price*. Baltimore: Johns Hopkins Press, 1958.

Nevile, J. W., "Professor Hicks' Theory of Investment and Postwar Investment Figures in Australia and the United States," *Economic Record*, Vol. 34, No. 68 (August 1958), pp. 249–253.

Simon, Herbert, "Theories of Decision-Making in Economics and Behavioral Science," *American Economic Review*, Vol. 49, No. 3 (June 1959), pp. 253–283.

Spiro, Alan, "Empirical Research and the Rate of Interest," *Review of Economics and Statistics*, Vol. 40, No. 1 (February 1958), pp. 52–58.

Steger, Wilbur A., "Countercyclical Corporate Tax Rates," *Southern Economic Journal*, Vol. 25, No. 1 (July 1958), pp. 97–101.

Terborgh, George W., "Business Investment for Stability and Growth," *American Economic Review*, Vol. 47, No. 2 (May 1957), pp. 132–134.

Weston, J. Fred, "The Management of Corporate Capital: A Review Article," *Journal of Business* (University of Chicago), Vol. 34, No. 2 (April 1961), pp. 129–139.

White, William H., "The Rate of Interest, Marginal Efficiency of Capital and Investment Programming," *Economic Journal*, Vol. 68, No. 269 (March 1958), pp. 51–59.

Index

277

ABSTRACT

Investment Decisions, Economic Forecasting, and Public Policy

This study is a part of a broader program of research in the area of "Profits and the Functioning of the American Economy" going forward at the Harvard Business School under the direction of Professor John Lintner. This program has consisted of a series of interrelated studies focusing on particular decisions of management in which profits play a key role either as a source of funds or as expected returns which provide incentives to take action.

This particular study focuses on the determinants of investment outlays of business corporations. It should be of primary interest to those parts of business organizations involved in general forecasting and especially forecasting of plant and equipment expenditures, and to other economists studying business investment and its implications for growth and stability.

The authors are John R. Meyer, Professor of Economics, Harvard University, and Robert R. Glauber, Doctoral Research Fellow, Harvard Graduate School of Business Administration.

The theory and measurement of investment behavior is one of the most controversial areas of professional economic study. The subject is inherently difficult and complex, the data available for performing empirical evaluations are not always of the highest quality or the type needed and specific theories, concepts, or views of investment behavior have become intimately associated with justifications for particular tax and fiscal programs. A number of unresolved issues, therefore, are encountered in discussions of business investment decisions and related policies for influencing these decisions. In large measure the more relevant and important of these issues can be summarized in a series of four questions:

1. To what extent is investment demand sensitive to changes in rates of interest?
2. What constitutes the best measure of the general level of investment demand?
3. Do business managements value money obtained from internal sources differently from external sources, and therefore is the supply of investment funds viewed as consid-

erably less elastic by business when external sources must be used?

4. To what degree are shifts in the demand for investment and the supply of funds available for investment positively synchronized?

The primary focus of this study has been upon obtaining empirical answers to these questions. Also, because of the strong policy orientation of the study, an attempt has been made to incorporate the search for these answers into a systematic forecasting model that could be better used for policy purposes.

The conceptual framework used for conducting this empirical search is provided by an "accelerator-residual funds" hypothesis about investment behavior developed from previous empirical studies of investment decisions and relationships. The essence of this theory is that a discontinuity in investment behavior occurs at the point where full utilization of productive capacity is achieved. An accelerator or capacity-output relationship is suggested as the key factor in establishing short-run investment budgets when capacity is fully utilized and, contrarily, the level of cash funds flowing into the firm from current operations is considered a prime determinant when capacity is less than fully utilized. In terms of the questions just posed, the hypothesis thus asserts that investment demands are expected to outpace the supply of internal funds in business upswings and that the main determinant of the level of investment demand at such time is some measure of capacity utilization. By contrast, in business downswings, it is hypothesized that a discontinuity becomes operative in the supply of funds function and that investment demand is more or less synchronized with the internal supply of funds.

This hypothesis is tested against two basically different types of data: cross-sectional and time-series. The cross-section samples are composed of observations on a number of individual firms at one point in time, while the time-series samples contain observations over time of aggregates of individual firms grouped by industrial or product sectors. The cross-section samples are constituted primarily of observations on large manufacturing firms and, in particular, large manufacturing firms in industries with relatively high capital intensity and investment rates during the years 1951–1954 inclusive. The time-series samples are taken primarily from conventional Fed-